The Wycliffe Cookbook

Wycliffe®
.org

Wycliffe Bible Translators
PO Box 628200
Orlando, FL 32862-8200
1-800-WYCLIFFE

The Wycliffe Cookbook

Design and layout by Sean Stark
Angela Nelson, Editor
Marlene Mohr and Sean Stark, Illustrations

First Edition January 1989
Second Edition September 1990
Third Edition February 2000
Fourth Edition January 2002
Fifth Edition December 2011

ISBN 978-0-938978-10-7

Printed in the United States of America
Visit Wycliffe's website at **www.wycliffe.org.**

Table of Contents

Acknowledgements

Many people have played significant roles in the development of this cookbook from its first printing in 1989. Some of those people have been Gaylyn Williams, Terry Whalin, Roger Garland, Shirley Strachan, Shirley Skomerza, Charlotte Horton, Roberta Coder, Gwen Bergman, Larry Clark, Kim Beaty, Vida Wolter, Shirley Johnston, Theresa Bohm, Elsie Kogler, Marlene Mohr, John Hamilton, Ken Harris, Carolynn Andrews, Ralph Eichenberger, Gordon Whitney, and Kathy Wacek.

For the 2011 edition, we are grateful for the contributions of Sean Stark (layout and graphic design), and Angela Nelson (editor), as well as strategic input from Matt Petersen, Katie Adams, Katie Drees, Ann Richardson, Kathy Zoetewey, Dustin Moody, Cindi Hampshire, and Kristie Frieze. The recipes and stories for this edition were submitted by Wycliffe members around the world.

About Wycliffe Bible Translators

Wycliffe was founded in 1942 by William Cameron Townsend, a missionary to the Cakchiquel Indians of Guatemala. Townsend caught the vision for translation when Cakchiquel-speaking men expressed their concern that the Bible was not available to them in the language they understood clearly. As a result, Townsend resolved that every man, woman, and child should be able to read God's Word in their own language.

To date, Wycliffe has played a part in completing more than seven hundred Scripture translations. Currently our efforts serve languages spoken in more than ninety countries. The majority of the remaining translation needs represent minority languages—relatively small people groups, many of which struggle to maintain their identity in the shadow of majority culture. Often these groups have no written language of their own, and many struggle to gain the literacy skills they need to prosper in the majority culture.

The benefits of translation and literacy for these minority language groups are many. They include better health as a result of access to medical information, economic growth due to the acquisition of marketable skills, and the preservation of culture thanks to a written history. Most importantly, Bible translation brings people closer to God Himself—the One who transforms hearts.

Our desire is that this cookbook will be another tool to help God's work around the world as our workers and their friends prepare food that is tasty, nutritious, and economical.

Preface

The scent of curry fills the street as smoke curls from a large, bubbling caldron. A woman with a long flowing robe and a caste mark on the center of her forehead stirs the liquid. In another part of the world, roasted corn tempts passersby as they look down and see a small grill with fresh ears of corn roasting. With a few coins they purchase one and continue shopping.

Because food is a critical part of any culture, this book was designed to help you prepare and enjoy a variety of foods in and from other lands. Recipes were chosen which can be used in any country, even in countries where food processors, microwaves, gas and electric stoves, and refrigeration are unknown. The goal of use in other cultures is incorporated into the fiber of this book. The recipes were chosen according to usage in cultures foreign to us. No fancy gadgets are necessary, such as food processors or microwaves, and few recipes call for refrigeration. The majority of the world doesn't have access to such things, and recipes that call for them would be useless.

Why Another Cookbook?

This book began originally as the Jungle Camp Cookbook, printed in and prepared for cooking in southern Mexico. Although now out of print, for years this cross-cultural cookbook helped Wycliffe members and other people in full-time Christian service around the world.

Many favorite recipes from the Jungle Camp Cookbook have been preserved in this book. Wycliffe members from around the world have submitted hundreds of new recipes, as well as variations on recipes from the old book. These have been tested, modified, and condensed. The recipes represent a broad selection from countries in the Pacific, Africa, Asia, and Latin America. Wycliffe's work has expanded through the past seventy years and this book represents that expansion with its broad spectrum of recipes.

Some Special Features of This Book

Missionary Stories From the Field: Throughout the book, enjoy fun anecdotes about food overseas, written by Wycliffe missionaries.

Tested Recipes: Each recipe has been carefully tested and modified, when necessary, for use at home and overseas.

New Recipes: Eighteen new recipes have been added to this edition of the Wycliffe Cookbook.

International Recipes: This book includes a variety of international recipes submitted by members of Wycliffe Bible Translators who serve around the world.

International Measurements: Conversions for international measurements are included in tables found on pages 260–261. Milliliters are used for all measurements instead of grams because the recipes are written according to volume rather than weight.

Options: Many recipes include one or more options after the recipe. These are either in italics or have a bold title. They include variations, substitutions, and additions to the recipe. If you don't have a particular ingredient, check the options for a possible substitution.

Substitutions: Several pages of substitutions are provided to help those living overseas (see pages 272–274).

Hints: Helpful hints are found in the front of nearly every section. For the novice or experienced cook, the suggestions will lend the invaluable experience of others.

Children's Section: This section includes both cooking and craft projects. If play dough is unavailable in your location, see how to make it in the Children's Corner.

Index: The main index at the back of the book contains all the main titles as well as the alternate recipes.

Tabs: On each section tab is a listing of the primary recipe types and corresponding page numbers.

Appendix: Contains special information for home or overseas, including alternate cooking methods, health precautions, food preservation, and pest control.

Quick Bread Hints

To keep muffins or cupcakes from burning around the edges: Fill one cup of muffin tin with water instead of batter.

To make tortilla crumbs: Grind fresh tortillas. Spread the crumbs on cookie sheets. Put in a warm place to dry or put in a slow oven, stirring frequently until crumbs are crispy and golden. Cool thoroughly. Store in a can with a tight-fitting lid.

To store muffins, biscuits, breads, and coffee cakes: Place in a cool, dry place. In the refrigerator they become stale more quickly. They keep in the freezer for 3 months, if tightly wrapped.

To use stale baked goods: If you don't need crumbs, just sprinkle them with water, place in a paper bag, and warm in oven at 250°F for 5–10 minutes. This will restore freshness.

To toast rice, wheat, corn, or other grains: Wash thoroughly and dry. Toast while still a little damp, stirring often on cookie sheets in the oven, or in a hot skillet until golden brown.

To make flour from rice, wheat, corn, or other grains: Wash thoroughly. Dry. Toast if desired. Grind dry grain in corn grinder with burrs adjusted to grind very fine. Sift if desired.

To prevent weevils in flour and in staples: Freeze for at least 24 hours before storing. Or place a bay leaf or two in the storage container.

Master Mix

Combine:
- 8 1/2 cups all-purpose flour
- 1 tablespoon baking powder
- 1 teaspoon baking soda
- 2 teaspoons cream of tartar, optional
- 1 tablespoon salt
- 1 1/2 cups powdered milk

Cut in:
- 2 1/4 cups vegetable shortening

Place in airtight container with tight lid, plastic container, or bag,

- omit baking soda, increase baking powder to 1/4 cup.
- omit powdered milk, but add milk if a recipe calls for water or milk.
- decrease shortening to 1 1/4 cups.
- High altitude: Increase flour 1/2 cup.
- For recipes using Master Mix, see index.

Cake Mix: Omit soda, cream of tartar, and milk. Increase baking powder to 1/4 cup, decrease salt to 1 1/2 teaspoons. (See Dessert Cake and Master Mix Cake.)

Whole Wheat Bread Mix: Substitute 4 1/2 cups whole wheat flour for all-purpose flour. Increase baking powder to 2 tablespoons.

Master Mix Biscuits

Stir with a fork until dampened:

- **2 cups Master Mix**
- **1/2–2/3 cup water or less**

On floured board, knead slightly, roll or pat to 1/4 inch, and cut biscuits. A small can with both ends cut out makes a handy biscuit cutter.

Place on baking sheet. Bake at 450°F for 12–15 minutes. Makes twelve medium-sized biscuits.

* *Use any options on Baking Powder Biscuits (see next recipe).*

Biscuits on a Stick: Select several green, skinned sticks which are about 1 1/2 inches in diameter. (Note: Only use sticks from trees or vines which bear edible fruit). Place 1/3 to 1/2 cup of dough over the end of each stick forming a "bowl" shaped biscuit. Bake by holding it over red coals, turning slowly to cook without burning. When cooked, remove from stick.

Fill "bowl" with honey, jam, or fruit, or sprinkle with cinnamon-sugar mixture.

Drop Biscuits: Increase water to 3/4 cup. Drop by spoonfuls onto baking sheet.

Baking Powder Biscuits

Combine:

- **2 cups flour**
- **1 tablespoon baking powder**
- **1/2 teaspoon salt**
- **2 tablespoons sugar, optional**

Cut in with fork or pastry blender:

- **1/4–1/3 cup shortening**

Add gradually to make a soft, but not sticky dough:

- **3/4 cup milk**

Dough should be of the consistency that can be rolled out easily. Handle dough lightly. Put dough on a lightly floured board. Knead lightly a few times. Roll or pat out 1/2–3/4 inch thick. Cut with a biscuit cutter or cut in squares. Bake on ungreased baking sheet at 425°F for 10–15 minutes. May use any type flour for half the flour.

Bacon Biscuits: Add 1/3 cup crisp bacon chips to flour and shortening mixture.

Cheese Biscuits: Add 1/2 cup grated cheese to flour and shortening mixture.

Cinnamon Rolls: Roll dough into oblong shape. Spread with margarine or oil. Sprinkle generously with brown sugar, cinnamon, and raisins or chopped nuts. Roll up tightly and seal by pinching edges of roll together. Cut roll into 1-inch slices. Place on a greased baking sheet. Bake at 400°F for 12–15 minutes until golden in color.

Cornmeal Biscuits: Use 2/3 cup cornmeal and 1 1/3 cups flour.

See page 240 for International Conversion Charts

Drop Biscuits: Increase milk to 1 cup. Drop by spoonfuls onto a greased baking sheet or into greased muffin cups.

Fried Biscuits: Place biscuits in greased skillet over low heat. Cover with lid. Brown on one side. Turn over and brown on other side. Serve with butter and syrup, if desired.

Jam Biscuits: Make a deep depression in each biscuit and fill with jam before baking.

Orange Biscuits: Use orange juice instead of milk.

Quick Biscuits: Substitute 1/3 cup oil for shortening and use 2/3 cup milk. Pour oil and milk all at once into flour. Stir with fork until mixture cleans sides of bowl and mounds into a ball.

Short Cakes: Add 2 tablespoons sugar. Melt 2 tablespoons margarine. Brush half the biscuits with margarine. Cover each with another biscuit. Bake as usual.

Tomato Biscuits: Use tomato juice instead of milk.

Cheese Straws

Combine:

- 1/4 cup soft butter or margarine
- 3/4 cup flour, white or whole wheat
- 1/2 teaspoon salt
- 1 teaspoon Worcestershire sauce or hot sauce
- 8 drops Tabasco (pepper) sauce, optional

Add:

- 1 cup grated cheddar or other cheese

Roll out thin and cut into straws or small biscuits. Put on trays and refrigerate 1 hour or until cold. Bake at 475°F for 10 minutes until brown.

Cheese Balls: Omit sauces and salt. Use only 2 tablespoons butter and 1/2 cup flour. Add 1/4 cup water. Roll stiff dough into small balls. Bake at 250°F for 15 minutes.

Brown Bread

Combine:

- 3 cups whole wheat flour
- 2 teaspoons baking soda
- 1 teaspoon salt
- 1/2 cup each, brown sugar, raisins, and chopped nuts
- 2 cups sour milk

Bake in greased pan at 325°F for 1 hour.

*   *In place of whole wheat flour use a combination of white flour and wheat germ or a mixture of cornmeal, whole wheat, and white flour.*

Zucchini Bread

Combine:

- 3 eggs
- 1 1/2–2 cups sugar

Add and mix well:

- 1 cup oil
- 1 teaspoon vanilla

Combine separately and add:

- 1 cup oatmeal, quick or rolled
- 2 cups flour
- 1 tablespoon cinnamon
- 1 teaspoon baking soda
- 1 teaspoon salt
- 1/4 teaspoon baking powder

Add:

- 2 cups unpeeled, raw, grated zucchini
- nuts, optional

Pour into 2 greased and floured loaf pans. Bake at 350°F for 1 hour.

* *Substitute grated carrots or beets for all or part of the zucchini.*

Favorite Corn Bread

Combine:

- 3/4 cup cornmeal
- 1 cup flour
- 1/3 cup sugar
- 1 tablespoon baking powder
- 3/4 teaspoon salt

Add:

- 1 cup milk
- 1 beaten egg
- 2 tablespoons melted shortening

Pour into greased 9x9 pan. Bake at 400°F for 20 minutes or cook in skillet over flame spreader (low heat) for 10–15 minutes.

See page 240 for International Conversion Charts

Banana Bread

Combine:

- 1/2 cup shortening or 1/3 cup oil
- 1 cup sugar
- 1/4 cup water

Add:

- 1–2 beaten eggs, optional
- 2–3 bananas, mashed
- 1 teaspoon lemon juice, optional

Combine separately and add:

- 2 cups flour
- 1/2 teaspoon salt
- 1 teaspoon baking soda
- 1/4–1/2 teaspoon cinnamon, cloves, or nutmeg
- 1 teaspoon vanilla
- 1/2–1 cup chopped nuts, optional

Pour into greased loaf or 9x9 pan. Bake at 375°F for 45–60 minutes.

* *If necessary, reduce sugar to 3/4 cup and omit shortening.*

* *Omit water, add 2 beaten eggs and 1 cup mashed bananas.*

* *Add any of these or a combination: 1 cup flaked coconut, 2 teaspoons nutmeg, 1 cup bran, 1/2 cup raisins, 1/3 cup chopped raw cranberries or other fruit.*

Apple Bread: Substitute 1 cup chopped apples or applesauce for bananas and 1/3 cup sour milk or orange juice for water.

Chocolate Banana Bread: Add 1/2 cup cocoa to the flour.

Master Mix Bread: Substitute 2 1/3 cups Master Mix (see page 9) for salt, soda, and flour. Use either banana, apple, or pumpkin options.

Pumpkin Bread: Substitute 1 cup cooked, mashed pumpkin or any yellow squash for bananas. Increase sugar to 1 1/2 cups. Add 1 1/2 teaspoons each, cinnamon and nutmeg, and 1/2 teaspoon ginger.

Corn Tortillas

Stir together in saucepan on low heat:

- 1 1/2 cups boiling water
- 1 cup cornmeal
- 3 tablespoons margarine
- 1 teaspoon salt

Remove from heat, cover for 5 minutes, then add until not sticky or stiff:

- 1 cup flour or more

Roll on floured board until very thin. Fry both sides in hot, ungreased skillet.

Flour Tortillas

Combine:

- **4 cups flour**
- **2 teaspoons salt**

Cut in:

- **6 tablespoons shortening or oil**

Add:

- **1 cup water**

Form a ball. Add more water if necessary, until bowl is clear of all dough. Knead well on floured board and make balls the size of an egg. Let stand for 15 minutes. Roll thin with a rolling pin to about the size of a salad plate. Place in hot ungreased skillet and cook for about 2 minutes on one side. Turn and cook 1 minute longer. Makes about 2 dozen.

Cornmeal Tortillas: Replace 1 cup flour with cornmeal.

Whole Wheat Tortillas: Use 2 cups each whole wheat and white flour.

Dumplings

Combine:

- **1 cup flour**
- **2 teaspoons baking powder**
- **1/2 teaspoon salt**

Add and stir:

- **1/2 cup milk**

Dip spoon into soup or gravy, then spoon in dumplings. Cover and cook 15 minutes. Dumplings cook better if placed on beans or stew vegetables so they don't sink to the bottom of the pan.

Cornmeal Dumplings: Reduce flour to 1/4 cup. Add 1 cup cornmeal, 1 egg, and 1 teaspoon melted shortening.

Fluffy Dumplings: Add 1 beaten egg and 1 1/2 teaspoons melted margarine or butter. Decrease milk to 1/3 cup.

Master Mix Dumplings: Substitute Master Mix (page 9) for flour, 1 teaspoon baking powder, and salt.

See page 240 for International Conversion Charts

Hush Puppies

Combine:

- 1/2 cup flour
- 1 1/2 cups cornmeal
- 1 teaspoon baking powder
- 3/4 teaspoon salt
- 3/4 cup milk
- 1/4 cup water
- 1 small onion, chopped, optional

Mold mixture into little cakes, about 1 tablespoon each, and fry in 1-inch of hot oil until browned on each side. Drain. Serve hot.

Whole Wheat Popovers

Combine and beat:

- 3 eggs, beaten until frothy
- 1 cup milk
- 3 tablespoons oil

Add and beat until smooth:

- 1/2 cup whole wheat flour
- 1/2 cup flour
- 1/2 teaspoon salt

Pour batter into 12 well–greased muffin cups, about 3/4 full. Bake at 375°F for 35 minutes or until puffed and brown. Serve immediately.

* *Hint: To lessen the possibility of the popovers sticking to the pan, place pan in oven to heat oil until very hot and then pour in the batter and bake.*

Fritters

Combine:

- 2 eggs, beaten
- 2/3 cup milk
- 1 tablespoon oil or melted shortening

Add:

- 1 cup flour, can be a mixture of flour
- 1/2 teaspoon salt
- 1 tablespoon sugar, for sweet fritters only

Add to or dip into fritter batter:

- Fruit, vegetables, or cooked meat, cut in pieces.
- Brown in hot deep fat at 375°F. Drain and serve with syrup or gravy.
- Separate egg whites and yolks. Beat egg whites until stiff. Fold into batter.

Fruit Fritters: Sprinkle with sugar and cinnamon, if desired.

Master Mix Fritters: Omit flour and salt. Add 1 cup Master Mix (page 9).

Banana Fritters: Omit oil, 1/2 cup flour, milk, and egg. Mash 1 large, ripe cooking banana and combine with flour and 1 teaspoon baking powder. Drop by spoonfuls into hot oil. Sprinkle with cinnamon and sugar if desired. Pan fry if desired.

Cake Doughnuts

Combine:

- 4 egg yolks or 2 whole eggs, well beaten
- 1 cup sugar
- 2 tablespoons soft shortening or oil
- 3/4 cup milk

Combine separately and add:

- 3 1/2 cups flour
- 4 teaspoons baking powder
- 1/2 teaspoon salt
- 1/4 teaspoon nutmeg
- 1/4 teaspoon cinnamon

Add more flour if necessary. Roll out and cut doughnuts. Fry in hot oil until brown. Drain over kettle, then on absorbent paper in a warm place. Serve plain, sugared, glazed, with grated coconut, or with crumbs.

* *For doughnut hints and glaze see Raised Doughnuts in Yeast Breads.*

Master Mix Coffee Cake

Combine:

- 3 cups Master Mix (page 9)
- 1/3–1/2 cup sugar

Add and fold together until blended:

- 1 egg
- 1 cup milk
- 1 teaspoon vanilla

Pour into a greased 9x9 pan. Sprinkle with any coffee cake topping. (Recipes following.) Bake at 400°F 25–30 minutes.

Orange Delight Coffee Cake: Substitute orange juice for milk. Increase sugar to 2/3 cup. Combine the following and sprinkle over unbaked cake: 1/2 cup each chopped nuts and sugar and 1 teaspoon each cinnamon and nutmeg.

Coffee Cake Toppings

Brown Sugar Topping: Combine 1/2 cup brown sugar and 1/4 teaspoon nutmeg.

Cinnamon Topping: Combine 2–4 tablespoons flour, 1/3 cup cookie, cake crumbs, or Master Mix (page 9), 1/3–1/2 cup white or brown sugar, 2–4 tablespoons shortening, 1–2 teaspoons cinnamon, and 1/2 cup chopped nuts.

Oatmeal Topping: Combine 1/2 cup oatmeal, 1/3 cup each brown sugar and chopped nuts, and 1 tablespoon oil.

See page 240 for International Conversion Charts

Peanut Topping: Combine 2 tablespoons oil, 1/3 cup brown sugar, and chopped peanuts.

Master Mix Muffins

Combine:

- **2 cups Master Mix**
- **2/3 cup water or milk**
- **2 eggs, beaten**

Mix well. Fill greased muffin pans 2/3 full. Bake at 425°F about 20 minutes. Makes 10–12 small muffins. Store in airtight container when cool.

Use any of the options for Muffins.

Coffee Cake

Combine:

- **2 cups flour**
- **1 tablespoon baking powder**
- **2/3–1 cup sugar**
- **1/2 teaspoon salt**
- **1 teaspoon cinnamon, optional**
- **1/3 cup powdered milk**

Stir in:

- **1 egg**
- **2/3 cup water**

Pour batter into greased 9 x13 baking pan. Sprinkle Coffee Cake Topping over the batter. Bake at 350°F for 45 minutes.

Bake cake without topping. When cake is done, spread top of warm cake with margarine or oil. Sprinkle with a mixture of cinnamon and sugar.

Apple Coffee Cake: Add 1/4 cup melted margarine or shortening and 1 1/2 cups finely chopped apples.

Fruit Coffee Cake: Arrange sliced or chopped fruit over batter.

Overnight Crunch Coffee Cake: Add 1 teaspoon soda, 2/3 cup butter, 1/2 cup brown sugar, and 1 egg. Omit water. Add 1 cup buttermilk, yogurt, or milk with 1 1/2 teaspoons lemon juice or vinegar added. Spread batter in pan. Top with any coffee cake topping. Refrigerate overnight, then bake.

Upside-Down Nut Coffee Cake: Melt 1/2 cup butter or margarine in a 9x9 greased pan. Stir into margarine 3/4 cup brown sugar, 3/4 cup chopped nuts, and 1/4 cup powdered skim milk. Drop batter by spoonfuls into the pan. Bake, then invert onto a heated platter. Serve hot or cold.

Muffins

Combine:

- **1–2 eggs, beaten**
- **1 cup milk or yogurt**
- **2–4 tablespoons oil or melted shortening**

Combine separately and add, stirring only until flour is moistened:

- **3/4 teaspoon salt**
- **1 tablespoon baking powder**
- **2–4 tablespoons sugar**
- **2 cups flour**

Be careful not to over mix. Batter will be a little lumpy. Fill greased muffin pans 2/3 full. Bake at 400°F for 20 minutes. Remove pans from oven and loosen muffins.

Use 9x9 square pan instead of muffin pans.

Add any of the following or a combination: 1/2–1 cup raisins, nuts or sunflower seeds; 1 cup finely chopped apples, blueberries, dates, crushed pineapple, cooked prunes or other fruit; 1 teaspoon cinnamon; 2–4 tablespoons more sugar; 1/2–3/4 cup grated cheese with 1/8 teaspoon paprika; 1/4 cup crisp bacon chips (also substitute bacon fat for oil); 3/4 cup candied orange peel, or finely cut lemon.

Applesauce Muffins: Substitute applesauce for milk. Increase shortening to 1/2 cup and sugar to 1 cup. Use 2 eggs. Add 1 teaspoon cinnamon, 1/2 teaspoon nutmeg, and 1 cup chopped nuts or raisins, optional.

Bran Muffins: Substitute 1 cup bran for 1 cup flour. Use 1/4 cup brown sugar for white sugar.

Cornmeal Muffins: Substitute 1 cup cornmeal for 1 cup flour.

Jelly Muffins: Fill muffin cups 1/3 full. In center of each put a scant teaspoon jelly. Continue to fill muffin cups 2/3 full.

Muffin Drop Biscuits: Drop batter on a greased baking sheet.

Oatmeal Muffins: Substitute 1 cup oats for 1 cup flour. Use sour milk. Soak oats in sour milk for 1 hour. Increase oil to 1/2 cup and use 1/3 cup brown sugar instead of white. Add 1/2 teaspoon baking soda. Decrease baking powder to 1 teaspoon.

Sour Milk Muffins: Decrease baking powder to 2 teaspoons. Add 1/2 teaspoon baking soda with dry ingredients. Use sour milk instead of sweet milk.

Soybean Muffins: Use half soybean flour.

Whole Wheat Muffins: Use half whole wheat flour. Reduce baking powder to 1 teaspoon. Add 1 teaspoon baking soda. Substitute 1 1/2 cups sour milk for milk.

    See page 240 for International Conversion Charts

Pancake Mix

Combine:

- **6 cups flour**
- **1 tablespoon salt**
- **3 tablespoons baking powder**
- **1/3–2/3 cup sugar, optional**
- **2 cups powdered milk**
- **1 cup wheat germ, optional**

* *Use half whole wheat flour, if desired.*
Increase baking powder to 6 tablespoons, if desired.

Master Mix Pancakes

Combine and beat until smooth:

- **2 cups Master Mix (page 9)**
- **1 egg**
- **1 1/4 cups milk or water**

Cook on hot greased griddle until surface is covered with bubbles. Turn and brown on the other side. Makes about 13 pancakes.

Double Master Mix and milk and use only 1 egg.

Cornmeal Pancakes: Use 1 1/2 cups Mix and 1/2 cup cornmeal, and add 3 tablespoons sugar, optional.

Eggless Pancakes: Omit eggs. Use 1 3/4 cups water and 2 tablespoons sugar, optional.

Master Mix Waffles: Add 2 tablespoons oil, if desired. Cook on hot waffle iron. Makes three 9-inch waffles. For lighter waffles: Add beaten egg yolk to milk. Fold in stiffly beaten egg whites.

Pancake Mix Pancakes

Combine:

- **1 egg, slightly beaten, optional**
- **1 cup water**
- **2 tablespoons oil, optional**
- **1 1/2 cups Pancake Mix (see previous recipe)**

Fry on hot griddle.

Omit egg and oil. Increase water to 1 1/4–1 1/2 cups.

Pancake Mix Waffles: Increase oil to 1/4 cup and cook on hot waffle iron.

Favorite Pancakes

Combine:

- **2 cups flour**
- **2 tablespoons sugar, optional**
- **4 teaspoons baking powder**
- **1 teaspoon salt, optional**

Combine separately and add:

- **2 eggs, beaten**
- **1 1/2 cups milk**
- **1/4 cup oil or melted shortening**

Stir quickly until blended. Do not beat. Cook on a hot greased griddle, turning when bubbly. Yields about 15 three inch pancakes.

Use any mixture of flours: whole wheat, white, oatmeal, rye, wheat germ, cornmeal, rice flour, millet, etc.

Apple Spice Pancakes: Add 1 cup grated apple, 1 tablespoon lemon juice, 2 tablespoons sugar, and 1/2 teaspoon cinnamon.

Banana Pancakes: Add to liquid 3/4–1 cup mashed ripe bananas, 1 tablespoon lemon juice, and 2 tablespoons sugar.

Cheese and Bacon Pancakes: Add 1/2 cup each grated cheese and crisp crumbled bacon.

Ham Pancakes: Add 1/2–1 cup ground or chopped ham.

Pineapple Pancakes: Use pineapple juice and powdered milk instead of the milk. When the batter is ready, add 1 cup pineapple.

Raisin Pancakes: Add 1 cup raisins. Serve with jam.

Waffles: Cook batter on heated waffle iron. If desired, separate egg yolks from whites. Keep yolks with milk mixture. Fold in stiffly beaten whites.

Rich Rice Pancakes

Combine:

- **3 cups cooked rice**
- **4–6 eggs, beaten**
- **1 teaspoon salt**

Drop by tablespoons in hot frying pan to form patties. Cook until golden brown on both sides. Serve with syrup.

Crêpes

Beat lightly:

- **2 eggs**
- **2 cups milk**
- **2 tablespoons oil**

Add and beat in:

- **2/3 cup flour—white, whole wheat, or combination**
- **1/2 teaspoon salt**

Lightly grease a frying pan, a non-stick pan, or a cast iron skillet. Pour about 1/4 cup batter into the hot pan for each crêpe. Tilt the pan to spread the batter into a thin round layer. Turn the crêpe when it is fully solidified and brown on one side. Loosen the edges before turning. Brown on the other side. You may not

See page 240 for International Conversion Charts

need to add more oil to the pan between crêpes. Stir the batter and scoop it from the bottom each time. Make filling. Fill each crêpe with a little filling. Roll up, top with more filling, and serve. Makes about 15 crêpes. Batter may be refrigerated or frozen.

Filling for Crêpes

Prepare:

- **2–3 cups white sauce**
- **Add any combination of the following:**
- **herbs: basil, thyme, rosemary, marjoram, etc.**
- **sautéed mushrooms, peppers or onions**
- **1 1/2 cups grated cheese**
- **1/2 cup Parmesan cheese**
- **2 cups chopped spinach and 1 teaspoon lemon juice**
- **1 cup tuna, cooked ground beef, sausage, or chicken**

Vegetable Crêpes: Make white sauce with any variations. Fill each crêpe with a little sauce and finely chopped cooked vegetables of your choice. Roll up and pour rest of sauce over crêpes. Use any combination of mushrooms, asparagus, broccoli, cauliflower, carrots, potatoes, onion, green pepper, peas, etc.

Fruit Crêpes: Fill with any chopped; lightly-sweetened fruit. Roll up and top with more fruit or whipped cream.

Welsh Griddle Cakes

Combine:

- **1 cup flour**
- **1/4 cup sugar**
- **1 teaspoon baking powder**
- **1/8 teaspoon salt**

Cut in:

- **1/4 cup shortening**

Add:

- **1/4 cup raisins**
- **2–4 tablespoons milk, enough to hold batter together**

Form small cakes approximately 2 inches across and 1/4–1/2 inch thick. Cook on floured griddle, over low heat, until brown and crusted on one side, then turn. When done the cakes should give a dry sound when tapped with the spatula. These are sweet biscuits—almost like English muffins. Serve with butter and honey or jam.

French Toast

Combine:

- 2 eggs
- 2/3 cup milk
- 2 teaspoons sugar, optional
- 1/4 teaspoon salt, optional
- 1/2–1 teaspoon cinnamon optional
- 1/4 teaspoon nutmeg, optional
- 1 teaspoon vanilla, optional

Dip in milk mixture:

- 6 slices of bread

Fry on hot griddle until golden on both sides. Serve with butter and syrup.

Maple Syrup

Combine in a pan and boil about 15 minutes:

- 4 cups sugar
- 2 cups boiling water

Remove from heat and add:

- 1 teaspoon maple or vanilla flavoring

See page 240 for International Conversion Charts

Yeast Bread Hints and Directions

For Sourdough Hints see page 33.

Temperature of liquid: If yeast is mixed directly with liquid, the liquid should be 105–115°F. If yeast is added to dry ingredients, the liquid should be 120–130°F.

If using raw milk: Be sure to scald and cool to warm before adding to yeast.

To knead dough: Place dough on lightly floured surface. Flour hands and form dough into a ball. Fold edges of dough toward center. Push dough down and away from you using the heels of your hands. Give dough a quarter turn and repeat folding, pushing, and turning until dough is smooth and elastic. Add more flour to board as needed to keep dough from sticking.

To raise dough: Return kneaded dough to oiled bowl. Turn several times to coat dough. Cover with cloth, set in warm place out of drafts, and let rise until double in bulk. Press fingers into dough. If impression remains, dough has risen sufficiently. Punch down dough by plunging fist into center and fold edges toward center. Shape dough into rolls, loaves, etc., and let rise again until double in size.

To check rising time: Put a small ball of dough in a glass of water. If you are going to be working away from the kitchen, take the glass of water with you. When the ball surfaces, the loaves are ready for the oven. This way you do not have to keep checking the dough.

To raise dough quickly: Put dough in microwave with a jar of 2–3 cups boiling water. Microwave on the lowest setting until double.

To shape loaves: Flatten dough for one loaf by pressing down and rolling lengthwise, pressing out air pockets. Fold both ends of dough into center. Repeat 3–4 times. Press out air each time. Roll into loaf. Tuck ends under loaf or roll dough into 10x12-inch rectangle then roll rectangle tightly into a long thin roll. Tuck ends under. Put in greased loaf pans.

To check if bread is baked: It should be well browned and shrink slightly from edge of the pan. A clean toothpick or uncooked spaghetti noodle inserted should come out clean. When bread is baked, remove from pan immediately and cool on rack to prevent a soggy crust.

To make a lighter loaf: Add ascorbic acid (100 mg vitamin C tablet, crushed) to the bread. This cuts the rising time in half and the bread keeps longer.

To make bread in hot, dry climates: Make a less rich bread. Do not use oil, milk, or egg. Rich breads go stiff and crumbly the second day.

Easy Yeast Bread

Combine:

- 4 cups flour, see options below
- 3/4 cup milk powder
- 2 tablespoons dry active yeast
- 1–3 teaspoons salt
- 3–6 tablespoons sugar, honey, or molasses
- 3–6 tablespoons margarine, shortening, or oil

Add and mix well:

- 2 3/4 cups lukewarm water
- 1 teaspoon maple flavoring, optional

Add:

- 3 1/2–4 cups white flour

Knead 10 minutes, grease, let rise until double. (See Hints, page 23.) Punch down, divide in half, and let rise in greased bread pans until double. Bake at 375°F for 30–40 minutes. Remove from pans to cool. Makes two loaves, or one loaf and 12–16 rolls, or 30 hamburger buns.

* *Note: Use this recipe only if you know your yeast is fresh.*

* *Use any combination of the following for flour: Whole wheat flour, cracked wheat, rye flour, unbleached white flour, oatmeal or oat flour, cornmeal, wheat germ, 1/2–1 cup bran, gluten flour, soy flour, sunflower seeds, raisins, granola, carob powder.*

* *Add any of the following or a combination: 1/4 cup honey, grated orange peel, 2 eggs, nuts and dried fruits, 1/2 cup bean sprouts.*

* *Use 3 cups warm milk for milk powder and water.*

Easy Oatmeal Bread: Omit water and milk powder. Combine 1 1/2 cups each oatmeal and boiling water. Add 1/3 cup each oil and honey. Add yeast, salt, and 1 cup yogurt. Then add flour using only 5–5 1/2 cups flour. Let rise in refrigerator (see Refrigerator Rise Bread below).

Quick Yeast Bread: After kneading dough, divide into three balls. Cover. Let stand 10–15 minutes. Mold into 3 loaves. Place into greased loaf pans. Cover and let rise 45 minutes. Bake. Keep dough warm throughout process.

Refrigerator or Slow Rise Bread: After kneading, let bread rest while greasing three 8 1/2 x 4 1/2-inch loaf pans with butter or margarine. *Do not* use oil as it will be absorbed during the long rise. Place dough in pans. Cover loosely with greased plastic wrap and place in refrigerator where they have room to rise and won't have to be moved. Allow to rise 5–24 hours. Then remove from refrigerator, take off plastic wrap and put in cold oven. Turn oven to 350°F. Bake for about 50 minutes. Test for doneness when crust is dark brown. Remove from pans to cool.

See page 240 for International Conversion Charts

Jungle Camp Yeast Bread

Combine and set aside until foam rises to top:

- **3 cups warm water**
- **2 tablespoons dry yeast**
- **1/3 cup sugar, honey, or molasses**

Add:

- **2 eggs**
- **1/3 cup soft shortening, butter, or oil**

Combine separately and add:

- **8 cups flour**
- **1 tablespoon salt**
- **3/4 cup milk powder**

When the dough begins to leave the sides of the bowl, turn it out onto a lightly floured board to knead. Knead until smooth and elastic and it doesn't stick to board. Place in a greased bowl. Cover with damp cloth and let rise in warm, draft-free spot 85°F until double (1 1/2–2 hours). Punch down. Let rise again until almost double in bulk (30–45 minutes). Form loaves, rolls, or coffee cake. Cover and let rest 15 minutes. Bake at 425°F for rolls or 375°F for loaves for 30–40 minutes. Makes 3 loaves, 4 dozen plain rolls, 1 large pan of rolls, or 1 coffee cake and 2 dozen plain rolls.

* *Use 1/2 wheat flour or any combination of flours from Easy Yeast Bread.*

* *Use warm milk in place of water and milk powder.*

Cheese Bread: Add 1 cup grated cheese and 1/4 cup Parmesan cheese to dough.

Dill Bread: Add 1 tablespoon dried dill weed and/or 1 tablespoon dill seed and 1/4 cup finely chopped onion.

Jiffy Pan Rolls: Omit eggs. Use sour milk in place of milk powder and water. Add 1/4 teaspoon soda. Decrease flour to about 6 cups. Knead dough 3 minutes. Shape into rolls or loaves. Let rise until double (about 1 1/2 hours), then bake. Can be used as a thick pizza crust.

Monkey Bread: Omit 1 tablespoon yeast, 2 eggs, and water. Reduce flour to 6 cups. Combine all ingredients. Add 1 cup boiling water or milk. Do not knead. Raise in covered bowl 1 hour, then turn out on floured board. Mix in just enough flour to form egg-size balls. Roll balls in melted margarine. Place in 2 tube pans or 9x9 pans. Pour margarine on top and raise until double. Bake at 350°F for 40 minutes.

Oatmeal Bread: Omit milk and eggs. Reduce shortening to 2 tablespoons. Use brown sugar instead of white. Combine 3 cups each boiling water and oats, cool to lukewarm, and add to sugar. Decrease flour to 6–6 1/2 cups.

Quick Sweet Dough: Increase yeast to 3 tablespoons and sugar and shortening to 1/2 cup each. Let rise 1/2 hour for first rising. Shape into rolls. Let rise another 1/2 hour, then bake.

Sweet Dough: Increase sugar and shortening to 1/2 cup each.

No-Knead Bread

In the evening, mix in a container that has a lid:

- 4 1/2 cups all-purpose flour
- 1/4 teaspoon instant yeast
- 1 1/2 teaspoons salt

Mix in until there is no more dry flour on the bottom of the container:

- 2 cups water

The dough will be lumpy and sticky. Cover with the lid and leave overnight.

In the morning, 12–18 hours later, the dough will be bubbly and will have risen to twice its original volume. Preheat the oven to 375°F. Lightly oil a bread pan and use a spatula to scrape the dough into it. Bake until the outside of the bread is nice and golden brown—about 30–45 minutes.

Loaf Recipes

Cinnamon Bread Loaf: Mix 1/4 of any Yeast Bread recipe. After the first rising, punch down and knead. Roll into rectangle 1/2-inch thick. Spread with softened butter and sprinkle with 1/4 cup sugar mixed with 1 teaspoon cinnamon. Roll like a jelly roll. Place in a buttered loaf pan, brush with melted butter, cover with a clean cloth, and let rise until double in bulk. Bake 30 minutes at 400°F.

Raisin Bread Loaf: Add 1/4 cup molasses or honey, 1 teaspoon, cinnamon and 1 cup raisins to any Yeast Bread recipe.

Sour Cream or Yogurt Braided Bread Loaf: Substitute sour cream or yogurt for milk or water in any Yeast Bread recipe. After dough rises first time, punch down, divide dough in half, and divide each half into 3 equal pieces. Cover and let rest 10 minutes. On lightly floured surface, roll each piece of dough to 18-inch long rope. Place the 3 ropes side by side on a large baking sheet and braid loosely from center to ends. Press rope ends together to seal. Cover and let rise until nearly double. Combine 2 beaten egg yolks with 4 teaspoons water and brush top of loaf with mixture. Bake at 350°F for 35–40 minutes.

See page 240 for International Conversion Charts

Glazes for Bread and Rolls

Combine and brush on dough just before baking:

- **1 egg yolk**
- **2 tablespoons sugar**
- **3 tablespoons water, milk, or fruit juice**

Or combine, beat, and brush on top of bread or rolls just before baking:

- **1 egg white**
- **1 tablespoon milk or water**

Or brush on when loaf is removed from the oven: melted butter or margarine.

Danish Pastry

Combine flour, sugar, and salt, then cut in butter:

- **5 cups flour**
- **1 teaspoon sugar and 1/2 teaspoon salt**
- **1 1/2 cups butter or margarine**

Add and mix well:

- **1 tablespoon dry yeast dissolved in 1/4 cup warm water**
- **3/4 cup cold milk**

Divide into 6 parts. Roll each part into thin rectangles. Spread jam or cooked fruit down the center third of the dough. Moisten edges, fold dough over jam and pinch together. Turn over. Slice top. Bake at 350°F for 25–30 minutes.

Roll Recipes

Bread Sticks: Make any Yeast Bread recipe (page 24) adding 2 tablespoons butter and 1 egg white. When ready to shape, roll the dough into a rectangle about 8x12 inches. Cut in half lengthwise, then into 16 snips. Roll under the palms of your hands on a board without flour to make smooth, even sticks 8–10 inches long. Arrange 1 inch apart on a cookie sheet. Let rise. Bake at 425°F for 5 minutes, then reduce heat to 350°F and bake 15 minutes. The slower baking makes the sticks crisp and dry.

Brown and Serve Rolls: Make any rolls. Bake at 250–275°F for 30 minutes. (They will still be pale in color.) Store in refrigerator up to 2 weeks or freeze indefinitely. Bake at 400°F until brown and serve.

Butter Rolls: Roll any Yeast Bread recipe (page 24) into a rectangle. Spread with softened butter. Cut in snips 2 inches wide. Stack evenly in a pile. Cut in 1-inch pieces and fit into buttered muffin tins.

Caramel Rolls: Simmer and stir over moderate heat until sugar dissolves: 1/4 cup butter, 3/4 cup brown sugar, 2 tablespoons dark corn syrup, and 1 tablespoon water. Pour into 9x13 pan. Put cinnamon rolls on top (page 28). Bake at 375°F for 25–30 minutes. Loosen from edges immediately and invert. Leave pan in place for one minute. Sprinkle with nuts if desired.

Cheese Sticks: Roll any Yeast Bread recipe into a rectangle 1/4-inch thick. Spread with butter, sprinkle with flour, and fold from ends to make 3 layers. Repeat three times and cut in finger-shaped pieces. Arrange on a cookie sheet, cover, and let stand 15 minutes. Bake at 425°F for 10 minutes. Remove from oven, brush tops with egg white, and dip in Parmesan cheese seasoned with salt and cayenne. Bake 5 more minutes.

Cinnamon Buns: Increase sugar to 1/2 cup. Add 1/2 teaspoon cinnamon and 1/4 cup raisins, if desired, to any Yeast Bread recipe. Flatten dough and cut into buns with a 3-inch cutter. Place on greased cookie sheet and allow to rise. Bake 20–30 minutes at 425°F.

Cinnamon Puffs: Add 1 teaspoon lemon juice and 1 egg to any Yeast Bread recipe. Decrease flour to 6 cups. Do not knead. Let rise until double. Spoon into greased muffin pans. Sprinkle cinnamon and sugar on top. Let rise until double. Bake at 350°F for 20 minutes.

Cinnamon Rolls: Use 1/2 mix of any Yeast Bread recipe. Roll 1/4-inch thick, spread with oil or shortening, and sprinkle with brown sugar and cinnamon. Add chopped nuts and raisins if desired. Roll up like a jelly roll. Cut in 3/4-inch pieces. Place in greased pan, close together. Let rise until double in bulk and bake 20 minutes at 400°F.

French Rolls: Form rolls from any Yeast Bread recipe. When nearly finished baking, brush with a beaten egg white mixed with 1 tablespoon water and 1/2 teaspoon vanilla. Sprinkle with sugar if desired.

Hard Rolls: Prepare any Yeast Bread recipe, add 1 egg white. Sprinkle a pan with cornmeal and arrange the shaped rolls on it 2 inches apart. Let rise and bake at 400°F with a pan of boiling water on the rack beneath the rolls. The oven should be kept steamy throughout the baking time.

Orange Rolls: Mix any Yeast Bread recipe and use orange juice in place of milk. Add 1 tablespoon grated orange peel. Roll dough into walnut-size balls and place 3 per greased muffin tin. Let rise, then bake. Frost with 1/4 cup orange or lemon juice and confectioner's sugar until thick enough to spread. Beat thoroughly.

Refrigerator Rolls: Use any Yeast Bread recipe. Place dough in a greased, covered bowl in refrigerator for at least 2 hours or up to 2 weeks. Remove from refrigerator, shape dough, let rise until double (about 1 1/4 hours), then bake as usual.

Sesame or Poppyseed Rolls: Brush any unbaked rolls with 1 egg white blended with 2 tablespoons water and sprinkle with seeds.

Upside-Down Orange Rolls: Combine to make orange filling: 1/2 cup sugar, 1 tablespoon grated orange rind, 1/4 cup orange juice and pulp, and 1/4 cup margarine. Cook 5 minutes then cool. Roll out 1/4 of any Yeast Bread recipe into a rectangle 1/4-inch thick and spread with enough orange filling to cover. Roll up and cut in about 1-inch pieces. Spread remainder of filling in greased baking pan. Place rolls on top of filling. Let rise until double in size. Bake 30–40 minutes at 375°F. Remove from pan immediately. Greased muffin tins may be used to bake the rolls.

Upside-Down Pecan Rolls: Roll 1/2 of any Yeast Bread recipe into a rectangle 9x13 inches; brush with margarine, shortening, or cooking oil; and sprinkle generously with brown sugar. Roll up as for jelly roll. Cut in 12 slices. Combine until crumbly and spread in greased baking pan: 1/2 cup softened margarine, 1 cup firmly packed brown sugar, 1 cup chopped nuts, and 1/4 cup powdered skim milk. Follow remaining directions as in Upside-Down Orange Rolls.

Coffee Cake Recipes

Apple Coffee Cake: Use 1/2 of any Yeast Bread recipe. Knead and spread in two greased layer cake pans or a 9x13 pan. Brush with melted butter. Peel 5 tart apples and cut in eighths. Press close together into the dough, sharp edge down. Sprinkle with 1/4 cup sugar mixed with 1/2 teaspoon cinnamon and 2 tablespoons currants or raisins. Cover and let rise. Bake 30 minutes at 350°F.

Christmas Stollen: Use 1/2 of any Yeast Bread recipe. After mixing and rising, turn the dough onto a floured board and pat or roll out flat. Cover with 1/2 cup slivered almonds, 1/4 cup candied fruit, 1 cup raisins, and 1 tablespoon grated lemon rind. Fold and knead the fruit into the dough. Flatten the dough into an oblong shape. Brush with melted butter and fold lengthwise. Press the edges together. Place on a greased baking sheet. Let rise to double in bulk. Bake at 375°F for 35 minutes. Frost and decorate with almonds and candied fruit.

Cincinnati Coffee Cake: Spread 1/4 of any Yeast Bread recipe in a 9x9 pan. Combine the following and sprinkle over dough: 1/4 cup sugar, 1 1/2 teaspoons cinnamon, 1 cup soft stale bread crumbs, and 4 tablespoons each melted butter and chopped blanched almonds. Bake at 375°F for 30–35 minutes.

Filled Coffee Cake: Combine 1 cup brown sugar, 1/2 cup softened margarine, and 1 cup nuts, finely chopped. Use 1/4 of any Yeast Bread recipe. Divide into 3 pieces and roll into 9-inch circles. Put one round in greased 9-inch pan and sprinkle with 1/3 of the filling. Put second round over filling and sprinkle with another 1/3 of the filling. Put third round on. Sprinkle top with remaining filling, pressing it into dough. Cover and let rise until light. Bake at 375°F for 35 minutes. Let stand 10 minutes before removing from pan.

Hungarian Coffee Cake: Form 1/2 of any Yeast Bread recipe into balls the size of walnuts and roll in 1/2 cup melted butter. Then roll in mixture of 3/4 cup sugar, 1 teaspoon cinnamon, and 1/2 cup finely chopped nuts. Place a layer of balls so they barely touch in well greased 9-inch tube pan. Sprinkle with a few raisins. Add another layer of balls and sprinkle with more raisins, pressing them in slightly. Let rise 45 minutes. Bake at 375°F for 35–40 minutes. Loosen from pan and invert pan so that butter-sugar mixture runs down over cake.

Streusel Cake: Spread 1/4 of any Yeast Bread recipe in a 9x9 pan. Combine 1/3 cup each of sugar, flour, and butter. Mix until crumbly. Spread over the dough, pressing in slightly with fingers. Let rise until double. Bake at 375°F for 35 minutes.

Bagels

Combine:

- **1 tablespoon dry yeast**
- **3 tablespoons sugar**
- **1 teaspoon salt**
- **1 cup warm water**

Add until kneadable:

- **3 cups flour**

Turn onto lightly floured surface and knead until elastic (8–10 minutes). Place in greased bowl and turn over so top of dough is also greased. Cover with clean towel and let rise in warm place 30–40 minutes. Punch dough down. Separate into 12 pieces. Shape into balls and work in sesame, poppy, or caraway seeds or minced onion, if desired. Stick your thumb through to make 1/2–1-inch hole (1–2 1/2 cm) to form bagel. Let bagels rise 20 minutes. Put 2–3 bagels at a time in a large pot of boiling water with 1 tablespoon oil. Let rise to top and turn over. Remove and sprinkle with salt, onion, or more seeds if desired. Bake on ungreased cookie sheet at 400–500°F for 15–20 minutes until brown on bottom.

Fruit Bagels: Add spices to 1/3–2/3 cup finely chopped fruits such as apples, raisins, strawberries, blueberries, peaches, and bananas.

Whole Wheat Bagels: Use half whole wheat flour and half white.

English Muffins

Combine and dissolve until foamy:

- **1/4 cup water**
- **1 teaspoon sugar**
- **1 tablespoon yeast**

Combine separately:

- **1/2 cup hot milk**
- **1 cup water**
- **1 teaspoon salt**

Add yeast and:

- **2 cups flour**

Beat well. Let rise until double in bulk, then add:

- **3 tablespoons oil**
- **2 cups flour**

Beat and knead well to ensure fine texture. Let rise until double in bulk again. Roll to 3/4-inch thickness. Let set. When dough begins to rise, cut into squares with a sharp knife or into 3-inch rounds. Bake 15 minutes on a hot greased griddle, turning several times during cooking. Makes 24–30 muffins.

* See also Sourdough English Muffins (page 35).

Raised Doughnuts

Combine and soften:

- 1 tablespoon dry yeast
- 1 cup warm water or milk, about 110°F
- 1/4 cup sugar

Add:

- 1 egg
- 1/4 cup margarine
- 3–31/2 cups flour
- 1 teaspoon salt

Mix well. Knead until smooth and pliable, about 5 minutes. Place in a greased bowl. Turn once to bring greased side up. Cover with a damp cloth. Let rise 1 1/2 hours or until double in bulk. Roll out on floured surface to 1/2 inch. Cut out with doughnut cutter. Let rise, uncovered, on floured surface for 40 minutes or until double. Fry in deep hot fat, 400°F. Turn when first side is golden brown. Drain. Serve plain, glazed, or brushed with butter and rolled in a cinnamon-sugar mixture. Makes 12 doughnuts.

* *To keep doughnuts from absorbing too much fat: Add more egg or a small amount of vinegar to the batter.*

* *To keep doughnuts from burning: Add a few potato slices to the oil.*

* *To make dough easier to handle: Place it in refrigerator 1 hour before rolling out.*

* *To cut doughnuts: Use tuna can for doughnuts and a bottle cap for holes.*

Baked Irish Doughnuts: Add 1/4 cup warm potato water, 1 egg, 1–1 1/2 cups each flour and cooked, mashed potatoes. Let rise the second time on a greased cookie sheet. Bake at 425°F for 10 minutes or until golden on top. Best served warm.

Potato Doughnuts: Add 1/2 cup mashed potatoes to dough.

Doughnut Glaze

Combine:

- 1/3–1/2 cup hot water or evaporated milk
- 1 cup confectioner's sugar
- 1 teaspoon vanilla

Dip doughnuts in glaze or brush onto doughnuts.

* *Omit water and add 1/3 cup mashed, ripe berries, and heat gently in a saucepan. Gradually stir in sugar. Remove from heat and add vanilla.*

English Muffin Loaf

Combine:

- **3 cups white or wheat flour**
- **2 tablespoons dry yeast**
- **1 tablespoon sugar**
- **2 teaspoons salt**
- **1/4 teaspoon baking soda**
- **2/3 cup milk powder**

Add and beat well:

- **2 1/2 cups hot water, about 120°F**

Stir in to make a stiff batter:

- **2 1/2–3 cups flour**

Pour into two greased loaf pans sprinkled with cornmeal. Sprinkle tops with cornmeal. Cover and let rise in a warm place for 45 minutes. Bake at 400°F for 25 minutes. Remove from pans, cool, and serve toasted.

* *Add one or more of the following before adding liquid: 2 tablespoons grated orange rind, 1/2 cup nuts or raisins, cinnamon.*

* *Substitute 2 1/2 cups hot milk for milk powder and water.*

* *Substitute 1/4 cup wheat germ for 1/4 cup flour.*

Herb Bread: Add 2–6 teaspoons mixed herbs (thyme, dill seed or weed, sage, basil, tarragon, oregano, pepper, caraway seeds). Omit cornmeal. For 1 teaspoon salt, substitute any seasoned salt.

Salted Crackers

Combine and dissolve:

- **1 tablespoon dry yeast**
- **1/4 cup warm water**

Combine separately and set aside:

- **1 teaspoon baking soda**
- **2 tablespoons warm water**

Combine separately:

- **4 cups flour**
- **1 tablespoon salt**

Add:

- **1 3/4 cups water**
- **soda mixture**
- **yeast mixture**
- **2/3 cup oil or melted shortening**

Add:

- **4 cups flour**

Knead until smooth. Divide into several small portions. Roll dough to 1/8 inch. Cut into squares. Prick with a fork. Sprinkle with salt. Bake at 350°F until lightly browned. Store in airtight container.

See page 240 for International Conversion Charts

Sourdough Hints

Advantages of Sourdough: Starter can be added to almost any recipe if soda is also added. The effect will be to make the bread or cake lighter and to give it a slightly sour flavor. Sourdough has a distinct and enjoyable flavor which cannot be achieved without starter. Starter will raise bread or pancakes at any temperature above freezing. Sourdough works well in outdoor cooking or skillet baking. Sourdough starter is easily transported. Sourdough bread keeps for a satisfactory length of time.

Disadvantages of Sourdough: Sourdough starter may go bad if you do not care for it well. In a warm climate without refrigeration, you must use the starter daily or cool it by evaporation. Every time you use the starter it must be replenished in order to maintain about 1 1/2 cups of starter.

To maintain the proper sourness: If starter is very sour, use more soda than the recipe calls for, and vice versa. A double leavening action exists in sourdough recipes from the reaction of acid (directly related to the sourness) with soda, and from the yeast action in the starter. The more sour your starter, the more soda you must add. Begin by using the suggested amount, which is based on average sourness. With experience you can judge the proper amount. Don't increase or decrease it more than 50 percent.

To control the rising time: If room or outdoor temperature is low, bread will rise more slowly. Allow plenty of time for your bread to rise well before baking. To make biscuits or pancakes for breakfast, combine the starter, flour, and liquid the night before. If the nights are exceptionally cold, start earlier in the afternoon to have it rise by morning. Cover the bowl and put it in a warm place to rise.

To determine the baking time: Some sourdough breads may require more cooking time than you expect. Sourdough pancakes cook more slowly than regular pancakes.

To skillet bake sourdough breads: (See alternate cooking methods.) For skillet baking, all bread doughs should be quite moist. It may be necessary to use slightly more liquid than the recipe calls for.

To maintain starter: Maintain about 1 1/2 cups of starter. Each time you use part of the starter, replenish it with a mixture of equal amounts of milk and flour. Leave at room temperature overnight or until it again becomes full of bubbles. Cover and store in a cool place or in the refrigerator. In a warm climate where refrigeration is not available, try to use starter every day. Refrigerator starter should be used at least once a week. If you do not use it for two or three weeks, spoon out and discard half of the starter and replenish it as described. Starter may be frozen. When removing it from the freezer, allow starter to be left at room temperature for 24 hours after thawing.

To transport starter: Mix with enough flour to make a soft ball. It can then be put into a container or plastic bag of flour for transporting. When the destination is reached, add liquid to make it into the original batter. Warmth will reactivate the starter.

Sourdough Starter

Place in glass jar or crock (not metal) and set at room temperature 24 hours:

- **1 cup milk**

Stir in:

- **1 cup flour**

Leave uncovered in a warm place, for 2–5 days, until full of bubbles and sour. It may be kept near the pilot light on a gas range. If dough starts to dry out, stir in enough tepid water to bring it back to the original consistency.

* *To speed process, cover jar with cheese cloth and place outside for several hours to expose dough to wild yeast cells floating in the wind.*

* *Use warm milk. Dissolve 1 tablespoon dry yeast in milk. Then add flour, 1 tablespoon sugar, and 1/8 teaspoon salt.*

Sourdough Corn Bread

Combine in a large bowl and mix thoroughly:

- **1 cup starter**
- **1 1/2 cups cornmeal**
- **1 1/2 cups evaporated milk**
- **2 beaten eggs**
- **2 tablespoons sugar**
- **1 cup flour**

Stir in:

- **1/2 cup warm, melted butter or oil**

- **1/2 teaspoon salt**
- **3/4 teaspoon soda**

Turn into a 10-inch greased frying pan or 9x9 pan. The batter will be thin. Bake 25–30 minutes at 450°F. Serve hot.

Sourdough French Bread

Combine in a large mixing bowl:

- **1 1/2 cups warm water**
- **1 tablespoon dry yeast**

Add:

- **1 cup starter**
- **4 cups flour, whole wheat gives the best texture**
- **2 teaspoons sugar**
- **2 teaspoons salt**

Stir vigorously for about 3 minutes with a wooden spoon. Turn into large greased bowl, cover with a towel, and let rise in a warm place until double in bulk, 1 1/2–2 hours. Combine and add to make dough stiff:

- **1 1/2 teaspoon soda**
- **1 cup unsifted flour**

Add to control stickiness:

- **1 cup unsifted flour or more**

Turn dough onto a floured board and begin kneading. Knead until satiny, about 5–8 minutes. Shape into two oblong loaves or one large round loaf. Place on a lightly greased cookie sheet, cover, and put in a warm place. Let rise to nearly double in size, 1–1 1/2 hours. Just before baking, brush outside with water and

   See page 240 for International Conversion Charts

slash with a sharp knife diagonally across top. Put a shallow pan of hot water in the bottom of the oven. Bake at 400°F for 45 minutes for oblong loaves, or 50 minutes for round loaves, until crust is medium dark brown.

* *Omit yeast. Leave at room temperature 18 hours or until doubled in size for first rising.*

* *Substitute 1/2 cup raw wheat germ for 1/2 cup (120 ml) flour.*

Sourdough English Muffins

Combine in bowl, cover loosely, and set at room temperature overnight:

- **1/2 cup starter**
- **1 cup milk**
- **2 cups flour**

Combine separately, then add to dough and mix thoroughly:

- **1 tablespoon sugar**
- **3/4 teaspoon salt**
- **1/2 teaspoon soda**
- **1/2 cup flour**

Turn dough out onto floured board. Knead 2–3 minutes or until no longer sticky. Add flour if necessary. Roll out 3/4 inch thick. Cut with cutter or glass. Place 1 inch apart on cookie sheet sprinkled with cornmeal. Sprinkle cornmeal on top, about 3 tablespoons in all. Cover and set aside to rise, about 45 minutes. Fry 8–10 minutes per side. Split and toast. Makes 12 muffins. Cook without oil in teflon pan.

Sourdough Biscuits: Substitute 1 teaspoon baking powder for soda. Roll out dough to 1/2 inch. Cut out biscuits with a cutter. Let rise on a greased baking sheet 1/2 hour. Bake at 375°F for 30–35 minutes.

Sourdough Cinnamon Rolls: Add 1 egg, 2 tablespoons sugar, and 1/4 cup soft butter after dough has set overnight. Then add 1 cup flour and 1 teaspoon baking powder. After kneading, roll out to 8x16 inches. Brush with 2 tablespoons butter. Sprinkle with 1/4 cup brown sugar, 1 1/2 teaspoons cinnamon, and 1/4 cup raisins, optional. Roll up dough. Cut 1 1/2 inches thick. Place in 9x9 greased pan. Cover and let rise in a warm place for about 1 hour. Bake at 375°F for 30–35 minutes.

Sourdough Cookies

Combine and set aside for 2 hours:

- 1/2 cup starter
- 1 1/2 cups flour

Meanwhile, cream:

- 1 cup butter or margarine
- 1 1/4 cups dark brown sugar

Add:

- 1 beaten egg

Combine separately and add:

- 1/2 cup flour
- 1/2 teaspoon soda
- 1/2 teaspoon salt

Stir in:

- 3 cups corn flakes, oats, or other cereal, crushed

Blend both mixtures together. Drop batter from a teaspoon onto a greased cookie sheet, 2 inches apart. Bake at 375°F for 15 minutes.

* *Add any of the following: 1/2–1 cup peanut butter, 1/2–3/4 cup nuts, 3/4 cup shredded coconut.*

Sourdough Muffins

Stir only enough to blend:

- 1/2 cup whole wheat flour
- 1 1/2 cups white flour
- 1/2 cup shortening
- 1/2 cup evaporated milk
- 1 egg
- 1 cup raisins
- 1 teaspoon salt
- 1 teaspoon soda
- starter to make mixture moist and hold together as muffins

Bake in greased muffin pans at 375°F for 30–35 minutes. Test before taking them out, because they bake slower than ordinary muffins.

See page 240 for International Conversion Charts

Quick Sourdough Biscuits

Mix until blended to make kneadable dough:

- **1 cup starter**
- **1/4 teaspoon soda**
- **1/2 teaspoon salt, optional**
- **1 egg**
- **1 tablespoon oil or melted shortening**
- **flour to make a stiff dough**

Knead until smooth. Roll and cut into biscuit-sized pieces. Let rise on greased cookie sheet an hour or more, if possible. Bake at 350°F for 15–20 minutes or until golden brown. Makes 10–12 biscuits.

Sourdough Rolls: Omit egg. Use 1/4 cup starter. Add 1/4 cup each powdered milk and water or 1/3 cup evaporated milk.

Crisp Sourdough Waffles

Combine, cover, and set in a warm place, 85°F and leave overnight:

- **3/4 cup sourdough starter**
- **1 1/2 cups warm water, about 110°F**
- **1 3/4 cups flour, unsifted**

In the morning, combine and add to sourdough mixture:

- **2 egg yolks (reserve whites)**
- **1/4 cup oil or melted butter**

Combine and set aside:

- **3/4 teaspoon salt**
- **3/4 teaspoon soda**
- **1 1/2 tablespoons sugar**

Gently fold in:

- **2 egg whites, beaten until stiff, but still moist**

Stir soda mixture into batter. Bake in a preheated waffle iron until well browned. Serve with syrup, fruit preserves, or whipped butter. Makes 4 large waffles.

* *Substitute half whole wheat flour, buck wheat flour, or cornmeal for flour.*

Sourdough Pancakes: Omit oil. Do not separate eggs. Mix well but don't beat. Cook in a greased skillet over medium heat. They take longer to cook than regular pancakes. Makes 12 pancakes.

See page 240 for International Conversion Charts

Dairy Product Hints

Eggs

To keep hard-cooked egg yolks from crumbling when slicing: Wet the knife between each cut.

To increase the stability of egg whites: Add cream of tartar or sugar.

To keep egg whites from collapsing when heated: Do not overbeat.

To make fluffier omelets: Add a pinch of cornstarch before beating.

To test eggs for freshness: Put each egg against a light. If the light shines through, the egg is good; if not, discard. Or shake egg. A bad egg will have a thumping sound.

To wrap eggs for transporting: Wrap corn husks or leaves around eggs, shape, and tie the ends with strips of husk.

To store eggs: Store on end, small end down, in dry bran or oatmeal. Keep in a cool place or refrigerator for up to 3 weeks.

Cheese

To preserve cheese: Melt some wax in a small can and spread on the cut end of the cheese each time a piece is cut off. It will last for at least six months. Or wrap individual pieces in cloth, sew up, and dip into hot paraffin. Or wrap cheese in a cloth dampened with vinegar and store in a cool place. Or spread cut surface with thin coat of butter after it is used.

To store cottage cheese: Place carton upside down to keep twice as long.

Margarine

To store margarine: Store for months in a large can arranged so that air can circulate between layers of wrapped cubes. Or buy cans of margarine.

To add flavor: Combine margarine or butter with shortening.

Milk

To use powdered milk in cooking: Mix powdered milk with dry ingredients and add the required amount of water.

To keep powdered milk from curdling: When boiled with brown sugar or panela add a small pinch of soda.

To make coffee cream from powdered or evaporated milk: Mix powdered milk with half the amount of water, or combine reconstituted powdered milk with evaporated milk.

To make milk from evaporated milk: Combine equal amounts of evaporated milk and water.

To keep scalding milk from scorching: Rinse pan with hot water first.

To use sweetened condensed milk: It does not sugar when heated, or form ice crystals in frozen desserts, and it thickens without heat when combined with lemon, orange, pineapple, or apple juice.

Hard-Boiled Eggs

Place in saucepan:

- **eggs, as many as desired**
- **water to cover eggs**
- **2 tablespoons vinegar or salt, keeps eggs from cracking**

Bring to a boil. Reduce heat and boil 12 minutes. Immerse immediately in cold water and peel.

* *If egg yolks have a grayish color, it means they have been overcooked.*

* *To save energy: Bring to boil, cover, turn off heat, set 15–20 minutes.*

Soft-Boiled Eggs: Boil 4–6 minutes. Remove egg from shell by cutting egg in half and scooping out egg into a dish.

Omelet

Heat in skillet and tilt pan to coat the sides:

- **1 tablespoon butter or margarine**

Beat together and pour into skillet:

- **2 eggs**
- **1 tablespoon water**
- **1/8 teaspoon each salt and pepper**

Cook over medium heat. Lift edges as eggs begin to set so uncooked egg will flow underneath. When set, spoon filling over omelet. Fold and top with filling. Serves 1.

For fluffier omelet: Beat egg whites separately and fold in.

Omelet Fillings: Use any combination of the following for filling:

- **1/4 cup shredded cheese**
- **2 tablespoons yogurt or sour cream**
- **1/3 cup sliced, fried vegetables: zucchini, mushrooms, onions, potatoes, carrots, celery, green peppers, bean sprouts**
- **1/3 cup cooked bacon, chopped ham, tuna, or sausage**

Egg Strips: Omit water. Cook as an omelet. When set, cut into strips. Serve with a cream sauce, or mix with oriental noodles or rice dishes, or sprinkle on top of a vegetable dish or salad.

Frittata: Fry onions and vegetables in skillet. May add 1/2–1 teaspoon each parsley, chives, and basil. Distribute onion mixture over bottom of pan. Add egg mixture. Cook covered on low until set.

See page 240 for International Conversion Charts

Scrambled Eggs: Add any of the Omelet Fillings to the egg mixture. Stir eggs frequently while cooking instead of letting set.

Scrambled Eggs and Tortillas: Cut 1–2 tortillas in eighths and fry in oil. Add to egg mixture and scramble. Add 1–2 tablespoons catsup, if desired, and any of the Omelet Fillings.

Easy Poached Eggs

Bring almost to boil in lightly greased skillet:

- water, about 1–inch deep
- 1/4 teaspoon salt

Break into cup, 1 at a time:

- eggs

Lower cup until close to surface of water and quickly slip egg into water. Repeat, arranging eggs side by side. Don't crowd. Cover skillet. Simmer until whites are solid, yolks of desired firmness. When eggs are done, slip slotted spoon or pancake turner under each. Lift out of water and tilt slightly against side of skillet to drain. To hold eggs together while poaching, add a few drops of vinegar or lemon juice to the cooking water.

Ranch-Style Eggs: Poach eggs in the following sauce: Fry 1 diced onion in 2 tablespoons cooking oil in skillet. Add 2 large cloves garlic, minced; 2 large diced tomatoes or 1 cup tomato sauce or juice; 1/4 teaspoon each salt and sugar, optional,; 1/2 teaspoon oregano, optional; and 1–2 chopped chilies, optional. Carefully spoon a little of the sauce over the eggs. Cover skillet. Simmer until eggs are of desired doneness.

Fried Eggs

Break gently into hot grease and fry until of desired doneness:

- eggs

Eggs Over: Cook 2–3 minutes until eggs are set on bottom. Carefully turn eggs and cook to desired doneness.

Sunny-Side-Up Eggs: Add 1 tablespoon water to pan. Cover and cook.

Skillet Breakfast

Fry in skillet until crisp and remove:

- 4 slices bacon, cut in half

Add to drippings in pan and cook until golden brown:

- 2 cups diced cooked potatoes

Outline potatoes into 4 wedges with bacon slices. Top wedges with:

- 4 eggs
- salt and pepper

Cover skillet and cook until eggs are set. Cut into 4 pie-shaped servings.

Baked Eggs

Combine in a pan and stir until smooth:

- **2 tablespoons butter or margarine**
- **2 tablespoons flour**
- **dash pepper**
- **1/2 teaspoon salt**
- **1 teaspoon prepared mustard**

Stir in and cook, stirring until smooth and thickened:

- **1 cup milk**

Add and stir until melted:

- **1 cup grated cheddar cheese**

Cover bottom of greased 9x9 baking dish with half of the cheese sauce. Carefully break, side by side, on cheese sauce:

- **6 eggs**

Cover with remaining sauce. Bake at 325°F for 20–25 minutes or until eggs are as cooked as desired. Serve from dish or on buttered toast. Serves 3–6.

* *Omit cheese sauce and sprinkle cheese in greased baking dish. Combine and add to dish 8 beaten eggs, salt, pepper, and 3/4 cup evaporated milk. Top with 1/2 cup grated cheese and bake.*

Deviled Eggs

Cover with water and boil 15 minutes:

- **6 eggs**

Put in cold water immediately to prevent darkening of the yolks. Peel and cut in half. Remove yolks and mash. Add to the yolks:

- **1/2 teaspoon salt**
- **pepper to taste**
- **1/2 teaspoon dry or prepared mustard**
- **2–3 tablespoons salad dressing, cream, or vinegar**

Fill whites with the mixture. Sprinkle with paprika, if desired.

* *Add any of the following to yolks: Cooked ham, chicken, tuna, bacon, parsley, pickle, Worcestershire sauce, browned onions, mushrooms, grated cheese, pimentos, chives, or celery.*

Picnic Eggs: Press deviled egg halves together and wrap each egg in square of waxed paper, twist ends to keep the halves in place.

See page 240 for International Conversion Charts

Bread and Cheese Soufflé

Combine:

- 3 cups bread crumbs
- 1 cup milk

Add:

- 2 eggs, beaten
- salt and pepper to taste

Place in a 9x9 baking dish and top with:

- 1 cup grated cheese

Bake at 450°F for 15 minutes.

Cheese Soufflé

Combine in saucepan and cook until smooth:

- 1/4 cup butter or margarine, melted
- 1/4 cup flour
- 1/4 teaspoon salt
- 1/8 teaspoon pepper

Add, boil, and stir 1 minute:

- 1 cup milk

Remove from heat and add:

- 1 tablespoon grated onion
- 1 teaspoon salt
- 1/8 teaspoon nutmeg
- 3 egg yolks, beaten
- 1 cup cheese, grated
- 1/4 teaspoon dry mustard, optional

Combine separately and beat until stiff:

- 3 egg whites
- 1/4 teaspoon cream of tartar, optional

Fold egg whites into sauce. Pour into greased 6 cup casserole dish. Set casserole dish in a pan of hot water about 1-inch deep. Bake at 350°F for 50–60 minutes until knife inserted half way between edge and center comes out clean. Serve immediately. Serves 4–6 people.

* *Add any of the following: 2 cups spinach or broccoli, cooked, drained, and chopped; 1/2–1 cup ham, chicken, tuna, sausage, or crisp crumbled bacon cooked and chopped, 2–4 cups cooked, drained corn. Omit cheese if desired.*

Tuna Soufflé: Omit white sauce and nutmeg. Add 1 cup tuna, 1/2 teaspoon paprika, and 1 teaspoon lemon juice. Soak 1 cup bread crumbs in 3/4 cup milk. Combine all ingredients except egg whites. Fold in beaten egg whites.

High Hat Tuna Soufflé

Dissolve until foamy:

- 1/4 cup warm water
- 1 tablespoon yeast

Add lukewarm mixture of:

- 1/2 cup scalded milk
- 1/4 cup shortening, melted
- 2 tablespoons sugar
- 1 teaspoon salt

Add:

- 2 egg yolks, reserve whites
- 1 cup flour

Beat until smooth, cover, and allow to rise until double in bulk.

In a casserole dish, combine:

- 1 1/4 cups cream of celery soup or medium white sauce
- 1 teaspoon celery salt, optional
- 1 cup tuna, drained
- 1 teaspoon onion, grated
- 1 tablespoon chopped pimento, optional

Beat until stiff and fold into risen batter:

- 2 egg whites

Top creamed tuna with batter and bake at 400°F for 40–50 minutes.

* *For tuna, substitute cooked sausage, ground beef, ham, bacon, chicken, broccoli, or spinach.*

Quiche

Prepare:

- 1 unbaked 9-inch pie crust

Layer any combination of the following in the pie crust:

- 1/2–1 cup sliced mushrooms, cooked
- 1/2 cup green peppers, diced
- 1/2 cup green onions, chopped
- 1 cup chopped and cooked bacon, ham, shrimp, crab, sausage, hamburger, tuna, zucchini, or spinach
- 1 cup cheese, grated

Beat together and pour into crust:

- 2–3 eggs
- 1 1/2–2 cups light cream, evaporated milk, or milk
- 1/2 teaspoon salt
- dash of pepper

Bake at 375°F for 45–50 minutes, until knife inserted in center comes out clean. Cool 5 minutes before serving.

* *Substitute for the light cream: yogurt, sour cream, whipping cream, or 1 1/4 cups cream of mushroom or chicken soup.*

Impossible Quiche: Omit crust. Grease 9–inch pie plate. Add 3/4 cup Master Mix (see page 9) to milk mixture. This forms its own crust. Or add 1/3 cup flour and 1 tablespoon oil.

See page 240 for International Conversion Charts

Evaporated Milk

Combine:

- **2 cups water**
- **1 cup milk powder**

* *To whip evaporated milk: Chill milk, bowl, and beater, then whip. To stiffen the whipped milk, add 2 tablespoons lemon juice for every cup of milk. Continue whipping long enough to blend juice.*

Reconstituted Powdered Milk

Combine and beat with a wire whip or rotary beater to make a smooth paste:

- **1 cup cool or lukewarm water**
- **1 cup powdered milk**

Gradually add while beating vigorously:

- **3 cups cold water**

* *Add for taste: 1/2 teaspoon vanilla and a dash of salt.*

Cottage Cheese

Heat to simmering over low heat:

- **8 cups milk**

Add a little at a time until milk curdles and separates:

- **vinegar, lime, or lemon juice**

Remove from heat and strain with cheese cloth or a tea towel (not terry cloth). Rinse. Add salt to taste and cream to consistency, if desired. Can be pressed into a "brick" or left crumbly. Will not dissolve or melt. If you begin with sour milk, you'll have a more sour taste.

* *Add any of the following: Salad dressing, parsley, nuts, pimento, or green pepper.*

Cream Cheese Substitute: Add cream and mix thoroughly.

Powdered Milk Cottage Cheese: Combine 2 cups water to each 1 cup powdered milk to make 3/4 cup (180 ml) cheese.

Sour Cream Substitute: Blend cottage cheese and add chives or fruit.

Ricotta Cheese: Just scald milk 150°F. Remove from heat. Add 1/4 cup lemon juice. Let mixture stand 2–12 hours outside refrigerator. Drain mixture in colander with 2 thicknesses of cheese cloth or a tea towel over a bowl. Stir occasionally so liquid goes through cloth. Refrigerate the drained liquid and use to make yogurt or in baking.

Cultured Buttermilk

Combine and leave overnight in warm place about 85°F:

- **4 cups milk**
- **1/4–1/2 cup previously cultured buttermilk**

Refrigerate as soon as milk reaches the desired level of acidity.

Sour Cream

Combine:

- **1 cup pasteurized cream**
- **1 1/2 cups pasteurized whole milk**
- **1/2 cup cultured buttermilk**

Stand 12–24 hours until thick enough to cling to spoon, then refrigerate.

Sweetened Condensed Milk

Blend in blender:

- **1 cup dry powdered milk**
- **2/3 cup sugar**
- **1/3 cup boiling water**
- **3 tablespoons melted margarine**

See page 240 for International Conversion Charts

Yogurt

Mix together thoroughly:

- **3 cups powdered milk**
- **4 cups cold water**

Add:

- **2 cups very hot water**
- **1/2–3/4 cup plain yogurt**

Place in warm, sterile jars, in pre-warmed oven at 200°F. Turn oven off and leave 3–6 hours, with pilot or light bulb on. Consistency should be like a custard. Refrigerate. Keep 3/4 cup yogurt as a starter for the next batch.

Other ways to let yogurt set: Place jar in a pot of lukewarm water in oven. Or wrap the jars in a thick blanket or 8 layers of thick bath towels. Or wrap jars in bath towels and put on a heating pad set on low.

Flavor yogurt with: jams, vanilla, honey, pre-sweetened drink mixes, nuts, granola, chopped fruits.

Use in place of sour cream or buttermilk: Add close to the end of the cooking time as yogurt separates when boiled. To prevent this separation when used in cooking, add 1 tablespoon cornstarch or whole wheat flour per 4 cups of yogurt .

Use as a tenderizer: Marinate meat or poultry overnight in plain yogurt.

Yogurt is easier to digest than other dairy products.

Eat yogurt after taking antibiotics: Some antibiotics kill off the beneficial intestinal bacteria. Yogurt replenishes this important bacteria.

Fresh Milk Yogurt: Heat milk to very warm, 115°F. Add starter.

Curdled Yogurt: Use it as you would soured yogurt. Yogurt may curdle if your water is too hot. It should not be fully boiling.

Soured Yogurt: If yogurt becomes sour, use it to make pancakes or cakes. Add a small amount of soured yogurt to begin a new batch and it will make a new creamy yogurt (the bacillus is still alive).

Yogurt Cheese: Strain yogurt in colander lined with cheese cloth or tea towel. Set over a bowl to drain for a few hours. Use in place of cream cheese or mix with mayonnaise or sour cream.

Cereal Hints

To crisp stale cereal: Place on baking sheets at 250°F for 10–15 minutes.

To store grains, nuts, and seeds: Place in dry, sealed containers. If they become moldy, discard them as they contain toxins.

To thicken a hot corn or wheat cereal: Add a little oatmeal and cook a few more minutes.

To make gruel for a baby or an invalid: Cook cereal twice as long and in 3 times the amount of water or milk.

To avoid gumming of cereal: Add cereal slowly to boiling water, stir constantly for the first 3 minutes, then place over boiling water and do not stir for the last few minutes of the cooking time.

To avoid lumps when reheating grains: Place it over boiling water and allow to heat thoroughly before stirring.

To increase food value of cereal: In the last few minutes of cooking, fold in 3 tablespoons dry skim milk and 2 teaspoons nutritional yeast or wheat germ.

To add variety to cereals: Add dates, figs, raisins, or cooked dried fruits, or serve with cold sliced fruits, cinnamon sugar mixture, sugar and cream, maple syrup, jam, or preserves.

To keep rice from sticking to the pan: Stir 1 tablespoon butter or margarine into the boiling water.

Cereal Cooking Chart

1 cup cereal and 1/2 tsp. salt	Water	Minutes at 5 lbs Pressure	Minutes Stove Top
Rice—brown	3 C	15–25	40–50
Rice—white	2 C	10	25–30
Barley, buckwheat, bulgur, cracked wheat, millet: soak 4–8 hrs.	3–4 C	20–30	60
Cornmeal, farina, hominy, oatmeal, cream of wheat, grits	2–3 C	3–5	5–20

See page 240 for International Conversion Charts

Chinese Porridge

Combine in a saucepan and bring to boil:

- 1 cup white rice
- 3 cups chicken broth
- 1/2 cup chopped chicken
- 1 teaspoon salt

Add:

- 1 inch ginger, cut into long thin threads

Porridge is ready when rice is soft with mushy appearance. Add water if needed. According to Asian culture, this is served for breakfast. Serves 6.

Grape Nuts

Combine:

- 3 1/2 cups graham or wheat flour
- 1 teaspoon salt
- 1 teaspoon soda

Add and mix thoroughly:

- 1 cup brown sugar or 3/4 cup syrup

Add and beat until smooth:

- 2 cups buttermilk or sour milk

Spread dough 1/4 inch thick on flat, greased pans. Bake at 375°F for 15 minutes or until crisp and a golden brown. Cool thoroughly. Grind coarsely in food chopper. Store in airtight container. May crisp in oven just before serving.

* *May be used as a topping for soups, salads, casseroles, and desserts.*

Granola

Granola can be made according to individual taste and the ingredients on hand. The only basic ingredients needed are oats, oil, and sweetener. The proportions depend on individual taste and how "healthy" you want it. Here is a basic recipe with many options.

Combine in large bowl 7–8 cups dry ingredients:

- 3–6 cups oatmeal
- 1/4–1/2 cup each of any of the following: wheat germ, whole wheat flour, bran, cornmeal, coconut, soy flour, milk powder, chopped nuts, sunflower seeds, sesame seeds
- 1–1 1/2 teaspoons spices: cinnamon, nutmeg, or allspice

Combine separately and add to dry ingredients:

- 1/2–3/4 cup oil, margarine, or butter, melted
- 1/2–3/4 cup honey, corn syrup, or brown sugar
- 1 teaspoon vanilla or other flavoring

Bake at 350°F for 30–45 minutes on large baking sheets until golden brown. Stir occasionally. After taking granola from oven, add any of the following, if desired:

- raisins, chopped dates, or any dried chopped fruits

Store in airtight containers.

* *Add any of following with wet ingredients: 1/4 cup orange juice, 1/2–1 cup peanut butter, 1/2 teaspoon maple flavoring.*

Granola bars: Make granola and add 1 beaten egg and 1/3 cup milk. Press granola into two well-greased 10x15–inch cookie sheets. Bake at 325°F until golden brown. Cut into bars immediately. Remove from pans when cool. Increase sweetener if desired.

Cornmeal Mush

Combine:

- 1 cup cornmeal
- 1/2–1 teaspoon salt
- 1 cup water

Stir into:

- 3 cups boiling water
- Cook, stirring constantly, until mixture thickens and boils. Cover and continue cooking over low heat for 10 minutes.

Millet Porridge: Substitute millet flour for cornmeal. Add 1 cup boiling water, 1/2 cup each powdered milk and sugar, and cinnamon or nutmeg to taste.

See page 240 for International Conversion Charts

Baked Oatmeal

Combine:

- 1/2 cup oil
- 1/2–3/4 cup white or brown sugar
- 2 eggs, beaten

Add:

- 3 cups uncooked oatmeal
- 1 1/2 teaspoon baking powder
- 1 teaspoon salt
- 1 cup milk

Pour into greased 9x9 pan and bake at 350°F for 35–40 minutes. Serve with warm milk, sugar, and cinnamon. Serves 6.

Oatmeal Cereal

Combine, stirring until blended:

- 2 cups water, boiling
- 1 cup oatmeal
- 1/2 teaspoon salt

Return to boiling point, cover, and boil for 3 minutes.

* *Substitute milk for water and simmer. Add 1 cup water, 1/2 cup wheat germ, and 1/4 cup raisins. When cooked stir in 2 tablespoons instant milk powder.*

* *To use rolled oats like instant oatmeal: Put in a bowl with raisins and milk powder and add boiling water. Let it sit for a minute and serve.*

Three Grain Cereal: Use 1/3 cup each cracked wheat, oatmeal, and bran. Double or triple and keep refrigerated. Reheat desired amount.

Wheat Cereal: Substitute bulgur or cracked wheat. Cook until tender.

Rice Cereal

Boil slowly 30 minutes stirring frequently:

- **4 cups milk**
- **1 cup rice**
- **1/2 teaspoon salt**
- **1/4 cup sugar, optional**
- **1 cinnamon stick or 1/2 teaspoon ground cinnamon**

For a thinner cereal (or pudding) use less rice or add more milk.

* *Use leftover cooked rice and add milk, sugar, and cinnamon stick.*

Desserts

See page 114 for this
Pumpkin Pie recipe.

Resurrection Cheesecake

Let me tell you about the time I made cheesecake. It took me three days. I made my own graham crackers for the graham cracker crust. I made the butter for the crust with cream I had skimmed from milk I had pasteurized myself. I made my own cream cheese. I started with powdered milk mixed with drinking water (boiled and filtered). Then I cultured it into yogurt. The third step was to drain it in a tea towel to make the cream cheese. I used eggs from my daughter's chickens. I used sugar bought from a wholesaler sixty miles away because the local sugar was mixed with sand. I baked the cheesecake with propane gas also brought from sixty miles away. The cheesecake was delicious. It was six inches across. It was a lot of work, but it was possible. Thinking back, I recognize how fortunate I was compared to the local women who would have had to milk a cow and pound grain that they had raised themselves into flour. And they had no oven to bake a cheesecake—they cook over wood fires. Something to think about next time we buy cheesecake.

From the kitchen of: —Juanita Matthews

Cake and Frosting Hints

* *For shortening and sugar hints, see page 85.*

Fill cake pan: Fill from 1/2–2/3 full except for fruit cakes which do not rise much. These may be filled 3/4 full.

To improve the taste of an inexpensive cake mix: Add 1 tablespoon of butter to the batter.

For a moister cake: Substitute mayonnaise for shortening.

To make cupcakes: Grease muffin tins and fill 1/2 to 2/3 full.

To use brown sugar in cakes: Add 1/2 teaspoon baking soda for each cup of brown sugar since brown sugar may cause a cake to fall flat because of its acidity.

To keep cooked frosting from sugaring: Add a pinch of cream of tartar before cooking.

To thicken cooked frosting: Beat it in the top of a double boiler. To keep frosting from hardening before spreading: Beat in a few drops of boiling water or lemon juice.

To substitute for boxed cake mix: Combine 2 cups flour, 1 1/2 cups sugar, 3 1/2 teaspoons baking powder, and 1 teaspoon salt. Cut in 1/2 cup hard butter.

Cake Pan Sizes

Recipes requiring from 1–1 3/4 cups flour: Use 7x10 inch, 9x9 inch, or 8x8 inch pan, or two 8-inch layers.

Recipes requiring from 2–3 cups flour: Use 9x13 inch or 10x12 inch pan, or two 9-inch layers.

Recipes requiring from 3 1/2–4 1/2 cups flour or recipes requiring from 2 1/2–3 1/2 cups flour and 6 or more egg whites: Use 10x14 inch pan or three 9-inch layers.

Steamed Cake

Put cake batter into a greased, metal mixing bowl or coffee can. Fill only 2/3 full. Cover with foil or something that can stand the heat. Place a rack in bottom of a large pan (may use a metal jar lid or an inverted pie tin). Put bowl with batter on rack and fill pan with 2–3 inches of boiling water. Put lid on pan. After the water comes to a boil, let simmer for the longest time called for by the recipe. Then test with a knife (or skewer). Cook longer as needed.

* *Any cake can be steamed in a pan on top of the stove or in a pressure cooker without the weight. It comes out light and moist.*

* *See also Alternate Cooking Methods: Skillet Cooking, page 242.*

Date Loaf Cake

Combine and let cool:

- **1/2 cup boiling water**
- **1/2 teaspoon soda**
- **1 cup dates, cut in pieces**
- **1 cup raisins**
- **1 cup sugar**
- **1/2 cup butter**

Add:

- **1 egg, beaten**

Stir in:

- **1/2 teaspoon salt**
- **1 1/2 cups flour**
- **1/2 cup chopped walnuts, optional**

Pour into a greased 9x9 pan and bake at 325°F for 1 hour or longer. This cake keeps well. Sprinkle with powdered sugar, if desired.

* *Increase water to 1 cup and simmer date mixture for 2 minutes.*

* *Substitute any chopped, dried fruit for dates and raisins.*

Fruit Cake: Add 1 cup mixed fruit and peel, dried fruit, or fruit topping. Add 1 teaspoon cinnamon and 1/2 teaspoon cloves.

Applesauce Cake

Combine:

- **1/3 cup oil**
- **1 cup sugar**
- **1 egg, optional**
- **1 cup unsweetened applesauce**

Add and mix thoroughly:

- **2 cups flour**
- **1 teaspoon soda**
- **1 teaspoon cinnamon**
- **1/4–1/2 teaspoon cloves or nutmeg**
- **1/4 teaspoon salt**
- **1/2–1 cup raisins or nuts, optional**

Bake in greased, floured 9x13 pan at 350°F 40 minutes.

* *Papaya, squash, green mango puree, or boiled mashed cooking bananas may be substituted for applesauce.*

Master Mix Applesauce Cake: Substitute 3 cups Master Mix, see page 9, for the flour, soda, and salt. Do not omit the egg.

Orange Cake: Omit applesauce and spices. Add 1 teaspoon baking powder, 1 cup milk, and grated peel from 1 large orange. Mix 2/3 cup each sugar and orange juice and pour over hot cooked cake.

See page 240 for International Conversion Charts

Apple Cake

Combine:

- **2 eggs, beaten**
- **2 cups diced, raw apples**

Add and mix:

- **2 cups sugar**
- **2 teaspoons cinnamon**
- **1/2 cup oil**

Add and mix well:

- **1 cup nuts, optional**
- **2 cups flour**
- **2 teaspoons soda**
- **1 teaspoon salt**
- **2 teaspoons vanilla**

Bake in a greased 9x13 pan 40–45 minutes at 350°F. Top with Lemon Cream Cheese Frosting or Apple Cake Topping.

Bundt-Pan Apple Cake: Add 1 cup each apples and flour and 1/2 cup oil. Bake in greased bundt pan at 350°F for 50–60 minutes. Top with whipped cream or powdered sugar.

Banana Cake

Combine and beat:

- **1/4 cup oil**
- **1 cup sugar**
- **1–2 eggs, slightly beaten**

Add:

- **1 cup mashed bananas**
- **1 teaspoon vanilla or lemon extract**

Combine separately:

- **1 1/4 cups flour**
- **1/2 teaspoon soda, or 1 teaspoon if sour milk is used**
- **1/4 teaspoon salt**

Add alternately to the first mixture:

- **1/2 cup milk, sweet or sour**

Beat well. Pour into well-greased 9x9 pan. Bake at 350°F for 20–30 minutes.

* *Add any of the following: 1 tablespoon lemon juice, 1/8 teaspoon cloves, or 1 1/2 teaspoons nutmeg.*

Master Mix Banana Cake: Replace oil, flour, soda, salt, and milk with 2 cups Master Mix (page 9) and 1/4 cup water.

Carrot Cake

Combine:

- **2 cups sugar**
- **1 cup oil**

Beat in, one at a time:

- **4 large eggs**

Combine separately, add, and mix well:

- **2 cups flour**
- **2 teaspoons baking powder**
- **2 teaspoons baking soda**
- **2 teaspoons cinnamon**
- **1 teaspoon salt**

Add and mix well:

- **3 cups grated carrots, zucchini, beets, or a combination**
- **1 cup nuts, optional**

Bake in greased and floured 9x13 pan at 350°F for 45 minutes. Turn off oven. Leave in oven for 5 more minutes.

* *To vary, use 1 cup crushed, drained pineapple for 1 cup carrots.*

Sponge Cake

Heat to just below boiling and set aside:

- **1 cup milk**
- **2 tablespoons oil or butter**

Beat until thick, 4–6 minutes on high speed:

- **4 large eggs**

Add:

- **2 cups sugar**

Combine and add:

- **2 1/2 cups flour**
- **2 teaspoons baking powder**
- **1/2–3/4 teaspoon salt**

Add and blend in slowly:

- **1 teaspoon vanilla**
- **heated milk and butter mixture**

Immediately pour into an oiled tube pan and bake 30–40 minutes at 350°F. Serve with sliced fresh fruit and whipped cream or jam.

* *In place of hot milk add 1/4 cup powdered milk and 1 cup boiling water with oil. Add 1/2 teaspoon almond extract.*

See page 240 for International Conversion Charts

One Egg Cake

Combine:

- 1/4 cup oil
- 1/2 cup sugar
- 1 egg, beaten

Combine separately:

- 1 1/2 cups flour
- 2 teaspoons baking powder
- 1/4 teaspoon salt

Mix dry ingredients alternately into first mixture with:

- 1/2 cup milk
- 1/2 teaspoon vanilla

Beat until mixed well. Place in greased and floured 9x9 pan and bake at 350°F for 25 minutes.

Cupcakes: Bake at 375°F for 20–25 minutes.

Yogurt Cake: Substitute plain or flavored yogurt for milk.

Eggless Spice Cake

Combine:

- 1/2 cup shortening
- 1 cup sugar
- 1 tablespoon molasses or brown sugar syrup, optional

Sift together:

- 2 cups flour
- 1/2 teaspoon each salt and baking soda
- 1 teaspoon each baking powder and cinnamon
- 1 teaspoon allspice or nutmeg, optional
- 1/4 teaspoon cloves, optional

Add dry ingredients alternately with:

- 1 cup sour milk

Beat and add:

- 1 cup raisins
- 1/2 cup nuts, optional

Pour into greased loaf pan or 9x13 pan. Bake at 350°F for 40–45 minutes.

Eggless Carrot Spice Cake: Add 1 1/2 cups grated carrots. Decrease shortening to 1/4 cup. Increase sugar to 1 1/3 cups and soda to 2 teaspoons. Add 1 1/3 cups water. Omit baking powder and sour milk. Boil carrots, shortening, sugar, and water slowly for 5 minutes. Cool and add remaining ingredients.

Master Mix Spice Cake: Use 2 cups Master Mix (page 9) and 2/3 cup water for shortening, flour, salt, baking powder, soda, and milk. Add 1 egg.

Angel Food Cake

Combine:

- **5 egg yolks, beaten**
- **1/2 cup cold water**
- **1 teaspoon vanilla**

Add gradually:

- **1 1/2 cups sugar**

Sift together 5 times, then add gradually:

- **1 1/2 cups flour**
- **1/2 teaspoon baking powder**
- **1/4 teaspoon salt**

Beat until stiff and fold in gently:

- **5 egg whites**
- **3/4 teaspoon cream of tartar**

Bake in ungreased tube or loaf pan at 325°F for 1 hour.

Master Mix Cake

Combine:

- **2 cups Master Mix or Cake Mix (page 9)**
- **3/4 cup sugar, omit sugar if using Cake Mix**

Add and beat until well mixed:

- **1/2 cup milk**
- **1 teaspoon vanilla**
- **1 egg, beaten**

Bake in greased 9x9 pan at 350°F for 30 minutes.

- **Add 1/4–1/2 cup raisins or chopped nuts.**

Chocolate Cake: Omit milk, add 5 tablespoons cocoa, 3 tablespoons oil, 2/3 cup water, and increase sugar to 1 cup.

Picnic Cake: Omit milk. Add 1/2 cup chopped dates, 1/2 teaspoon baking soda, and 3/4 cup boiling water. Set aside to cool. Beat mix, egg, vanilla, and 1 teaspoon cinnamon 4–5 minutes. Add date mixture, beat 2 more minutes, and pour into pan. Top with 1/3 cup each brown sugar, nuts, and chocolate chips.

Pineapple Upside-Down Cake: Combine and spread in bottom of pan 3 tablespoons margarine and 1/2 cup brown sugar. Add pineapple slices. Pour cake batter on top. Invert baked cake on platter.

Pound Cake: Add 1/4 cup each vanilla pudding and oil, and 1 egg. Bake at 375°F in a greased and floured loaf pan for 30–40 minutes.

Spice Cake: Add 1/2 teaspoon each nutmeg and cinnamon and 1/4 teaspoon cloves.

White Cake: Omit egg, add 2 egg whites beaten 2–4 minutes.

See page 240 for International Conversion Charts

Dessert Cake

Layer in a greased 9x9 pan:

- 2 cups chopped fruit with juice or pie filling
- 2 cups Cake Mix (page 9)

Drizzle with:

- 1/2 cup melted butter or margarine

Top with:

- 1/2–1 cup coconut, optional
- 1/2–1 cup chopped nuts, optional

Bake at 350°F for 45 minutes.

Philly Christmas Cake

Sprinkle into a greased 9x9 pan or a tube pan:

- 1/2 cup finely chopped nuts

Combine separately:

- 1 cup cream cheese
- 1 cup margarine
- 1 1/2 cups white sugar
- 1 1/2 teaspoons vanilla

Add and mix well:

- 4 eggs, beaten

Gradually add:

- 2 cups flour
- 1 1/2 teaspoons baking powder

Combine separately and then fold into batter:

- 1/4 cup flour
- 1 cup candied fruit
- 1/2 cup chopped nuts

Pour in prepared pan and bake at 325°F for 1 hour. Cool and frost, if desired. This cake keeps well either frozen or in the refrigerator.

Fiesta Fruit Cake

Combine in a bowl and mix well:

- 2 cups chopped nuts
- 1 1/2 cups candied fruit, chopped
- 3/4 cup sifted flour
- 3/4 cup sugar
- 1/2 teaspoon each salt and baking powder

Add and blend:

- 3 eggs, beaten
- 1 teaspoon vanilla

Place mixture into a 9x9 pan that has been greased and lined with wax paper or greased and floured. Bake at 300°F for 2 hours. This cake may be kept indefinitely in the freezer or refrigerator.

Nut Cake: Use more nuts in place of some of the candied fruit.

Cake Decorator's Frosting

Beat with electric mixer for 15 minutes:

- 7 cups powdered sugar
- 1 1/4 cups shortening
- 1 teaspoon each salt and vanilla
- 1/2 cup milk or water

Add food coloring as desired. Oil based colors work best. Store in a sealed container for up to 3 weeks in refrigerator or indefinitely in freezer. Frost cakes at room temperature.

* *Add any of the following: 1 teaspoon lemon juice, 1/2 teaspoon almond extract or butter flavoring, 1 envelope dream whip (makes icing creamier), 1/2–1 cup cream cheese, cocoa powder to taste, 1/4 cup light corn syrup.*

Powdered Sugar Frosting

Combine:

- 4 cups powdered sugar
- 1/3 cup soft margarine or butter
- 1/4 teaspoon salt, optional
- 1 teaspoon vanilla or other flavoring

Add milk 1 tablespoon at a time until icing is the right consistency:

- 2-4 tablespoons milk

Chocolate Frosting: Add 1/4 cup cocoa or more to taste.

Coconut Frosting: Use coconut milk for liquid and sprinkle with coconut.

Coffee Frosting: Substitute liquid black coffee for milk and vanilla.

Cream Cheese Frosting: Add 1/3–1/2 cup cream cheese.

Lemon Cream Cheese Frosting: Add 1/2 cup cream cheese and 1–3 tablespoons lemon juice to taste.

Low Sugar Cream Cheese Frosting: Add 1 cup cream cheese, and 1 tablespoon each lemon juice and rind. Decrease sugar to 1/4 cup.

Spice Cake Frosting: Use maple for flavoring and coffee for milk.

Yogurt Frosting: Use yogurt for milk. Add more lemon juice if desired.

See page 240 for International Conversion Charts

Seven-Minute Frosting

Combine in top of double boiler:

- 1 egg white
- 3/4 cup sugar
- 2 tablespoons water
- pinch of salt
- 1/4 teaspoon cream of tartar

Stir until sugar dissolves. Place over briskly boiling water. Beat with rotary beater until stiff enough to stand up in peaks, 6–10 minutes. Remove from heat and flavor as desired. Beat further if not thick enough to spread.

* *Substitute 1 teaspoon light corn syrup for cream of tartar.*

Marshmallow Frosting: After removing from heat, add 8 marshmallows cut into small pieces. Continue beating until icing is the right consistency.

Easy Caramel Frosting

Cook over low heat 2 minutes, stirring constantly:

- 1/2 cup margarine
- 1 cup brown sugar, firmly packed

Add and continue to stir until mixture comes to a boil:

- 1/4 cup milk

Remove from heat, cool, and gradually add until right consistency:

- 1 3/4–2 cups powdered sugar

Creamy Frosting

Combine gradually, blend thoroughly, and cook until thick, then cool:

- 1/4 cup flour
- 1 cup milk

Cream together separately until fluffy:

- 1 cup sugar
- 1 cup margarine

Add and beat well:

- 3/4 teaspoon salt
- 1–2 teaspoons vinegar
- 1 tablespoon vanilla or other flavoring

Add cooled, cooked mixture and beat a little longer until well-blended and creamy.

* *For margarine use 2/3 cup shortening or half each margarine and shortening.*

Coconut Topping

Combine:

- **6 tablespoons margarine, melted**
- **1/2 cup brown sugar**

Add and mix well:

- **1/2 cup cream, evaporated milk, or fresh milk**

Add:

- **1 teaspoon vanilla**
- **1/2–1 cup coconut**
- **1 cup chopped nuts, optional**

Spread over top of warm cake and put under the broiler until bubbly (this takes only a few minutes), or bake at 350°F for 10 minutes.

* *Increase sugar to 2/3 cup and omit milk and vanilla.*

Cooked Coconut Topping: Reduce margarine to 2 tablespoons and add 1–2 tablespoons flour. Combine all ingredients and cook over medium heat until thick. Spread on warm cake. Do not broil.

Apple Cake Topping: Omit coconut, nuts, cream and 2 tablespoons margarine. Add 2 tablespoons white or wheat flour and 1 cup water.

Chocolate Fudge Frosting

Boil in saucepan to soft ball stage (see page 69) 236°F:

- **1 cup sugar**
- **1/4 cup cocoa**
- **2 tablespoons butter, margarine, or oil**
- **1/4 cup milk or water**
- **1/8 teaspoon salt**

Remove from heat and add:

- **1 teaspoon vanilla**

Beat immediately until glossy and of a spreading consistency for frosting.

Brown Sugar Frosting or Fudge: Omit cocoa. Substitute panela or brown sugar for white sugar.

Fudge: Beat longer until it loses its gloss. Spread in a greased pan. When cool, cut into squares.

Peanut Butter Fudge: Omit butter and add 1/4 cup peanut butter. Omit cocoa, if desired, and follow directions for fudge.

Candy and Cookie Hints

For shortening and sugar hints, see desserts.

To keep fudge from being hard or sugary: Add a little milk to soften it and recook to the right temperature.

If fudge won't set: Scrape it back in a pan, add a teaspoon or two of water, and cook until it reaches the proper test for doneness or add a little cream of tartar before cooking.

To remove cookies or brownies that stick to the cookie sheet: Hold the sheet over a stove burner or return to the oven for a moment.

Candy Temperatures

Temperature	Stage	Description of syrup placed in cold water
236°F	Soft ball	Ball flattens
244°F	Firm ball	Does not flatten
254°F	Hard ball	Can be molded
270°F	Soft crack	Not brittle threads
300°F	Hard crack	Hard brittle threads

Quick Fudge and Frosting

Combine, stir, and cook until thick:

- **1 3/4 cup sweetened condensed milk**
- **1/4–1/2 cup powdered cocoa**
- **1/8 teaspoon salt**

Remove from heat and add:

- **1 teaspoon vanilla**
- **chopped nuts or marshmallows, optional**

Pour on cookie sheet and cut in squares when cool, or spread over cake.

Sugar Peanuts

Combine in pan, cook, and stir until syrup is hard to stir, about 45 minutes:

- **5 cups peanuts, with skins**
- **3 cups sugar**
- **2 cups hot water**
- **1/8 teaspoon cinnamon, optional**
- **1/8 teaspoon red food coloring, optional**

Spread on a greased cookie sheet or wax paper to dry.

Never-Fail Fudge

Combine:

- 1–1 1/2 cups chocolate chips or chopped candy bars
- 1 cup nuts, chopped
- 1/2 cup butter, margarine, or shortening
- 1 tablespoon vanilla
- 2 tablespoons cocoa, optional
- 1/8 teaspoon cream of tartar, optional

Combine separately and bring to a boil, stirring constantly:

- 10 large marshmallows
- 2/3 cup evaporated milk
- 2 cups sugar

Boil for 6 minutes over low to medium heat. Pour over first ingredients in bowl and stir until butter is melted. Pour into greased 9x9 pan and put in a cool place to set.

* *For firmer fudge, use vegetable shortening rather than butter or margarine.*

* *Add a pinch of cream of tartar to fudge to keep it from sugaring.*

Coconut Fudge: Spread coconut on bottom of pan. Top with fudge.

Peppermint Fudge: Sprinkle broken peppermint candy over top of fudge.

Marshmallows

Boil to soft ball stage (see page 69), 236°F, then remove from heat:

- 3/4 cup water
- 2 cups sugar

Combine separately and let set for 2–5 minutes, then add to sugar:

- 2 tablespoons unflavored gelatin
- 1/2 cup cool water

Cool for 10–15 minutes, then add:

- 1/2 teaspoon salt
- 1 teaspoon vanilla

Beat on high speed until very stiff. Pour into greased 9x13 pan or drop by small spoonfuls onto greased baking sheet. When cooled and hardened, cut and shake a few pieces at a time in powdered sugar.

* *Instead of greasing pan, dust it with a mixture of 1 tablespoon cornstarch and 2 cups powdered sugar. Save remaining mixture and roll the marshmallows in it.*

* *Add food coloring or any flavoring in place of vanilla, such as lemon or coconut or 1/4 teaspoon mint or berry extract.*

Apple Candy: Substitute 1 1/4 cups applesauce for first water. Add 1 cup chopped nuts with vanilla.

Marshmallow Cream Sauce: Do not pour mixture into pan, but use it as a topping on ice cream or in recipes calling for marshmallow cream.

See page 240 for International Conversion Charts

Caramels

Combine and cook to firm ball stage (see page 69), 244°F:

- 1 cup margarine or butter
- 2 1/4 cups packed brown sugar
- 1 1/4 cups sweetened condensed milk, cream, or milk
- 1 cup light corn syrup

Remove from heat and immediately stir in:

- 1 teaspoon vanilla
- 1 cup chopped nuts, optional
- 3 tablespoons instant coffee crystals, optional
- 1 teaspoon finely shredded orange peel, optional

Quickly pour caramel mixture into a buttered, foil-lined 9x9 baking pan. When firm use foil to lift out of pan. Use buttered knife to cut candy into 1-inch squares. Wrap candies in clear plastic wrap.

Quick Caramels: Omit all ingredients except sweetened condensed milk. Combine sweetened condensed milk and 3 tablespoons margarine and cook to soft ball stage (see page 69). Pour onto greased dish, cool, and cut.

Nut Brittle

Stir over low heat until a caramel color:

- 2 cups sugar, white or brown
- 1/2 teaspoon salt

Add and stir until dissolved:

- 1 cup sugar
- 2 cups chopped nuts
- 2 tablespoons butter

Spread out on greased baking sheet. Cool and break into serving sizes.

* *To vary: Omit 1 cup sugar and add 1 cup each corn syrup and water. Combine all ingredients except butter. Cook to a hard crack stage (see page 69) 300°F, stirring occasionally. Remove from heat. Add butter, 1 teaspoon vanilla, and 1/2 teaspoon soda.*

Honey Peanut Butter Candy

Mix together and knead;

- 1/2 cup peanut butter
- 1/4–1/2 cup honey, syrup, or sweetened condensed milk
- 1 cup milk powder
- 1 cup raw oatmeal, optional
- 2 tablespoons cocoa, optional
- 1/4 teaspoon maple flavoring, optional
- 1/8 teaspoon salt, optional

Roll into 1-inch balls and roll in:

- toasted sesame seeds, coconut, crushed cereal flakes, or nuts

Keeps in hot, humid climates without refrigeration for 2 days.

* *Spread candy in greased pan and cut into squares or form into rolls and slice.*

Christmas Delights

Grind or finely chop:

- 1 cup dates or other dried fruit
- 1 cup nuts
- 1/2 cup coconut

Add:

- 2 teaspoons cream or milk
- 1 tablespoon vanilla

Form into balls, roll in brown sugar, then powdered sugar or roll in shredded coconut that has red or green food coloring added.

See page 240 for International Conversion Charts

Cracker Jack and Jills

Boil for 5 minutes, stirring constantly:

- 2 cups brown sugar
- 1/4–1/2 cup corn syrup
- 1 cup margarine

Remove from stove and add:

- 1/2 teaspoon salt
- 1/2 teaspoon baking soda
- 2 teaspoons vanilla
- 1/8 teaspoon cream of tartar, optional

Pour over:

- 32 cups popped corn
- 2 cups peanuts, optional

Bake on cookie sheet at 200°F for 1 hour, stirring every 15 minutes. Spread on table top or foil to cool. Store in airtight containers.

Popcorn Balls

Combine in saucepan:

- 2 cups brown or white sugar, or a combination
- 1/4 cup molasses, corn syrup, or honey
- 2 tablespoons vinegar
- 1/4 cup butter or shortening

Boil to soft crack stage (see page 69) 270°F. Do not burn. Pour over:

- 16 cups or more popped corn

Stir as little as necessary to coat most of the kernels. Shape into balls. Do not press hard, but mold gently so kernels will not be crushed.

* *To keep popcorn fresh and eliminate non-poppers: Soak it in water a few minutes, drain, and dry thoroughly, or keep popcorn in the freezer.*

* *Use 1/2 cup corn syrup and 1/4 cup molasses for 1 cup of sugar.*

* *Omit molasses and use 1/4 cup brown sugar and 2 tablespoons water. Pour cooked candy mixture onto small pieces of waxed paper for individual candies, or pour over fruit, coconut, or nuts.*

Butterscotch Candy: Substitute water for molasses. Decrease vinegar to 1 tablespoon. Omit popcorn. Pour into buttered pan. Cool. Cut into squares.

Puffed Rice Balls or Puffed Wheat Balls: Heat in oven about 10 cups of puffed rice or wheat to use in place of popcorn, and pour on syrup.

Candied Orange Peel

Remove all pulp from oranges and soak orange rind for 24 hours, completely covered and weighted down, in salt water made by combining 1 tablespoon salt for each 4 cups water. Drain and rinse well. Cover with cold water and bring to a boil. Drain and repeat 3 more times (4 times in all). Drain, cool, and cut in desired strips. Measure cut rind.

Combine in pan:

- **4 cups orange rind**
- **4 cups sugar**
- **1/2 cup water**

Mix well and boil until almost no syrup remains, stirring frequently (about 3 hours), reducing heat as necessary to keep from burning. Shake or roll in sugar while still hot. Cool on wire rack.

Candied Grapefruit Peel: Use grapefruit and make as above.

Candied Fruits and Nuts: Use peeled, sliced fresh or dried fruits or nuts. Combine the following and boil to a hard crack (see page 69) 300°F: 2 cups sugar, 1 cup boiling water, and 1/8 cup vinegar or 1/2 teaspoon cream of tartar. Place pan over boiling water and drop fruit or nuts into syrup and boil until almost no syrup remains. Remove fruit or nuts with fork or tongs and cool on a greased surface.

Cookie Mix

Combine:

- **8 cups flour**
- **2 1/2 cups sugar**
- **2 cups brown sugar**
- **4 teaspoons salt**
- **1 1/2 teaspoons baking soda**

Add and work in:

- **3 cups shortening**

Store in airtight container.

* *See Cookie Mix Cookies, page 75.*

See page 240 for International Conversion Charts

Swiss No-Bake Cookies

Combine:

- 1 1/4 cups unsweetened chocolate, grated or ground in blender
- 1 1/4 cup sugar
- 2–4 teaspoons water, to make mixture stick together
- 2 1/2 cups nuts ground in blender or chopped fine
- 1/2–1 teaspoon almond or vanilla flavoring

Roll out with rolling pin to 1/4-inch thick. Cut into shapes with cookie cutters, or cut into rectangles. Dry in oven at 150–200°F or on racks for 1–2 days.

* *Use peanuts or hazelnuts and add 1 teaspoon almond flavoring.*

* *Use candy bars and decrease the sugar by 1/2 cup or to taste.*

Cookie Mix Cookies

Combine:

- 3 cups Cookie Mix, page 74
- 1 teaspoon milk, more if necessary
- 1 1/2 teaspoons vanilla
- 1 egg

Drop by teaspoonfuls onto greased baking sheets. Sprinkle with sugar if desired. Bake 10–15 minutes at 375°F until edges are golden. Frost if desired. Makes about 24 cookies .

* *Add any or a combination of the following: 1 cup nuts, raisins, gumdrops, chocolate chips, butterscotch chips, dates, grated coconut, 1 tablespoon orange peel, 2 cups oatmeal.*

Master Mix Cookies: Substitute Master Mix (page 9) for Cookie Mix. Add 1 cup sugar. Increase milk to 3 tablespoons for shaped or rolled cookies and 1/2 cup for drop cookies. Use any of the other options with this option.

Chocolate Cookies: Add 2 tablespoons cocoa and increase milk to 2 tablespoons. Frost if desired.

Lemon Cookies: Add 1 teaspoon grated lemon peel, 1/8 teaspoon almond flavoring, and 1/3 cup chopped nuts, if desired. Shape dough into a roll 2 inches in diameter. Cover with plastic wrap and chill 3–4 hours or overnight. Cut roll into thin slices. Bake on ungreased baking sheets 8–10 minutes.

Oatmeal Banana Cookies: Decrease Cookie Mix to 2 cups. Add 1 large mashed banana, 2 tablespoons sugar, 1/4 cup each sunflower seeds and wheat germ, and 3/4 cup oatmeal.

Peanut Butter Cookies: Add 1/2–1 cup peanut butter and 1/4 cup brown sugar. Shape into 1-inch balls. Flatten with a fork.

Spice Cookies: Add 1 teaspoon cinnamon, 1/4 teaspoon allspice, and 1/2 teaspoon cloves. Add 1/2 cup molasses or honey if using Master Mix.

Snickerdoodles: Add 1/4 teaspoon baking soda and 1 teaspoon cream of tartar. Omit milk. Shape dough into balls. Roll in a combination of 2 tablespoons sugar and 1 teaspoon cinnamon. Flatten balls slightly. Bake 8–10 minutes until lightly browned.

Sugar Cookies: Add 6 tablespoons flour. Roll out to 1/8–1/4 inch thickness on floured surface. Bake 8–10 minutes.

Layered Bars

Layer in order given in a 9x9 pan:

- 1/2 cup butter or margarine, melted
- 1 cup graham cracker or cookie crumbs
- 1 cup each chocolate chips, coconut, and chopped nuts
- 1 3/4 cups sweetened condensed milk

Bake at 350°F for 30 minutes. Cut into bars.

Basic Dough for Cookies

Combine:

- 1 cup shortening
- 2 cups sugar
- 3 eggs

Add:

- 1/3 cup milk
- 2 teaspoons vanilla

Add:

- 5–5 1/2 cups flour
- 1/2–1 teaspoon salt
- 1 tablespoon baking powder

Divide and chill if desired. On ungreased baking sheet, drop dough by spoonfuls and bake at 400°F for 8–10 minutes. Can be refrigerated and used when needed. Keeps 2–3 weeks.

* Add 1/2–1 cup of any of the following to 1/4 recipe: chocolate chips, chopped nuts, raisins, or coconut.

Chocolate Cookies: Add 1/4 cup cocoa to 1/4 recipe above.

Filled Cookies: Roll out dough to 1/4-inch and cut with a glass. Put a little filling on one cookie. Put another cookie on top, pinch edges together, and bake. Fill with any of the following: nuts, raisins, jam, chocolate chips, mint patties, peanut butter or jellybeans.

Orange Cookies: Decrease eggs to 2, flour to 4 cups, and baking powder to 1 teaspoon. Add 1 teaspoon baking soda and the juice and grated rind of one orange. Omit milk. Add 1 cup sour milk. Drop by spoonfuls or spread in a greased 9x13 pan to make bars.

Spice Cookies: To 1/4 recipe add 1/4 teaspoon cloves, 1 teaspoon cinnamon, and 1/2 teaspoon nutmeg. Roll in sugar before baking.

Rolled Cookies: Roll out to 1/4 inch and cut with cookie cutters.

Snickerdoodles: Decrease baking powder to 1 teaspoon. Add 1 teaspoon cream of tartar. Form dough into balls. Roll in mixture of 3 tablespoons sugar and 1 teaspoon cinnamon. Place on baking sheet. Flatten slightly.

See page 240 for International Conversion Charts

Sugar Cookies

Cream:

- 1/2 cup soft butter or oil
- 1 cup sugar
- 1 egg or 2 yolks
- 1 tablespoon milk or cream
- 1/2 teaspoon vanilla

Add:

- 2 cups flour
- 1/2 teaspoon salt
- 1 teaspoon baking powder

Mix well. Drop by teaspoonfuls onto greased baking sheet. Bake at 400°F for 10–12 minutes. (See Rolled Sugar Cookies below.)

* *Add any of the following: 1/2 cup grated coconut or chopped nuts, 1 teaspoon baking soda or lemon juice, or 2 teaspoons grated lemon rind.*

Butter Cookies: Omit milk, vanilla, salt, and baking powder. Increase butter to 1 cup, decrease sugar to 1/2 cup, and use only 1 egg yolk.

Honey Drop Cookies: Substitute honey for sugar.

Refrigerator Peanut Cookies: Add 2 teaspoons peanut butter and 1 cup chopped peanuts. Shape dough into 2 rolls. Wrap and refrigerate until firm, then slice and bake on greased baking sheet.

Rolled Sugar Cookies: Add 1/4–1/3 cup flour until consistency to roll out. Roll out to 1/8–1/4-inch thickness on floured surface. Cut into desired shapes. Bake 8–10 minutes.

Macaroons

Beat until stiff:

- 3 egg whites
- 3/4 –1 cup sugar

Add:

- 1 cup chopped nuts, optional
- 1 cup butterscotch, chocolate chips, or coconut

Preheat oven to 425°F. Drop macaroons by spoonfuls onto greased cookie sheets. Put in hot oven. Turn off oven and leave for 8–12 hours.

Coconut Macaroons

Combine:

- 4–5 cups coconut
- 1/8 teaspoon salt
- 1 2/3 cups sweetened condensed milk
- 1 tablespoon vanilla

Drop by spoonfuls on greased baking sheet. Bake at 375°F for 5–8 minutes. Makes 24 macaroons.

* *To vary: Use only 3 cups coconut and 2 cups chopped peanuts or other nuts and 1/2–1 teaspoon almond flavoring.*

No-Bake Chocolate Oatmeal Cookies

Boil together for 5 minutes:

- 1 1/2–2 cups sugar
- 1/4–1/2 cup cocoa
- 1/3–1/2 cup shortening or margarine
- 1/2 cup milk
- 1 teaspoon salt

Remove from heat. Immediately add:

- 3 cups oatmeal
- 1 1/2 teaspoons vanilla
- nuts, optional

Drop by tablespoons on waxed paper to cool or spread on cookie sheet to harden. Cut into bars.

Chocolate Chip Cookies

Cream:

- 1 cup margarine or shortening, softened
- 1/2 cup each sugar and brown sugar
- 1 teaspoon vanilla
- 2 eggs, beaten

Combine and add gradually:

- 1 teaspoon baking soda
- 2 1/4 cups flour
- 1 teaspoon salt

Add:

- 3/4–1 cup chocolate chips
- 1/2 cup chopped nuts, optional

Drop by spoonfuls onto ungreased cookie sheets or spread on cookie sheet or 9x13 pan to form bars. Bake at 375°F for 8–10 minutes for drop cookies, 20 minutes for pan cookies on cookie sheet, or 40 minutes for cookie bars. Cut while still hot.

See page 240 for International Conversion Charts

Flapjack Cookies

Combine:

- 2 cups oatmeal
- 1 cup brown sugar
- 1 teaspoon salt
- 1/3 cup plus 1 tablespoon oil or melted shortening

Pat mixture into a lightly greased pan. Bake at 350°F for 10–15 minutes until mixture bubbles. Cool slightly and cut into pieces. Do not remove from pan until flapjack is cold.

* *Add to mixture 1 egg, 2 teaspoons vanilla, 2 tablespoons milk, chopped nuts, and 1/2 cup more brown sugar, if desired.*

* *Add shredded coconut, cinnamon, dates, nuts, or raisins.*

Frying Pan Cookies

Combine:

- 1/2 cup milk
- 1 egg, slightly beaten
- 1 teaspoon vanilla
- 1 1/4 cups raisins
- 2/3 cup oil

Combine separately and add:

- 1 cup sugar
- 1/4–1/2 teaspoon salt
- 3 1/2 cups flour
- 1 1/2 teaspoons baking powder

Make into patties as thin as possible and fry in covered skillet over low to medium heat until bottoms brown. Turn over and cook until brown.

Peanut Butter Cookies

Combine:

- 1/2 cup soft shortening or half butter
- 1/2–1 cup peanut butter
- 1/2 cup sugar
- 1/2 teaspoon vanilla
- 1/2 cup brown sugar
- 1 egg

Add:

- 1 1/4–1 1/2 cups flour
- 1/2 teaspoon baking powder
- 3/4 teaspoon baking soda
- 1/4 teaspoon salt

Chill dough. Roll into balls the size of large walnuts. Place 3 inches apart on lightly greased baking sheet. Flatten with fork dipped in flour. Bake at 375°F for 10–12 minutes. Makes about 36 cookies.

* *Substitute 1/4 cup evaporated milk for egg.*

Honey Peanut Butter Cookies: Follow recipe above, except use only 1/4 cup shortening and for brown sugar use 1/2 cup honey.

Master Mix Peanut Butter Cookies: Substitute 1 3/4–2 cups Master Mix, page 9, for shortening, flour, baking powder, soda, and salt.

Ginger Snaps

Combine:

- 1/2 cup shortening
- 1 egg, beaten
- 2 tablespoons syrup, honey, or molasses
- 1 cup brown sugar

Sift together and add:

- 2 cups flour
- 1 teaspoon baking soda
- 1/2 teaspoon salt
- 1 1/2 teaspoons ginger
- 1/2–1 teaspoon cloves
- 2 teaspoons cinnamon

Roll into small balls the size of walnuts. Roll each ball in sugar. Bake on greased sheet at 350°F for 10–15 minutes. Makes 36–48 cookies.

Rolled Gingerbread Cookies: Add 1/2–1 cup flour and knead on floured board until firm enough. Roll out thin, cut and bake. Cookies may be iced or decorated.

Butterscotch Bars

Combine:

- 1 cup brown sugar
- 1/4 cup oil or margarine

Add:

- 1 egg
- 1 teaspoon vanilla

Combine separately and stir in:

- 1/2 cup flour
- 1 teaspoon baking powder
- 1/2 teaspoon salt
- 1/2 cup nuts

Pour in greased 9x9 pan. Bake at 350°F for 30 minutes.

Butter-Nut Bars: Increase margarine to 1 cup, flour to 2 cups, and vanilla to 2 1/2 teaspoons. Save egg white, beat until frothy, and spread over dough in pan. Sprinkle with chopped nuts and bake.

See page 240 for International Conversion Charts

Cereal Cookies

Cream:

- 1 cup sugar
- 1 cup brown sugar
- 1 cup shortening

Add:

- 2 eggs
- 1 teaspoon vanilla

Combine separately and stir in:

- 1/2–1 teaspoon salt
- 2 cups flour
- 1 teaspoon baking soda
- 1/2 teaspoon baking powder

Add:

- 2 cups oatmeal
- 2 cups wheat, corn, or bran flakes, or rice crispies, optional

Drop by tablespoons onto greased baking sheets or roll in balls and press flat with fork. Bake at 375°F for 12 minutes. Makes 6 dozen.

* *Add any of the following: 1 cup raisins, chocolate chips, nuts, or coconut; 1/2 cup peanut butter or sunflower seeds; 1/4 teaspoon cloves, 1 teaspoon cinnamon, 1/2 teaspoon nutmeg.*

Bar Cookies: Press cookie mixture into greased 9x13 pan. Bake 10–15 minutes. Cut and remove from pan while warm.

Crisp Rolled-in-Oats Cookies: Omit 1/2 cup each white and brown sugar, soda, baking powder, and flakes. Increase flour 1/2–1 cup. Form balls the size of walnuts and roll each in oats until completely coated. Bake at 350°F for 20 minutes.

Crunchy Jumble Cookies: Omit oatmeal. Use 2 cups rice crispies. Add 1–2 cups each chocolate chips and raisins.

Eggless Oatmeal Cookies: Omit 1 cup sugar, eggs, cereal, and baking powder. Add 1/4 cup boiling water to sugar mixture.

Eggless Oatmeal Peanut Butter Cookies: Make changes as above except use 3/4 cup shortening and 1/4 cup peanut butter.

Peanut Butter Bars

Boil:

- 1 cup sugar
- 1 cup light corn syrup

Remove from heat and stir in:

- 1 cup peanut butter
- 6 cups rice crispies or other dried cereal

Press into greased 9x13 pan, then melt and pour over:

- 3/4–1 cup butterscotch chips
- 3/4–1 cup chocolate chips

Cool and cut into bars.

Sandies (Mexican Wedding Cakes or Russian Tea Cakes)

Combine:

- **1 cup margarine**
- **1/3 cup sugar**

Add and mix well:

- **2 teaspoons water**
- **2 teaspoons vanilla**
- **2 cups flour**
- **1 cup chopped nuts, optional**

Chill 1–2 hours, if desired. Roll into 1/2-inch balls or into a long roll and cut into 1/2-inch pieces. Bake at 325°F for 25 minutes on ungreased cookie sheet. Cool, then roll in powdered sugar.

Favorite Brownies

Melt in saucepan, then cool:

- **4 squares unsweetened chocolate**
- **1 cup margarine or shortening**

Add and beat until thick:

- **4 eggs, well beaten**
- **2 cups sugar**

Add:

- **1 teaspoon vanilla**

Fold in just until blended:

- **1 cup flour**
- **1/4 teaspoon salt**
- **1–2 cups chopped nuts, optional**

Pour into a greased 9x13 baking pan. Bake at 350°F for 25–30 minutes, or until shiny and firm on top. Do not overbake. Middle should be fudge-like. Cool completely, then cut into squares. Makes about 24 brownies. Frost if desired.

* *Use for chocolate: 3/4 cup cocoa and 1/4 cup shortening.*

Fudgy Brownies: Substitute 2/3 cup oil for margarine or shortening. Omit 2 eggs. Add 1/2 cup boiling water with oil, 1/2 teaspoon baking soda, and 1/3 cup flour.

Peanut Butter Brownies: Omit 1 egg. Add 1/2 cup peanut butter.

No-Shortening Brownies: Omit margarine or shortening.

See page 240 for International Conversion Charts

Lemon Bars

Combine:

- 1 cup flour
- 1/2 cup butter or margarine
- 1/4 cup powdered sugar

Press into 9x9 pan and bake at 350°F for 20 minutes.

Combine and pour over hot crust:

- 2 eggs, beaten until light and fluffy
- 1 cup sugar
- 1/2 teaspoon baking powder
- 1/4 teaspoon salt
- 2–3 tablespoons lemon juice
- 2 tablespoons flour

Bake about 25 minutes longer until crust is light brown.

* *Use a 9x13 pan for thinner bars. Decrease baking time.*
* *Double the recipe and bake in 10x15 jelly-roll pan.*
* *Freeze and eat without thawing.*

Fresh Fruit Bars

Cream together:

- 1 cup shortening or butter or 3/4 cup oil
- 1 1/2 cups white or brown sugar
- 2 eggs

Add:

- 1 teaspoon salt
- 2 teaspoons baking powder
- 3 cups flour

Mold 3/4 of dough on regular-sized cookie sheet. Make sure the dough is pressed against the sides to the top. Spread sliced fruit or jam very thin over dough. Roll out remainder of dough and make strips. Make a lattice crisscrossing dough over the fruit. Sprinkle with 1/2 cup sugar. Bake at 375°F until dough is a light brown. Slice in squares.

Jam Bars: Omit eggs and use only 1 1/2 cups of flour and add 1 1/2 cups oats. Press mixture into greased 9x13 pan and spread with favorite jam. Bake at 400°F for 20–25 minutes. Cool. Cut into bars.

Coconut Jam Bars: Press dough into 9x13 pan. Spread with jam. Combine the following and spread on top of jam: 1 cup sugar, 2 tablespoons butter or margarine, 1 beaten egg, 1/8 teaspoon salt, 1 teaspoon vanilla, and 2 cups coconut. Bake at 350°F for 45 minutes. Cool. Cut into bars.

Graham Crackers

Cream together:

- 1 cup sugar
- 2 cups brown sugar
- 1 cup shortening or oil
- 1 teaspoon vanilla

Combine separately:

- 2 cups flour
- 4 cups graham flour or wheat flour
- 1 teaspoon soda
- 2 teaspoons baking powder
- 1/2 teaspoon salt
- 2 teaspoons cinnamon, optional

Add dry ingredients alternately with:

- 1 cup milk, sweet or sour

Mix thoroughly. Roll out on a lightly floured board and cut in squares. Place 1 inch apart on a greased baking sheet. Bake at 350°F until golden in color.

Graham Cracker Pie Crust: Roll out 1/4 of the dough and shape to fit a 9-inch pie pan. Bake at 350°F for 15 minutes.

Sugar-Free Graham Crackers: Omit sugars and milk. Use oil in place of shortening. Add 2–3 bananas, blended, or 3/4 cup apple juice concentrate. To make concentrate, boil apple juice until thick.

Master Mix Coconut Bars

Combine:

- 2 cups Master Mix (page 9)
- 1 1/2–2 cups brown sugar
- 1 cup coconut
- 1 cup chopped nuts, optional

Add:

- 2 eggs
- 1 teaspoon vanilla
- 2/3 cup water, optional for softer bars

Batter will be stiff. Spread in greased 9x9 pan. Bake at 350°F for 25 minutes. Cut into bars.

Cookie Mix Bars: Substitute Cookie Mix, page 74, for Master Mix, page 9. Omit sugar.

Date Bars: Substitute dates for coconut.

Master Mix Brownies: Omit coconut. Add 3 squares melted chocolate or 1/2 cup cocoa, and 3 tablespoons shortening.

Dessert Hints

To make powdered sugar: Put granulated sugar through a corn mill and grind until it is as fine as desired. Adjust the mill so that it is only necessary to grind once. Or blend in a blender.

To make brown sugar: Add a little water to panela and boil until of the right consistency. If panela is quite dirty, strain the syrup. Mix the panela syrup with white sugar until it is the color of brown sugar. Or add a few drops of maple flavoring to white sugar. Stir and continue adding a little maple flavoring until the color of light brown sugar. Taste is a little different, but this works very well when brown sugar is not available. Or stir 2 tablespoons molasses into 1 cup white sugar.

To a recipe that is too sweet: Add a few drops of lemon juice or vinegar.

To enhance flavor: Always add extracts when mixture is cool.

To keep unsweetened chocolate from sticking to the pan when melting: Put chocolate in a custard cup and melt over hot water (not boiling). Or put chocolate on a little waxed paper in the top of double boiler. Or grease the pan in which chocolate is to be melted with shortening or margarine first.

To remove burned taste from pudding: Add a small, peeled, whole onion and cook a few minutes.

To make good custard: Use low heat. High heat causes eggs to curdle and this causes lumpy, thin custards. Use heavy saucepan or double boiler and stir constantly. Custard is cooked when you lift your spoon from the mixture and the spoon does not show through the mixture.

To measure honey or syrups: Oil the cup and rinse with hot water before measuring.

To substitute for shortening or margarine: Use cooking oil, but cut down the amount. Or substitute mayonnaise for shortening.

To measure shortening: For 1/2 cup of solid shortening, fill the cup half full of cold water, then drop in pieces of the shortening until the water reaches the top of the cup. Drain off water. The remaining shortening measures the correct amount. If you want 3/4 cup of shortening, put 1/4 cup of water in a measuring cup and then add enough shortening to bring the water level up to 1 cup, etc.

To measure spoonfuls of shortening: Dip spoon in hot water before measuring.

To improvise for a rolling pin: Use a long round bottle.

To keep granulated sugar from lumping: Place a couple of saltine crackers in the container and cover tightly.

To keep brown sugar from becoming hard, or to soften brown sugar that has hardened: Place in a glass jar with a tight-fitting lid and place a piece of bread or half an apple inside the jar.

To remove lumps from brown sugar for immediate use: Place in a shallow pan and bake at 250°F for 15 minutes.

To soften sugar with large crystals for baking: Heat sugar with water or other liquid (from recipe) until softened. Then add to recipe.

Pudding Mix

Combine:

- **2 1/2 cups dry milk powder**
- **1 1/2 cups sugar**
- **1 1/4 cups flour**
- **1 teaspoon salt**

Store in tightly covered container. Use this with Pudding Mix puddings and Pudding cakes.

Chocolate Pudding Mix: Add 1 1/2 cups cocoa. Use with Chocolate Syrup from Mix, page 99.

Pudding Mix Vanilla Pudding

Combine and cook, stirring until thickened:

- **1 1/4 cups Pudding Mix**
- **1 egg**
- **2 1/2–3 cups water**

Remove from heat and add:

- **1 1/2 teaspoons vanilla**

* *Use options on Vanilla Pudding.*

Pudding Mix Chocolate Pudding: Add 3 tablespoons cocoa and 2 tablespoons sugar to dry Pudding Mix.

Pudding Mix Rice Pudding: Add 2 cups cooked rice and 1/2 cup raisins to cooked pudding.

Baked Caramel Pudding

Spread over bottom of greased 9x9 pan:

- **1/2–1 cup brown sugar**

Dot with:

- **3 tablespoons butter**

Combine and pour over butter:

- **1 teaspoon vanilla**
- **1 1/2 cups boiling water**

Sprinkle with:

- **3/4 cup chopped peanuts or other nuts**

Combine separately and drop into pan:

- **1 1/2 cups Master Mix (page 9)**
- **1/2 cup each milk and brown sugar**
- **1 teaspoon vanilla**

Bake at 350°F for 40 minutes.

See page 240 for International Conversion Charts

Vanilla Pudding

Combine in pan:

- **5 tablespoons cornstarch**
- **1/3 cup sugar**
- **1/4 teaspoon salt**

Add and cook, stirring until thickened:

- **2 1/3 cups milk**

Beat separately until light:

- **1 egg**
- **2 tablespoons sugar**

Pour a little hot mixture over egg. Add to entire mixture and simmer 5 minutes, then add:

- **1 tablespoon margarine**
- **2 teaspoons vanilla**

Cook until thick.

* *Add 2/3 cup powdered milk with the dry ingredients and use water in place of milk.*

Chocolate Mint Pudding: Add 2 tablespoons each of cocoa and sugar and 1/2 teaspoon mint extract.

Chocolate Pudding: Add 2 tablespoons each cocoa and sugar (30 ml) to cornstarch mixture.

Coconut Pudding: Use coconut milk for milk. Omit egg, sugar, and margarine. Heat but do not boil. Stir constantly until thickened.

Date Pudding: After cooking, add 1/2–1 cup chopped dates.

Mocha Pudding: Add 2 tablespoons each cocoa, sugar, and instant coffee to cornstarch mixture.

Tapioca

Combine and let stand 5 minutes:

- **1 egg, slightly beaten**
- **1/3 cup sugar**
- **3 tablespoons tapioca**
- **1/8 teaspoon salt**
- **2 3/4 cups milk**

Cook over medium heat, stirring constantly until mixture comes to a full boil and is slightly thickened, about 6–8 minutes. Pudding thickens as it cools. Remove from heat and stir in:

- **1 teaspoon vanilla**

Serves 4–5.

* *If local tapioca is used, it may require longer soaking.*

Sweet Potato Pudding

Combine:

- **4 cups grated raw sweet potatoes or yellow squash**
- **1/2 teaspoon ginger**
- **1/2 teaspoon cloves**
- **3/4 cup brown sugar**
- **2 teaspoons grated lemon peel**
- **1 teaspoon cinnamon**
- **1 teaspoon salt**
- **3/4 cup melted butter or margarine**

Add and pour into greased bread pan or casserole dish:

- **4 eggs, beaten**

Sprinkle with:

- **1 cup chopped nuts, optional**

Bake at 350°F for 1 hour.

Baked Custard

Combine:

- **2 eggs or 4 egg yolks, beaten slightly**
- **1/4 cup sugar**
- **1/4 teaspoon salt**
- **1/2 teaspoon vanilla**

Scald and gradually stir into egg mixture:

- **2 cups milk**

Do not scald if using powdered milk. Cook by one of the following methods:

Pressure Cooker Method: Pour mixture into greased cups or small, empty, greased cans (tuna cans are just right for individual servings). Sprinkle with a little nutmeg. Set them on rack in pressure cooker with 1/2 cup water in the bottom of pan. Bring cooker up to 5 pounds of pressure and time 1 minute. Let pressure return to zero without attempting to cool the cooker.

Oven Method: Pour mixture into a greased casserole dish or baking pan. Sprinkle with a little nutmeg. Set in a pan filled with hot water halfway up side of dish. Bake at 350°F for 1–1 1/2 hours, until knife inserted halfway between edge and center comes out clean.

See page 240 for International Conversion Charts

Rice Pudding

Heat:

- 1 3/4 cups milk
- 1/4 cup sugar

Add and cook over low heat, stirring occasionally until slightly thickened:

- 1/2 cup or more each cooked rice and raisins
- 1–2 eggs, beaten
- 1/8 teaspoon salt
- 1 tablespoon flour or cornstarch, optional
- 1/2 teaspoon cinnamon
- 1/4 teaspoon nutmeg, optional

Add, sprinkle with cinnamon, and serve warm or cold:

- 1/2 teaspoon vanilla

Glorified Rice

Combine:

- 2/3 cup milk powder
- 1/3 cup water or juice
- 2–3 tablespoons flavored gelatin, optional
- 1/2 teaspoon vanilla
- sugar to taste

Combine separately and add to above:

- 2 cups cooled, cooked rice
- 2/3 cup drained crushed or chunk pineapple, or other fruit

- 1 banana, sliced and quartered, optional
- maraschino cherries and marshmallows, optional

Baked Bread Pudding

Combine:

- 4 cups each hot milk and bread crumbs or cubes

Add and mix together:

- 2/3 cup sugar
- 1/8 teaspoon salt
- 1 egg, slightly beaten
- 1 teaspoon vanilla
- 1 cup raisins

Grease pan and bake at 350°F 1 hour. Top with frosting or cream.

Chocolate Bread Pudding: Add 3 tablespoons cocoa.

Fruit Bread Pudding: Add mangos, pineapple, persimmons, or other fruit.

Steamed Bread Pudding

Combine:

- **2 cups dry bread crumbs**
- **1/2 cup each white and brown sugar**
- **1 tablespoon flour**
- **1/2 teaspoon cloves**
- **1 teaspoon cinnamon**
- **1/8 teaspoon salt**
- **1 cup raisins, nuts, or other fruit**

Combine separately and add:

- **1/2 cup sour milk or yogurt**
- **1 teaspoon baking soda**
- **1 egg**
- **1 tablespoon oil**

Pour into greased coffee can or suitable container, then place in a pan filled with 2–3 inches of water. Cover with lid. Or place in a pressure cooker with pressure valve open. Steam 1–1 1/2 hours. Serve hot, with or without a glaze or fruit sauce.

* *Use options for Baked Bread Pudding.*

Finnish Fruit Tart

Combine and pour into a greased skillet or 9x9 pan:

- **2 eggs**
- **1 cup sugar**
- **1 1/4 cups flour**
- **1 teaspoon baking powder**
- **1/4 cup melted butter, margarine, shortening, or oil**
- **1/8 teaspoon salt**

Arrange over batter:

- **2–2 1/2 cups sliced or chopped fruit**

Sprinkle with:

- **cinnamon and sugar**

Bake at 375°F for 30–45 minutes.

* *Fruits that work well are: apples, stewed raisins, peaches, chopped dates, nuts, and pineapple.*

* *Omit eggs. Add 1/4 cup margarine and 2/3 cup milk.*

Fruit Crumble: Omit eggs, 1/4 cup flour, and baking powder. Substitute 3/4 cup brown sugar for sugar. Spread half of the crumb mixture in bottom of greased pan. Spread with fruit and 1/2–3/4 cup juice. Cover with remaining crumb mixture.

Upside-Down Fruit Cobbler: Substitute 1/2 cup milk for eggs. Omit vanilla. Pour 1 cup juice over fruit. Add 1/4 cup sugar if using cooked berries.

See page 240 for International Conversion Charts

Applesauce

Combine and cook slowly, stirring frequently, until apples are tender:

- **6–8 medium apples, peeled and chopped**
- **1 cup water**
- **1/8 teaspoon salt, optional**

Add:

- **1/2–1 cup sugar**
- **3/4 teaspoon cinnamon or 1 cinnamon stick**
- **a few drops lemon juice, optional**

Cook a few more minutes until of sauce consistency. Mash apples with potato masher, if desired.

Mock Applesauce: Use ripe cooking bananas or green mangos.

Empanadas (Mexican Fried Pies)

For crust, blend:

- **2 cups flour**
- **2 teaspoons baking powder**
- **3/4 teaspoon salt**

Cut in:

- **1/2 cup shortening**

Add:

- **1/2 cup milk**

Roll dough very thin. Cut into 4–5-inch circles. Use any of the fillings listed below. Always thicken and cook the filling so that only the crust needs to cook. Place a large spoonful on each square and fold to close. Press edges together with a floured fork. Bake at 400°F for 20 minutes or fry in 1 inch of hot oil. Turn to brown both sides, drain, and serve warm. Pies may be sprinkled with sugar and cinnamon.

Fruit Filling: Any sweetened, cooked, or canned fruit thickened with cornstarch. Stewed apple slices with sugar, cinnamon, and cheese bits. Mincemeat, preserves, and cottage cheese. Sliced bananas and jelly. Pineapple and brown sugar.

Meat Filling: Combine and brown 1–2 tablespoons oil, 1 medium onion, minced, 1 cup ground beef, 1 teaspoon chili powder, 1/4 teaspoon each cumin seeds and cayenne pepper, salt, and pepper.

Apple Goody Dessert

Combine and place in a greased 9x9 pan:

- **5 cups diced apples or any fruit**
- **1 teaspoon cinnamon**
- **1 cup sugar**
- **1/2 cup chopped nuts**
- **1/2 cup water**

Combine and spread over apples:

- **3/4 cup flour**
- **1/4 teaspoon baking soda**
- **1/4 teaspoon baking powder**
- **3/4 cup oatmeal**
- **3/4 cup brown sugar**
- **1/3 cup melted shortening or butter**
- **1/2 cup chopped nuts, optional**

Bake at 350°F for 30–40 minutes.

Apple Crisp: Omit 1 cup sugar, water, soda, and baking powder.

Cream Puffs

Heat to a rolling boil in saucepan:

- **1 cup water**
- **1/2 cup butter**

Add and stir vigorously over low heat until mixture forms a ball:

- **1 cup flour**
- **1/4 teaspoon salt**

Cool about 5 minutes, then beat in one at a time until smooth:

- **4 eggs**

Drop from spoon onto ungreased baking sheet in 8–10 mounds, 3 inches apart. Bake at 400°F for 30–40 minutes or until puffed, golden brown, and dry. Allow to cool slowly, away from drafts. Cut off tops with a sharp knife. Scoop out any soft dough. Fill with whipped cream, ice cream, custard, pudding, or any fruit filling and serve with or without a sauce. Use immediately or refrigerate. Makes 8–10 large puffs.

Hot Fudge Pudding Cake

Combine:

- 1 1/4 cups flour
- 3/4 cup sugar
- 2 teaspoons baking powder
- 1/4 teaspoon salt
- 2 tablespoons cocoa

Combine separately and stir into dry mixture:

- 2 tablespoons butter or margarine, melted
- 1/2 cup milk
- 1 teaspoon vanilla

Pour into a greased 9x9 pan.

Mix together and spread over cake:

- 2 tablespoons cocoa
- 1/2 cup brown sugar
- 1/2 cup sugar

Pour over cake:

- 1 1/4 cups boiling water

Bake at 350°F for 1 hour. Serve warm or cool. May serve with whipped cream. It comes out of pan with cake on top and pudding on bottom.

Caramel Pudding Cake: Use brown sugar for all sugar and omit cocoa, or use a package of caramel pudding mix for topping.

Lemon Pudding Cake: Omit cocoa and substitute 2–4 tablespoons lemon juice, or use a package of lemon pudding mix for topping.

Master Mix Pudding Cake: Substitute 1 1/2 cups Master Mix, page 9, for flour, baking powder, salt, and butter. Can use with other options.

Pudding Mix Pudding Cake: Substitute 1/3 cup Chocolate Pudding Mix, page 86, for cocoa and sugars topping. Increase water to 2 cups.

Vanilla Pudding Cake: Use 2 teaspoons vanilla in place of cocoa. Use 1/3 cup Pudding Mix for topping, if desired.

Gingerbread

Combine:

- 1/2 cup sour milk or water
- 1/3–1/2 cup oil
- 1 egg

Combine separately, add, and beat thoroughly:

- 1 cup brown sugar or molasses
- 1 1/2 teaspoons soda
- 2 teaspoons ginger
- 2 cups flour
- 1/2 teaspoon salt
- 4 tablespoons oil
- 1/2 teaspoon cinnamon, optional
- 1/4 teaspoon each of cloves and nutmeg, optional

Place in a greased and floured 9x13 pan. Bake at 325°F for 30 minutes. Serve with lemon sauce or whipped cream. Bake with fruit as an upside-down cake, if desired.

Steamed Gingerbread: Set cake pan in a pan of hot water, cover, and bake.

Fruit Pizza

Combine with fork until it resembles coarse meal:

- 1 1/2 cups flour
- 1/4 cup sugar
- 1/4 cup margarine or butter

Stir in with a fork:

- 1/4 cup oil

Stir in 1 tablespoon at a time until dough leaves side of bowl:

- 3 tablespoons cold water

Grease baking sheet. Shape dough into a ball on baking sheet and flatten to an 11-inch circle. Bake at 375°F for 12–14 minutes. Cool 10 minutes, then carefully move to wire rack to finish cooling. When cool, slide onto serving plate. Combine and beat until smooth:

- 3/4 cup soft cream cheese, yogurt cheese, or tofu
- 1/4 cup sugar
- 1/2 teaspoon vanilla

Spread mixture over crust. Arrange in circles around crust, any combination of sliced fruit. Combine in a saucepan:

- 1 teaspoon cornstarch
- 1 tablespoon water
- 1/4 cup orange juice
- 3 tablespoons powdered sugar

Bring to a boil, stirring constantly. Boil 1 minute. Cool. Spoon over fruit. Refrigerate no longer than 2 hours.

* *Replace cream cheese mixture with a thick, cooled pudding.*

Fried Banana Dessert

Combine, coat bananas with mixture, and deep fry until brown.

- 4 1/4 tablespoons cornstarch
- 1 egg
- 5 tablespoons flour
- 5 tablespoons water
- 4 bananas, split

Combine and heat:

- 5 tablespoons brown sugar, white sugar, or honey
- 2 tablespoons water
- 1 tablespoon oil
- 1 teaspoon vanilla, optional

Roll deep fried bananas in above hot sugar mixture. Sprinkle with sesame seeds or chopped nuts, or roll in sugar.

* *To vary, use any fruit.*

Coffee Whip

Whip until thick:

- 1/2–1 cup evaporated milk, chilled

Dissolve separately:

- 1 tablespoon hot water
- 1–2 teaspoons instant coffee granules

Dissolve separately:

- 2 tablespoons water
- 1 1/2 teaspoons gelatin powder

Whisk into the evaporated milk:

- coffee mixture
- gelatin mixture
- 2 tablespoons sugar

Sprinkle with chopped nuts or chocolate sprinkles. Chill 2–3 hours before serving. Serves 2–3 people.

Chocolate Whip: Omit coffee. Add 1–2 tablespoons each cocoa and sugar.

Fruit Whip: Omit coffee. Add 1 cup chopped fruit and more sugar, if desired.

Lemon Whip: Omit coffee. Add 1 tablespoon lemon juice and 1–2 tablespoons sugar.

Mocha Whip: Add 1–2 tablespoons each cocoa and sugar.

Frozen Lemon Cream

In a chilled bowl, beat until stiff:

- 1 2/3 cups evaporated milk, chilled

Slowly beat in:

- 3/4 cup sugar

Slowly add and beat until very stiff:

- 1/3 cup lemon juice
- grated rind of one lemon

Roll until fine crumbs:

- 12 graham crackers or cookies

Put 1/2 the crumbs in bottom of 9x13 pan. Spread milk mixture over crumbs. Add remaining crumbs to top. Cover tightly and freeze.

Freezer Ice Cream

Combine:

- 4 cups half-and-half
- 3/4–1 cup sugar
- 1 tablespoon vanilla
- dash of salt

Crank in ice cream freezer until set. Makes about 8 cups.

* *Replace sugar with 1 1/2 cups sweetened condensed milk. Reduce milk to 3 cups.*

* *Substitute for half-and-half any or a combination of the following: milk, cream, or evaporated milk.*

* *Add any of the following to ice cream: 1/2–1 cup coconut, marshmallows, any chopped nuts, chocolate chips, crushed peppermint, or chopped candy; 2 tablespoons dissolved instant coffee, cooked mashed pumpkin, 1/2 teaspoon mint flavoring and green food color, 1 teaspoon almond extract and red food coloring, 1/4 cup lemon juice and yellow food coloring, 1 cup whipped cream or chocolate syrup.*

Fruit Ice Cream: Add 1–2 cups chopped fresh or canned fruit.

Fruit Sherbet: Omit vanilla. Add 2 bananas mashed or blended and juice of 2 oranges and 2 lemons. Use non-fat milk, whole milk, or half-and-half.

Powdered Milk Ice Cream: Replace half-and-half with 2 1/2 cups milk powder and water to make 4 cups.

Refrigerator Ice Cream: Freeze in metal bowl until almost solid. Beat well. Freeze. Beat again if desired.

See page 240 for International Conversion Charts

Vanilla Ice Cream

Freeze in metal or plastic container until almost firm:

- **1 3/4 cups evaporated milk**

Combine separately and heat:

- **1/3–1/2 cup water**
- **1 1/2 teaspoons plain gelatin**

Add, turn off heat, and stir well. Sugar will not dissolve completely:

- **2/3 cup sugar**

Add and beat at high speed until 8 cups in volume:

- **frozen evaporated milk**

Add and stir:

- **1–2 teaspoons vanilla**

Freeze. Do not beat a second time.

* *For additions to vanilla ice cream, see Freezer Ice Cream, page 96.*

* *Substitute 1 cup milk powder and 1 1/2 cups water for evaporated milk.*

* *Use 1 3/4 cups sweetened condensed milk for milk and sugar.*

Chocolate Ice Cream: Decrease water to 1/4 cup and increase sugar to 1 cup. Combine and add to hot sugar mixture: 2 tablespoons each cocoa and hot water.

Easy Ice Cream: Omit water, gelatin, and 1/3 cup sugar. Beat mixture until stiff. Freeze until partially set. Beat again and freeze.

Gelatin Ice Cream: Omit plain gelatin and sugar. Add 1/3 cup flavored gelatin and 3 tablespoons sugar.

Flavored Drink Mix Ice Cream: Beat in 1 package of flavored drink mix or other drink mix.

Pudding Ice Cream: Make Easy Ice Cream using 1/2 cup sugar. Add cooked and cooled pudding before beating.

Caramel Cream

Place unopened cans of sweetened condensed milk in a kettle and add sufficient water to completely cover the cans. Boil gently for 1–3 hours. Cook longer if thicker consistency is desired. Be certain the cans remain completely covered with water during the entire process. Caramel Cream may be kept unrefrigerated several days, if the can is not punctured.

Quick method: Put unopened cans of sweetened condensed milk on rack in pressure cooker. Add water until it comes up 1/2 inch on cans. Close cooker. Pressure 10 minutes at 10–15 pounds of pressure. Do not attempt to cool cooker, but allow pressure to return to zero.

Sherbet

Dissolve:

- 1/3 cup flavored gelatin, any flavor
- 1 cup boiling water

Add and mix well:

- 1/2 cup sugar
- 2 cups milk
- 1 cup cream
- 1/4 cup lemon or lime juice, or more to taste

Freeze until nearly firm. Beat until creamy. Freeze again. Makes about 4 cups.

Frozen Yogurt: Omit milk, cream, and lemon juice. Add 2 beaten eggs. Increase sugar by 1 cup. Add 2 cups plain yogurt.

Fruit Juice Ice: Substitute orange juice or any mixture of juices for the milk and cream. Omit lemon juice for a milder ice. Freeze in ice cream freezer or refrigerator freezer.

Lemon Ice Cream: Omit gelatin, water, and cream. Increase milk to 4 cups and sugar to 1 1/2 cups.

Tropical Fruit Slush

Mash or blend until smooth:

- 2 cups fresh fruit, cut into small pieces
- 4 cups fruit cocktail (reserving liquid) or other fresh fruit

Heat:

- 2 cups juice from canned fruit or other fruit juice
- 1 cup orange juice, concentrate if available

Pour into large flat container and mix. When slightly cool, add:

- 1/2–1 teaspoon flavored fruit extract, optional

Mix well and freeze. Thaw to slush before eating.

* *Replace orange juice with 7–Up, Sprite, or other lemon-lime soda.*

* *Omit canned fruit and replace the juice with 2 cups each water and sugar, or honey to taste.*

Tropical Fruit Ice Pops: Pour fruit mixture into popsicle molds.

See page 240 for International Conversion Charts

Frozen Fruit Yogurt

Combine and freeze until firm:

- **4 cups plain yogurt**
- **1 cup fruit, sweetened and chopped**

Chocolate Syrup

Combine in a pan:

- **1 1/2 cups sugar**
- **1/2–1 cup cocoa**
- **1/8 teaspoon salt**

Gradually add to make a smooth paste:

- **1 cup hot water**

Boil for 4 minutes. Cool and add:

- **2 teaspoons vanilla**

Chocolate Milk: Add 1–2 tablespoons syrup to cup of milk.

Hot Fudge Sauce

Combine in pan:

- **1 cup sugar**
- **1 cup evaporated milk**
- **1/4 cup cocoa**
- **dash salt**
- **3 tablespoons margarine**

Stir over heat with a wire whip, until thick. Then add:

- **1 teaspoon vanilla**

* *Use 1 square unsweetened chocolate for cocoa and omit 1 tablespoon margarine.*

Chocolate Sauce from Mix: Substitute 1/2 cup Chocolate Pudding Mix, page 86, for cocoa, salt, and sugar. Add 1/4 cup sugar. Use milk or water for evaporated milk. Cook until thick, stirring constantly.

Lemon Sauce

Combine:

- 1/2 cup sugar
- 1 1/2 tablespoons cornstarch

Slowly add and cook until thick:

- 1 cup boiling water

Remove from heat and add:

- 2–4 tablespoons lemon, lime, or pineapple juice
- 1–2 teaspoons grated lemon rind, optional
- pinch of salt
- 1 tablespoon butter or margarine

Serve over pudding, ice cream, or cake.

Fruit and Nut Hints

To add flavor to fruit: Serve or prepare them with candied peels, ginger, and spices, or add lemon or lime juice to fruits or fruit fillings.

Ways to use fresh fruit: Baking, compotes, as a topping, puréed for drinks, in salads, puddings, ices, gelatin desserts, custards, creams, or as a garnish.

Do not use fresh pineapple, figs, papaya, or kiwi in gelatin.

For fruit ices: Freeze puréed or whole fruit and shave into chilled bowls.

Fresh fried fruit: Fry and use as a dessert, a side dish, or a garnish.

To juice lemons or oranges: Heat to get more juice.

To remove membranes from citrus fruits: Soak in boiling water for five minutes before peeling, and the white pulp will come off perfectly.

To keep pineapple: Cut slices from the bottom as you need them. Wrap the unused portion, with the top growth attached, in plastic wrap.

To make citrus rind for seasoning cakes and frostings: Wash and grate just the outside layer (not the white membranes). Place in a tightly covered glass jar and store in the refrigerator or dry in the oven at 200°F.

To prevent fruit discoloration: Sprinkle peeled fruit with lemon juice.

To ripen fruits: To ripen apricots, nectarines, peaches, plums,

See page 240 for International Conversion Charts

pears, and avocados, place them in a paper bag and close it loosely. Ripen bananas and melons at room temperature. Ripen tomatoes away from direct sun.

To cut fruits in small pieces: Use scissors rubbed with butter. To avoid wrinkled baked apples, slit in a few places before baking.

To plump raisins: Boil in water for a few minutes.

To make dried bananas: Dry unpeeled, ripe cooking or eating bananas in the sun for 4–5 days. Take in at night. Turn daily. Or peel bananas and cut in slices. Place on cookie sheets, cover with cheese cloth. Dry in the sun 2–3 days. Or dry peeled, sliced bananas in oven at 200°F until dry.

To store bananas: Fresh, peeled bananas may be put in a glass jar with a tight lid and kept this way for a week or more. No refrigeration is necessary.

Bananas may be diced and used as a substitute for dried fruit.

To roast peanuts: Roast in a deep roasting pan at 200°F for 1–2 hours. Stir often, then place in a clean cloth sack and rub between hands to remove skins. Blow off the skins and store in dry, covered glass containers.

Do not attempt to roast cashew nuts as they give off a poisonous gas.

To make peanut butter: Grind peanuts in a corn grinder, running through 2–3 times. Add salt and cooking oil to the desired taste and consistency.

To blanch almonds: Cover with cold water in a pan, bring to a boil, strain, run cold water over, and dry on a cloth. The skins will slip off easily.

To freshen stale vegetables, fruits, and nuts: Pour boiling water over them, then spread in a shallow pan and heat in the oven, stirring often.

Chart for Cooking Fresh and Dried Fruits

Cut Fruit	Minutes	Water	Minutes at Stove top 15 lbs. Pressure
Apples—baked	24–30 oven	1/2 C	3
Apples—fresh	5–10	1/2 C	2
Apples—dried	20–30	2 C	6
Apricots, peaches, pears, figs—fresh	3–5	1 C	1
Apricots, peaches, pears—dried	40	2 C	10
Figs—dried	60	2 C	15

Preparing Exotic Fruits

Coconut: Open coconut by first removing the outer husk with a strong knife. To save the liquid, hold coconut over a bowl and punch holes in the "eyes" and drain off the liquid. Open the inner hard brown shell by using a hammer to tap in a line around the middle of the coconut. Give an extra tap when you reach the place you began tapping. Or place coconut in a shallow pan and bake at 300 degrees for 45 minutes. If coconut does not crack, tap it with a hammer. Remove the meat from the shell with a small spatula or knife, peel off the brown skin, and prepare as desired.

Grated Coconut: Grate by hand or in a blender. Keeps 3–4 days refrigerated, but indefinitely if put into the freezer in a tight container. Or place on a cookie sheet, dry, and store in a tight container. Coconut may be sugared before or after drying.

* *Grated coconut may be used in granola, cakes, cookies, candies, breads, and biscuits, in the place of flour.*

* *To freshen grated coconut, soak it in fresh milk and add a pinch of sugar, or place coconut in a sieve that is set over boiling water and steam.*

Coconut Milk: Combine 3 cups boiling water or coconut liquid and 4 cups freshly grated coconut. When water is cool enough, squeeze the soaked, grated coconut into the water with your hands about 20 times to extract "milk." Put the coconut milk through a strainer and store in the refrigerator or freeze it for later. It is best to freeze coconut milk, as it sours easily. Yields 2 cups. Coconut milk is used in cooking meats and fish, in desserts, in baking, or as a milk substitute.

Coconut Cream: Bake coconut milk at 200°F until set. Cool and use as cream on fruits or cereal.

Cherimoya: This heart-shaped fruit with a tough green skin is best when it is a uniform green color. If it is brown, it is too ripe. Allow this fruit to soften at room temperature. It has the flavor of a mixed fruit sherbet. Peel, slice, and serve. Or scoop out, remove seeds, and blend as a drink. Or use in a sherbet or with other fruits in a compote.

Fresh Dates: Store in refrigerator away from aromatic foods or freeze. Add to cakes, shakes, cookies, or serve plain or stuffed with nuts, cream cheese, candied orange peel, celery, water chestnuts, or jicama.

Fresh Figs: These are highly perishable so eat soon after purchasing. Serve for breakfast peeled and sliced in cream, orange juice, pineapple juice, or sprinkled with lime or lemon. Use for salads and desserts. Spoon lemon sherbet into a dish and add sliced figs, top with grated coconut, and garnish with mint.

Guavas: Refrigerate when soft. Clean, stem, slice, puree in a blender, squeeze through several layers of cheesecloth to remove seeds, and add sugar to taste and food coloring, if desired. Use in sherbets, drinks, or sauce. Freeze remainder until needed.

Kiwi: Ripen at room temperature, then refrigerate. Rub off fuzz or peel and slice. Use as a garnish for cream pies, puddings, mousses, or as a breakfast fruit with fresh lime juice and sugar sprinkled on top. Kiwi is excellent with cottage cheese in a salad or combined with other fruits, especially bananas.

Kumquats: You must eat the skin with the fruit to give the sweet and sour taste. Kumquats keep well and are great in fruit salads or candied. They are high in vitamin C.

Loquats: Wash, peel, remove seeds, and slice. Serve in fruit salads or make jam. Loquats keep well.

See page 240 for International Conversion Charts

Mangos: Ripen at room temperature. Chill before peeling and slice away from the seed. Use in short cake, upside-down cake, cobblers, pies, sherbets, and as mango mousse.

Mango Mousse: Simmer 8 cut, unpeeled mangos for 30 minutes, force through a fine sieve, cool, and fold into whipped cream, coconut cream, or ice cream. Top with powdered sugar if desired.

Green Papaya: Slice, cube, and cook as any vegetable, or cook as applesauce. Or use in cooking stews or boiled meats as a meat tenderizer.

Ripe Papaya: Peel, slice, and sprinkle with a little fresh lime juice, or use in sherbets for dessert. For a salad, fill with crab, shrimp, or any curried meat, or combine lettuce, endive, papaya, and grapefruit. Papaya or poppy seed dressing are excellent to use with this salad. Use papaya seeds in a dressing or in any meat marinade.

Persimmons: Refrigerate or freeze as soon as soft. To serve soft persimmons, place stem end down on a plate and cut through the top and spoon out the pulp. Serve slices on cereal or combine with other fruits. To use frozen, hold under water and slip off the skins. Use in your favorite recipe or slice while still frozen for a taste like a fine sherbet.

See page 240 for International Conversion Charts

Pie and Pastry Hints

To cut in shortening: Cut into flour using two knives, a fork, or a pastry blender. Shortening is cut in until it is the size of a pea and water is added slowly, using just enough to hold the dough together. Puff pastry is much faster as floured shortening is pinched and the water is added all at once.

To keep dough for later use: Place on floured board, flour, divide into two parts (one slightly larger) fold over, and place these in a plastic bag and refrigerate until needed.

To roll out dough: Roll the larger piece first to 1/8-inch thickness and trim slightly larger than pan. Keep board and rolling pin floured. Fold pastry in half, lay it across the ungreased pie pan, and unfold.

To flute the pie edge: Use the dough that hangs over the rim and pinch it between your thumb and forefinger to make a wavy pattern around the rim.

To make a single crust pie: Flute the edge. Prick the crust with a fork in several places if the crust is to be baked before filling. If the crust is to be used with a juicy pie filling, brush the crust with the white of an egg, melted butter, or apricot jam before baking, then bake at 425°F for 10 minutes. This will prevent the crust from becoming soggy when it is filled.

To make a two-crust pie: Fill the bottom crust, then roll out the top crust to 1 inch larger than the pan. Moisten the bottom rim with water and place top crust on top of pie, flute edges, gash with knife to let steam escape, and insert two 3-inch pieces of macaroni in gashed place to absorb juice.

To make a lattice top: Cut long narrow strips of dough with knife or pastry wheel and place across top. Moisten rim where strips touch bottom crust.

To make a pie shell: Place rolled dough on the bottom of an inverted pie pan, prick it, and allow it to relax in the refrigerator for 2 hours before baking. Bake shell at 425°F for 10–12 minutes.

To keep crust for custard pie firm: Use heated milk and shorten baking time.

To keep custard from separating: Beat hard for five minutes after cooking.

Five-Minute Puff Pastry

Combine and shake to cover thoroughly with the flour:

- **3/4 cup cold, firm shortening, cut into small cubes**
- **4 cups flour**
- **1/8 teaspoon salt**

Pinch floured cubes lightly to flatten, then add:

- **1/2 cup ice water**

Mix lightly with knife to cut in water and place dough on floured board. Roll out dough and place in pie pan. Follow directions under Pastry Hints. This dough works well for wrapping meats or turnovers, as well as for pie crusts.

Butter Crust

Combine and mix just until dough forms:

- 1/2 cup butter or margarine
- 2 tablespoons sugar
- 1 cup flour

Crumble 1/3 cup of mixture in small baking pan. With floured fingers, press remaining mixture in pie pan. Bake crust at 350°F 12–15 minutes until golden. Bake crumbs 10 minutes until crispy. Stir crumbs twice while baking. Cool crust and fill with desired filling. Sprinkle with crumbs.

* *Stir 1/4 cup finely chopped nuts or coconut into ingredients.*

Crumb Pie Crust

Combine:

- 1 1/2 cups corn flakes, oatmeal, crushed cookies, or graham crackers
- 1/2 cup chopped nuts, optional
- 1/4 cup shredded coconut, optional
- 1/3 cup melted butter, margarine, or cooking oil
- 1/4 cup honey or sugar
- 1/8 teaspoon salt, optional
- 1/4 teaspoon nutmeg, optional
- 1/4 teaspoon vanilla, optional

Press into bottom and sides of pie plate for crust. For crumbs, put 1/2 the mixture in cake pan. Bake both at 350°F for 10–15 minutes. Or fill unbaked crust with pie filling and bake as directed for pie. This is a good substitute for graham cracker or crumb crust.

See page 240 for International Conversion Charts

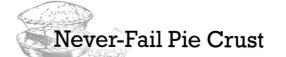

Single Pie Crust

Combine:

- **1 1/3 cups flour**
- **1/2 teaspoon salt**

Cut in until fairly coarse:

- **1/2 cup shortening**

Add a tablespoon at a time and toss with fork:

- **3 tablespoons water**

Roll out dough to fit pie pan. For crust baked without filling, prick it first with fork. Bake at 425°F for 10–15 minutes. For uncooked crust follow the recipe for baking time and temperature.

Lemon Crust: Add 1 tablespoon lemon juice, 1/2 teaspoon finely grated lemon peel, and 1 tablespoon sugar.

Nut Crust: Add 3 tablespoons finely chopped nuts.

Quick Oil Pie Crust: Mix ingredients in pie pan, substitute 1/3 cup oil for shortening, and press into pie pan with fingers.

Never-Fail Pie Crust

Combine:

- **3 cups white flour**
- **1 1/4 cups soft shortening**
- **1 teaspoon salt**

Combine separately and add:

- **1 egg, well-beaten**
- **5 tablespoons water**
- **1 tablespoon vinegar or lemon juice**

Blend with a fork until well moistened. Divide mixture into 4 balls and wrap balls in plastic or foil wrap. Store in freezer or roll out into pies now. Always available for quick use and it thaws in a few hours. This crust also keeps for 2 weeks in the refrigerator. Excellent for one or two crust pies or for cheese and vegetable pies. This is so easy to handle and can be patted into pie pan for a one crust pie. Follow directions under Pastry Hints for baking.

Rich Baked Pastry: Substitute 1/2 cup milk for egg, water, and vinegar. Combine 2–3 tablespoons milk and 1 beaten egg and paint this mixture on the crust before baking.

Banana Coconut Cream Pie

Make crumb pie crust. Line crust with:

- sliced bananas
- a little sugar

Cover bananas with:

- undiluted coconut cream (see page 102)
- cinnamon, sprinkled on top

Bake at 350°F until coconut cream sets.

Vanilla Cream Pie

Combine:

- 2/3 cup sugar
- 1/4–1/2 teaspoon salt
- 5 tablespoons cornstarch

Stir in gradually:

- 3 cups milk

Cook over moderate heat stirring constantly until mixture thickens. Boil 1 minute. Remove from heat and slowly stir half the hot mixture into:

- 3 egg yolks or 2 whole eggs, beaten slightly

Blend into hot mixture in saucepan. Boil gently for 5 minutes, stirring constantly. Remove from heat and add:

- 1 tablespoon oil or margarine
- 1 1/2 teaspoons vanilla

Pour into baked shell. Cool. Add crumb topping, meringue, nuts, or fruits.

Banana Cream Pie: Arrange sliced bananas on the top of the crust before pouring in the cream filling.

Chocolate Cream Pie: Increase sugar to 1 1/4 cups. Add 6 tablespoons cocoa and 2 teaspoons oil.

Coconut Cream Pie: Add 1–2 cups grated coconut to filling.

Peanut Butter Cream Pie: Combine 1 cup peanut butter and 1 1/2–2 cups powdered sugar until crumbly. Spread in baked pie shell. Spread cream filling on top. May sprinkle a few peanut butter crumbles on top. Use Chocolate Cream filling, if desired.

See page 240 for International Conversion Charts

Easy Coconut Custard Pie

Combine and beat with beater for 1 minute or blend 15 seconds:

- **4 eggs**
- **6 tablespoons margarine or butter**
- **1/2 cup flour or Master Mix (page 9)**
- **2 cups milk**
- **3/4 cup sugar**
- **1 teaspoon vanilla**

Add:

- **1 cup grated coconut**

Pour into greased and floured 9-inch pie pan. Bake at 350°F for 50–60 minutes. Pie forms its own crust

* *Use 1/4 cup oil for margarine and add 1/2 teaspoon salt.*

* *Sprinkle with nutmeg or cinnamon before baking.*

* *Substitute 1 cup cooked rice, raisins, drained canned fruit, or bananas for coconut. Bake in 10-inch pie pan.*

Lemon Meringue Pie

Combine in medium saucepan:

- **1 1/2 cups sugar**
- **3 tablespoons each flour and cornstarch**

Gradually stir in:

- **1 1/2 cups water**

Cook over medium heat until thick and bubbly, stirring occasionally. Reduce heat. Cook 2 minutes more. Add slowly:

- **3 egg yolks, beaten (reserve whites)**

Remove from heat, cook, and stir 2 minutes more. Then add:

- **2 tablespoons margarine**
- **1/2 teaspoon finely grated lemon peel**

Gradually stir in:

- **1/3 cup lemon juice**

Pour into a baked 9-inch pie crust and top with Meringue (see page 110). Bake at 350°F for 15 minutes or until Meringue is cooked.

Lemon Chess Pie: Omit cornstarch and water. Add 2 tablespoons cornmeal. Decrease flour to 2 tablespoons. Add 1/4 cup milk and 1 egg. Do not separate eggs. Decrease lemon juice to 1/4 cup. Do not cook mixture. Pour into unbaked crust. Bake at 375°F for 35 minutes or until set.

Lemon Meringue Pudding: Pour into a greased 9x9 pan. Top with Meringue and bake.

Lemon Pudding: Pour into bowl and do not bake.

Condensed Milk Lemon Pie

Combine and stir until mixture thickens:

- 1 2/3 cups sweetened condensed milk
- 1/2 cup lemon juice
- 1 teaspoon grated lemon rind
- 2 egg yolks, optional

Pour into a baked 9-inch pie crust. Top with Meringue (recipe follows). Pile beaten egg whites over filling and seal at edge. Bake at 350°F about 15 minutes, until brown. Chill and serve.

Meringue

Beat until soft peaks form:

- 3 egg whites at room temperature
- 1/2 teaspoon vanilla
- 1/4 teaspoon cream of tartar

Add gradually:

- 6 tablespoons sugar

Beat until stiff and glossy peaks form. Spread over warm filling, making sure it touches the pastry on all sides. Bake at 350°F for 15 minutes. Cool at room temperature. Meringue covers a 9 or 10-inch pie. Can be used with any cream or fruit pie.

* *For a smaller meringue use 2 egg whites and 1/4 cup sugar.*

Shoo-Fly Pie

Combine until crumbly and sprinkle 1/3 of mixture in unbaked pie crust:

- 1 1/2 cups flour
- 1 cup brown or white sugar
- 2 teaspoons cinnamon
- 1/4 teaspoon salt
- 1/4 cup shortening

Dissolve:

- 1/2 cup hot water
- 1/2 teaspoon baking soda

Add, then pour into crust:

- 1/2 cup molasses

Put remaining crumbs on top. Bake at 400°F for 10 minutes, until set, then 350°F for 30 minutes. This pie is best when served warm.

* *Add cinnamon, cloves, ginger, or other spices, if desired.*

Crustless Shoo-fly Pie: Omit crust. This is like gingerbread.

See page 240 for International Conversion Charts

Whipped Lemon Pie

Dissolve:

- 1/3 cup lemon gelatin
- 3/4 cup boiling water

Cool slightly, add, and chill until semi-firm:

- 1 cup orange juice

Whip gelatin mixture, then fold in:

- 1 cup whipping cream or evaporated milk, whipped

Pour into a 9 or 10-inch baked graham cracker or crumb crust. Top with baked crumbs. Chill several hours before serving.

* *Use any combination of gelatin and juice.*

Whipped Orange Pie: Use orange gelatin in place of lemon gelatin.

Whipped Pineapple Pie: Use pineapple juice in place of orange juice. Add 1 cup crushed pineapple and 1/3 cup cream cheese.

Candied Apple Pie

Arrange in a 9-inch unbaked pie crust:

- 2 cups cooked, sliced apples

Combine separately and spread over apples:

- 1/2 cup margarine or oil
- 1 cup brown sugar
- 1 cup flour

Bake at 325°F for 50 minutes.

Baked Apple Pie

Combine, toss lightly, and pour into a 9-inch unbaked pie crust:

- **5 cups sliced apples**
- **3/4–1 cup sugar**
- **2 tablespoons flour**
- **3/4 teaspoon cinnamon or nutmeg**
- **1 tablespoon lemon juice**
- **1/4 teaspoon salt**

Dot with:

- **2 tablespoons butter or margarine**

Top with pie crust. Seal and flute edges. Bake at 425°F for 40–45 minutes until juice is bubbly in center.

* *For an 8-inch pie decrease the following: Fruit by 1 cup, sugar by 1/4 cup, flour by 1 tablespoon, spice by 1/4 teaspoon, lemon juice by 1/2 teaspoon, and margarine by 1 tablespoon.*

* *For a 10-inch pie increase ingredients by the same proportions decreased in the 8-inch pie; don't increase margarine. Cook 5 minutes more.*

Apricot or Peach Pie: Use apricots or peaches in place of apples. Increase flour to 1/3 cup. Bake 30–35 minutes.

Blueberry Pie: Use blueberries for apples. Increase flour to 3 tablespoons, add dash of cinnamon, and bake at 425°F for 35–40 minutes.

Boysenberry or Blackberry Pie: Use boysenberries or blackberries in place of apples. Increase flour to 1/3 cup. Omit lemon.

Cherry Pie: Use cherries in place of apples. Increase sugar to 1 1/4 cups and increase flour to 1/4 cup, omit cinnamon and lemon juice and add 1/2 teaspoon almond extract, optional.

Green Papaya Pie: Use cooked or uncooked green papaya for apples.

Pineapple Pie: Use pineapple in place of apples. If fresh, chop in small pieces and cook for 5 minutes. Add 1/2 cup shredded coconut, optional.

Rhubarb Pie: Use rhubarb for apples. Increase sugar to 2 cups. Substitute cornstarch for flour.

Mock Apple Pie

Combine in a saucepan and boil gently for 15 minutes:

- **2 cups each, water and sugar**
- **2 teaspoons cream of tartar**

Stir in, then set aside to cool:

- **2 tablespoons lemon juice**
- **1 lemon rind, grated**

Arrange in 9-inch unbaked pie crust:

- **34 crackers, sliced cooking bananas, or green mangos**

Pour the cooled syrup over the crackers, dot generously with butter or margarine, and sprinkle with cinnamon. Cover with top crust and bake at 425°F for 30 minutes, until crust is crisp and golden. Serve warm.

See page 240 for International Conversion Charts

Unbaked Fresh Fruit Pie

Bake:

- 9-inch pie crust

In a saucepan combine:

- 1/2–1 cup sugar
- 3 tablespoons cornstarch

Gradually add and mix until smooth:

- 1 1/2 cups any fruit juice

Bring to a boil and cook one minute. Remove from heat, stir in:

- 1 tablespoon lemon juice
- 1 teaspoon grated rind, optional

Cool completely. Fold in:

- 4–6 cups assorted cut-up fresh fruit

Turn into crust and chill 4 hours.

Unbaked Berry Pie: Use 1 1/2 cups crushed berries for juice.

Unbaked Lemon Pie: Omit fruit. Double sauce. Pour into baked pie crust.

Fresh Fruit Yogurt Pie

Combine in saucepan and heat until granules disappear:

- 1/2 cup milk
- 1 tablespoon unflavored gelatin

Combine in a bowl, add to gelatin, and chill until set:

- 2 cups plain yogurt
- 1 teaspoon vanilla
- 1/2 cup honey

Wash and chop:

- 2 cups fresh strawberries or other fresh fruit

Mix half the fruit with gelatin mixture and pour into cooled crust. Arrange the remaining fruit on pie for decoration. Chill until set.

Lazy Pie

Melt in one 10-inch or two 8 or 9-inch pie pans:

- 1/2 cup shortening or margarine

Combine and pour over shortening:

- 1 cup each sugar and flour
- 1 teaspoon baking powder
- 1/8 teaspoon salt
- 2/3 cup milk

Drop over batter, do not mix:

- 2 1/2 cups chopped fruit
- 1/2–3/4 cup fruit juice, optional

Bake for 25 minutes at 350°F or use skillet cooking method (see page 242). Bake 35–40 minutes for uncooked apples.

Raisin Pie

Soak 2 hours or boil 10–15 minutes:

- 3/4 cup raisins
- 2 1/4 cups water

Combine separately:

- 1 3/4 cups sugar
- 4 1/2 tablespoons flour

Add and cook until thickened, stirring occasionally:

- 1 egg, well beaten
- 3 tablespoons lemon juice or pineapple juice, optional
- 1/8 teaspoon salt

Add raisins and liquid. Cool. Pour into baked crust.

Pumpkin Pie

Combine and beat with beater:

- 2 cups cooked, mashed pumpkin
- 1/2 teaspoon salt
- 1 2/3 cups evaporated milk
- 2 eggs, beaten slightly
- 3/4 cup sugar
- 1 teaspoon cinnamon
- 1/2 teaspoon nutmeg
- 1/2 teaspoon ginger, optional
- 1/4 teaspoon allspice or cloves
- 1 tablespoon oil

Pour into:

- 9-inch unbaked pie crust

Bake at 375°F about 1 hour or until knife inserted into center of pie comes out clean.

* *Use mashed cooked squash, sweet potatoes, cooking bananas, carrots, or chayotes in place of pumpkin.*

* *Bake filling in well-greased pan (omit the pastry).*

* *Add more spices to taste.*

See page 240 for International Conversion Charts

Cheesecake

Prepare Butter Crust, reserving 1/3 cup crumbs for top of cake. Bake both crumbs and crust according to directions. Cool.

Combine until creamy:

- 1 cup cream cheese, softened
- 1/3–2/3 cup sugar

Add, one at a time, beating well after each addition:

- 3 eggs

Blend in:

- 1 cup milk
- 1 teaspoon vanilla
- 1 teaspoon lemon juice, optional

Pour into crust. Bake at 375°F 40–45 for minutes. When baked, sprinkle with crumbs. Chill several hours before serving.

* *Substitute 1 3/4 cup tofu or cottage cheese for cream cheese. Blend until creamy. Add 2 tablespoons oil or margarine.*

Rich Cheesecake: Omit milk and increase cream cheese to 3 cups and sugar to 3/4 cup.

Pecan Pie

Combine and mix well:

- 1 cup light corn syrup
- 1/2 cup sugar
- 1/2 teaspoon each salt, cinnamon, and vanilla
- 3 tablespoons each flour, and margarine or butter
- 3 large eggs, beaten
- 1 cup pecans, almonds, or other nuts

Use a 9-inch unbaked crust. Bake at 350°F for 1 hour.

Fudgy Pecan Pie: Add 1/3 cup cocoa and 1/4 cup margarine.

Oatmeal Pie: Omit cinnamon, flour, and pecans. Add 1 cup sugar, 1 tablespoon vanilla, 3 tablespoons margarine, 1 1/2 cups shredded coconut, 1 1/4 cups oatmeal, and 3/4 cup milk. Pour into 10-inch deep dish pastry shell. Bake at 350°F for 45–55 minutes until browned and set. Serves 8–10.

Nut-Crunch Pie

Combine:

- **2 egg yolks**
- **1/2 cup sugar**
- **1 cup pecans or other nuts**
- **1 cup graham cracker or cookie crumbs**
- **1 teaspoon vanilla**

Combine separately and fold in:

- **2 egg whites, beaten until stiff**
- **1/2 cup sugar**

Pour into greased 9-inch pie pan. Bake at 350°F for 30 minutes.
Top with whipped cream if desired.

See page 240 for International Conversion Charts

Entrées

See page 151 for this Fried Chicken recipe.

Tastes Like Chicken

In our northern Ghanaian village, people often gave us gifts of food when we helped them out. After driving a woman to the clinic several hours away, we were given some very dark and stiff-as-a-board smoked antelope. Knowing it was meat, our four-year-old daughter was so excited that she danced along beside me as we walked the path home. On the way she asked, "Mommy, can you make chicken out of it?" I'm good at adapting recipes, but not that good!

From the kitchen of: _____ —Ginia Cahill

Main Dish Hints

To soak beans overnight: Place in water and let stand overnight.

To shorten bean soaking time: Combine beans, water, and 1 tablespoon soda. Boil 2 minutes, remove from heat, cover, and let set 1 hour.

To cook beans: After soaking, drain, apply fresh water, and add 1–2 teaspoons salt. Bring beans to boil, reduce heat, and simmer over low heat until tender. Add 1 tablespoon oil or shortening to reduce foam. Cooked beans freeze well.

To cook lentils: Simmer 1 cup dry lentils, 2 1/2 cups water, 1 bouillon cube, and 1 teaspoon salt for 30 minutes.

To cook beans in crockpot: Place soaked beans on high for 5 hours or on low for 10 hours.

To season bean, add any of the following: 1–2 teaspoons salt or 1 bouillon cube (less if using beans in another recipe), garlic powder or 1 garlic clove (minced or whole), browned onions (add to beans the last 10 minutes).

To avoid "boil overs" while cooking beans, macaroni, or spaghetti: Add 1 tablespoon cooking oil or shortening to the water.

To make rice whiter and fluffier: Add 1 teaspoon lemon juice or a pinch of rosemary to each 4 cups of water while cooking.

To wash grains like rice, beans, wheat: Wash several times until the water runs clear. The chaff and the bugs will float and can be poured off.

To protect dried grains and beans from insects during storage: Spread a thin layer on baking sheet and heat for 30 minutes in an oven set from 140–160°F. Or place in freezer that maintains a temperature of 0°F for four days. Or put a dried hot pepper or bay leaf in jar.

To enhance flavors of beans, casseroles, main dishes, soups, or any food lacking in flavor or richness: Add bouillon cubes or consommé powder to the liquid in recipe. Caution, bouillon cubes and consommé powder are salty and should he used as part of the salt required in recipes.

Cooking Chart for Dried Vegetables

Two cups dried vegetables yields about 5 cups cooked.

Vegetable	Hours Soak	Cups of Water	Pressure	Stove Top
Beans, navy, black-eyed peas	6	6	30 minutes	2 hours
Lentils, split peas	no	4	15 minutes	30–45 minutes
Lima beans	2	4	15 minutes	40–50 minutes
Peas, whole, black beans	2–4	6	25 minutes	1 hour
Soybeans	6	6	45 minutes	2–3 hours

Complementary Proteins

Certain foods can be combined to make complete proteins that are richer in protein than meat alone. The following groups of food combine to make complete proteins:

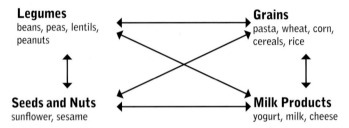

Legumes
beans, peas, lentils, peanuts

Grains
pasta, wheat, corn, cereals, rice

Seeds and Nuts
sunflower, sesame

Milk Products
yogurt, milk, cheese

Following are examples of meals made with combined proteins:

1. **Grains and Milk Products:** Bread made with milk or served with cheese; cereal with milk; cheese sandwiches; rice and cheese casserole; rice pudding; pasta with cheese; oatmeal with milk.

2. **Grains and Legumes:** Tortillas with beans; peanut butter sandwich; pea or bean soup with wheat toast; lentils with rice; rice and bean casserole.

3. **Seeds and Legumes:** Bean soup with sesame seeds; roasted seeds with peanuts or soybeans.

4. **Milk Products and Legumes:** Legume soups made with milk; cheese sauce with legumes; peanut butter sandwich with milk.

5. **Grains and Seeds:** Breads made with added seeds or seed sprouts; rice with sesame seeds.

Soybean Products

Dried soybeans are soaked, ground into a thick purée, and cooked. This cooked purée is separated into soy pulp and soymilk.

Tempe is dried soy pulp. Tofu or tahu is pressed soymilk curd. Tofu yields 10 grams of protein for every 100 calories. This is more than whole milk, eggs, or steak. Tofu keeps 1 week in refrigerator, if under fresh water. You can also freeze tofu and keep it indefinitely by slicing it into usable sizes, wrapping these in plastic wrap or foil, and freezing. To defrost, pour boiling water over the curd, dry, and pull into "chicken-like" strips.

See page 240 for International Conversion Charts

Uses for Tofu:

Puréed	Mashed	Cubed
dips	with scrambled eggs	soups
cakes	as scrambled eggs	stews
sauces	as cheese in lasagna	salads
cheesecake	meatloaf and rice dishes	

Casserole Toppings

Sprinkle any of the following over casseroles before baking:

- 1 tablespoon melted butter, 1/4 cup each dry bread crumbs and shredded American or cheddar cheese.
- 2 tablespoons butter and 1/2 cup crushed dry cereal.
- 1/2 cup crushed potato chips and 1/4 cup wheat germ.
- crushed soda crackers, french-fried onion rings, crisp bacon, nuts, or shoestring potatoes.

Pasta

Combine:

- 8 cups rapidly boiling water
- 1 cup macaroni or noodles
- 1 teaspoon salt
- 1 tablespoon butter, margarine or oil, optional

Boil until tender but still firm: 5–6 minutes for thin pasta, 9–12 minutes for medium, 14–15 minutes for medium thick, and 18–25 minutes for very thick. Drain and rinse, optional. May be served with white sauce, onions, meat, cheese, or vegetables.

* *To reheat plain leftover pasta or rice: Rinse first in cold water to remove excess starch, then drop into boiling water, heat 5 minutes, and drain.*

Homemade Noodles

Beat slightly:

- **1 egg**

Add and knead:

- **1/4 teaspoon salt**
- **2/3 cup flour**

Let stand covered for 30 minutes. Roll out very thin and spread on cloth to partially dry. Dough should not be sticky, but also should not be so dry that it will break or be brittle. Roll in a tight roll. Cut into very fine strips or threads. Toss lightly to separate. Spread out on board to dry, or cover a chair with a cloth and hang strips to dry completely, or let them dry curled up. When thoroughly dry, put in covered jars for future use. Store in freezer if possible. Drop by handfuls into boiling water or soup 5 minutes before serving.

Macaroni and Cheese

Layer in a greased casserole:

- **4 cups cooked macaroni**
- **1 1/4 cups cheese, diced or grated**

Sprinkle each layer with salt and pepper and dot with:

- **2 tablespoons margarine or oil**

Combine and pour over macaroni:

- **1–2 eggs, beaten**
- **2 cups milk, or more if thinner consistency is desired**

Sprinkle with paprika, if desired. Bake at 375°F for 40 minutes. Serves 5–6.

* *Add any of the following: 1 cup tuna, cooked beef, chicken, turkey, ham, or sliced hot dogs; 2 tablespoons chopped green pepper or onion; 1/2 cup cooked mushrooms; 1–2 chopped tomatoes; 1–2 cups cooked peas, green beans, carrots, or spinach.*

Creamy Macaroni and Cheese: Omit eggs. Stir 3 tablespoons flour into 3 tablespoons hot melted margarine. Add 1/2 teaspoon salt. Add milk and stir until mixture thickens. Add cheese and macaroni.

Quick Macaroni and Cheese: Just add cheese and small amount of hot milk to hot cooked macaroni. Cook a few minutes until cheese is melted.

See page 240 for International Conversion Charts

Eggplant in Coconut Milk

Have on hand an adequate amount of:

- **cooked noodles or other pasta, or leftover cooked rice**

Heat a skillet over high heat for 1 minute. Add:

- **2 tablespoons olive oil**

When the oil starts to smoke, add:

- **1 medium eggplant, peeled and diced into 1/2 inch cubes**
- **1 sweet red bell pepper, chopped**

Sear the eggplant and pepper for 5 minutes, stirring to prevent burning. Add:

- **1/2 teaspoon powdered cumin**
- **1/4 teaspoon garam masala (see page 152) or curry powder**
- **cayenne pepper to taste**
- **1/2 teaspoon salt**
- **1/2 teaspoon ground black pepper**

Pour into the skillet:

- **1 cup coconut milk**

Reduce heat and cook uncovered 10–15 minutes, stirring occasionally until the eggplant is soft and cooked and the coconut milk has thickened. Stir in:

- **1 teaspoon balsamic vinegar**
- **3 tablespoons chopped fresh parsley**

Serve eggplant warm over noodles or rice. Serves 4.

* *This recipe also works well with other vegetables like potatoes, carrots, or broccoli.*

* *If you leave the eggplant skin on, add a little extra balsamic vinegar to cut the bitterness.*

Stir-Fry Vegetables, Meat, and Noodles

Fry:

- **1 onion, sliced**
- **1 garlic clove, minced**
- **salt and pepper to taste**

Add and fry:

- **2 cups thinly sliced seasoned meat, cooked or uncooked (500 ml)**

Stir-fry separately over high heat:

- **3 cups thinly sliced vegetables—celery, carrots, or peppers**

Combine and reheat:

- **meat**
- **vegetables**
- **cooked macaroni, rice, or noodles**

Fry until firm, then cut into strips:

- **2–3 eggs, slightly beaten and seasoned**

Spread egg on meat mixture. Serve with peanuts, soy sauce, fish sauce, or Tabasco. Serves 8–10.

Perfect Rice

Combine in a pan and fry 2–3 minutes:

- 1–2 tablespoons shortening or oil
- 2 tablespoons onion, sliced, optional

Add and bring to a boil:

- 1 cup rice
- 2 cups boiling water
- 1/2–1 teaspoon salt

Cover, turn heat very low, and cook without stirring for 18–20 minutes, or longer for larger quantities.

Asian Rice: Omit oil and onion.

Rice Curry

Combine:

- 3 cups cooked rice
- 4–6 beaten eggs, optional
- 1 1/2 cups milk, optional
- 1/8 teaspoon black pepper
- 1/2–1 teaspoon each curry powder and salt

Bake at 350°F for 30 minutes or until egg is well done.

* *Add curry powder to water when cooking rice and omit milk and eggs.*

Spanish Rice

Fry until it begins to brown:

- 1 cup uncooked rice
- 3 tablespoons oil, shortening, or bacon fat, or 4 bacon strips

Add and fry until onion is transparent:

- 1 small onion, chopped
- 1 garlic clove, chopped

Add and allow to cook for a few minutes:

- 2 diced tomatoes or 3 tablespoons tomato sauce

Add:

- 3 cups water
- 1 teaspoon salt

Cover and cook without stirring over low heat 30 minutes or until rice is tender and liquid is absorbed.

* *Add any of the following or a combination, with the onion: 1–2 cups cooked chicken, ground beef, ham, or tuna; 1 cup chopped carrots, green beans, or peas; 1/4 teaspoon cumin or thyme or 1/2 teaspoon chili powder.*

See page 240 for International Conversion Charts

Easy Dinner-in-a-Casserole

Combine:

- 1 cup rice, uncooked
- 2 cups boiling water
- 2 tablespoons chopped parsley
- 1/4 cup chopped green pepper, optional
- 1 teaspoon salt
- 2 cups chopped tomatoes
- 1 cup tuna
- 1 onion, chopped
- 1 tablespoon Worcestershire sauce, optional
- 2 stalks chopped celery, optional

Pour mixture into greased casserole. Bake at 375°F for 1 1/2 hours without stirring. Or cover and simmer in skillet on low for 45–60 minutes.

* *For tuna use cooked chopped chicken, beef, sausage, pork, or alligator.*

Chicken and Rice: Omit tomatoes and tuna. Add 2–4 tablespoons dry onion soup mix or 1 1/4 cups condensed cream of chicken soup. Arrange rice mixture into greased 9x13 pan. Place chicken pieces that have been dipped in melted butter on top. Bake at 300°F for 1 1/2–2 hours.

Cuban Hamburger and Rice: Omit tuna. Fry green pepper, onion, 3 garlic cloves, and 2 cups ground beef. Add 1 teaspoon cumin, 1/4 cup lemon juice, and 1/4 teaspoon oregano. Substitute 3/4 cup tomato sauce for tomatoes.

Ceylonese Rice

Combine in skillet and stir frequently until brown (about 5 minutes):

- 1/4 cup oil
- 2 cups cooked rice
- 1 1/2 cups thin carrot strips
- 1 cup onion, chopped
- 1 bunch onion tops or scallions, chopped
- 1/2 cup raisins

Add and simmer 5 minutes:

- 2 cups water, bouillon, or broth
- 1 cup peas, cooked
- 1–2 teaspoons salt, decrease if you use bouillon

Combine separately and cook lightly:

- 1 tablespoon butter
- 1 cup cashews, pecans, or other nuts

Add nuts to rice mixture, toss lightly, and serve.

Tasty Rice Casserole

Combine in a baking dish:

- 3 cups cooked rice
- 1 cup any cooked vegetable desired
- 1–2 cups cooked meat, fish, or poultry
- 1–1 1/2 cups white sauce
- 1 1/2 teaspoons grated onion or 1/2 cup browned onion
- 1/3 cup parsley or celery, optional
- 1 garlic clove, minced, optional
- 1 teaspoon Worcestershire sauce, optional

Top with:

- 1/4 cup grated cheese

Bake at 350°F for 30 minutes.

* *Omit white sauce. Add 2 well-beaten eggs, 1 cup milk, 1/4 cup oil, 1 teaspoon salt, and 1 cup cheese. If desired, separate eggs and beat whites until stiff; fold into mixture.*

High Protein Squares: Decrease rice to 1 cup. Omit vegetable. Increase cheese to 3/4 cup and combine with rice mixture. Add 2 beaten eggs. Bake in well-greased 9x9 pan. After baking let stand 5 minutes. Then cut into squares. Serves 6.

Oriental Fried Rice

In large skillet or wok, cook without stirring until set:

- 1 tablespoon hot oil
- 2 eggs, beaten

Cut into strips and set aside. Then combine in skillet and cook 4 minutes:

- 1/2 cup diced, cooked ham, pork, beef, chicken, or shrimp
- 1/2 cup chopped mushrooms, optional
- 3 tablespoons chopped onion, green onion, if available
- 3 tablespoons soy sauce
- 1–2 teaspoons oil

Stir in:

- 4 cups cooked rice

Serve with egg strips, leftover or fresh vegetables, and soy sauce.

Indonesian Fried Rice (Nasi Goreng): Omit soy sauce and add 1/2 teaspoon black or white pepper; 1 teaspoon each paprika, garlic powder, ground coriander, cumin, and turmeric; 2 teaspoons sava galangal root; 1/2 teaspoon sereh powder, lemon grass, or citronella; 2 1/2 teaspoons salt and Tabasco, dried chili pepper flakes, or fresh hot pepper to taste. Garnish with egg strips.

See page 240 for International Conversion Charts

Golden Oats and Herbs

Combine in a large skillet:

- 3 tablespoons melted butter or margarine
- 1 1/2 cups oatmeal
- 1 egg

Cook, stirring constantly until oats are browned, separated, and dry.

Add:

- 3/4 cup broth
- 2 tablespoons parsley
- 1/2 teaspoon oregano
- 1/2 teaspoon basil
- 1/4 teaspoon salt

Cook and stir until liquid evaporates, 2–3 minutes. Serves 3–4.

Bean Loaf

Combine, place in greased loaf pan, and bake at 375°F for 45 minutes:

- 3 cups cooked beans, mashed
- 1 small onion, minced
- 3 tablespoons fat
- 1 cup bread crumbs
- 1 egg
- 1 1/2 teaspoons salt
- 1 cup evaporated milk

Black Beans with Pork

Combine and cook until tender:

- 2 cups black beans, soaked overnight
- 8 cups water
- 2 cups pork rind, cut in pieces
- 2 cups boneless pork, cubed
- 1/2 medium onion
- 2 1/2 teaspoons salt
- 2 tablespoons oregano

Serve with tortillas and arrange on a platter with:

- 2 lemons, sliced
- 1/2 onion, diced
- 2 minced green chilies, optional

Black Bean Soup: Add water, lemons, onion, and chilies directly into soup.

Refried Beans

Combine and simmer until tender, stirring frequently:

- 1 cup beans, soaked overnight
- 4 cups water
- garlic and salt to taste
- 2 tablespoons shortening

Heat in skillet:

- 1/2 cup bacon drippings or lard

Add beans to fat gradually, mashing them thoroughly. Add liquid from beans if needed. Serve with enchiladas, eggs, or any other Mexican dish. Cubes of cheese and onion may be folded into refried beans.

* *It is important to have the grease or lard very hot before adding the beans. The hot fat tenderizes the beans and makes them easy to mash.*

Baked Beans

Combine:

- 3 cups cooked white navy or small brown beans
- 1–2 medium onions, browned
- 1 cup tomato sauce or catsup
- 3 tablespoons brown sugar and/or 1/4 cup molasses
- 2 tablespoons prepared mustard or 1 tablespoon dry mustard
- 1/2 cup pork, bacon, or other cooked meat, optional

- 2 teaspoons salt
- pepper to taste

Serve immediately or bake 3 hours at 325°F to improve flavor.

Sunbeam Special

Combine and fry:

- 1–3 teaspoons oil
- 1 tortilla

Turn once and put on top:

- grated cheese
- chopped chilies, optional
- refried beans

Cover with:

- 1 tortilla

Turn immediately. Then pour over tortilla:

- 1 egg, beaten

Egg will run over the edges of the tortilla making the yellow part of a sunflower with the tortilla as the center. When fried on one side, turn and fry on the other side. Serve with tomato or hot sauce.

See page 240 for International Conversion Charts

Dahl Palak
(Lentils with spinach)

Lentils are best if cooked in a pressure cooker, but can also be cooked on a stove in a pan with a tight-fitting lid.

In a bowl with water, soak:

- **1 cup yellow lentils which look like small yellow split peas**

Presoak lentils for 1 hour if you are using a pressure cooker, or 3–4 hours if you are using a stovetop pan. Drain. Cook the lentils until soft, using either a pressure cooker or a stovetop pan.

If using pressure cooker: Add enough water to cover lentils, plus about 1 inch more. Cover and cook on high. When first whistle blows, reduce heat and cook for about 5 more whistles, or about another 15 minutes. Remove from heat and release handle. When lid drops in, check that lentils are soft and not too dry. If dry, add water to give a sauce-like consistency. If lentils aren't soft enough, add water as needed and pressure cook for about 5–10 minutes more.

If using stovetop pan with lid: Cover lentils with water to depth of 1-inch, as above, and cook tightly-covered over medium heat until lentils are soft (40–50 minutes), adding water as needed to ensure the lentils become soft but do not dry out.

After cooking, drain the lentils and remove from the pressure cooker or pan. In the pressure cooker or pan, heat:

- **1 tablespoon olive or other cooking oil**

Add:

- **1 teaspoon cumin seeds, also known as jeera**

Let seeds toast in the pan until they begin to darken. Add and cook till the onion starts to get translucent:

- **2 garlic cloves, minced**
- **half of a medium onion, chopped**

Add and cook until softened:

- **half of a green bell pepper, chopped**

In a dish or bowl, thoroughly mix together:

- **1/4 to 1 teaspoon ground red pepper**
- **1/4 teaspoon ground turmeric**
- **1/2 teaspoon ground coriander**
- **1/4 teaspoon ground ginger, optional**
- **1/2 teaspoon sea salt**

Stir this spice mixture into the pressure cooker or pan.

Next stir in:

- **1 medium tomato, chopped**

Add the cooked lentils to the mixture in the pressure cooker or pan. Stir gently.

Add:

- **1 cup finely chopped fresh spinach**

Cook while stirring for 5 minutes. Sprinkle dahl with chopped cilantro if desired. Serve hot with steamed rice or rotis (soft flatbreads similar to wheat tortillas). Serves 4.

Lentil Cheese Savory

Combine and simmer in covered saucepan for 15 minutes:

- 1 cup lentils
- 2 1/4 cups cold water

Add and simmer 30 minutes more:

- 1/2 teaspoon salt
- 2 cups chopped tomatoes or 1 cup sauce

Fry separately:

- 1/4 cup margarine
- 1 large onion, sliced

Add:

- 1 cup grated cheese
- lentil mixture

Place in greased 9x9 pan and cover with:

- 1/2 cup dry tortilla crumbs or buttered bread crumbs

Bake at 350°F for 20 minutes. Delicious hot or cold.

Lettuce Wraps

Add a splash of the following to a sauté pan:

- sesame or vegetable oil

Stir-fry in the oil for 5 minutes:

- 1 cup of tofu, cubed, or 1 cup fresh zucchini, diced
- 4 green onions, chopped fine
- 2 cloves of garlic, minced
- 1/2–1 teaspoon peeled fresh ginger, finely diced

Add:

- 1 tablespoon of satay sauce or coconut milk, optional

Let filling cool.

Mix the following in a bowl or blender:

- 1/2 teaspoon peeled ginger, chopped fine
- 1/4 cup ground peanuts or peanut butter
- 1/8–1/4 cup soy sauce
- 1/4 cup sesame oil
- 1/4 cup water
- 1 clove garlic, minced
- 1/4 cup chopped green onions
- chopped cilantro leaves to taste, optional
- 1 teaspoon fresh lemon or lime juice

Pour sauce over the stir-fried wrap filling and stir to combine. Chill the filling for about 30 minutes.

Immediately before serving the wraps, stir into the chilled, prepared filling:

- 1/3 cup or more of fresh carrots, finely diced

See page 240 for International Conversion Charts

- 1/3 cup or more of pear, apple, or water chestnut, chopped fine

To assemble the wraps, set out:

- 12–16 washed, large lettuce or cabbage leaves (cabbage can be blanched to soften)

Place some of the wrap filling in each leaf and sprinkle with:

- crushed ramen noodles

Roll to form wraps. Serve wraps with rice and cucumber sticks on the side. Serves 6–8.

* *For meat eaters, chicken can replace the tofu or zucchini.*

Soy Burgers

Combine and blend well:

- 2 cups cooked and drained soybeans
- 2 cups cooked rice
- 2 tablespoons oil
- 1/4 cup onion, chopped fine
- 1/2 cup grated cheese
- 2 beaten eggs
- 1 tablespoon soy sauce or 1 teaspoon salt
- 1/2 teaspoon basil, optional
- 1/2 cup whole wheat or white flour

The mixture should be thick enough to drop from a spoon. If not add more flour to make it stick together better. Heat a little oil in skillet over medium heat. Drop batter by large spoonfuls onto skillet to make burger-size patties. Fry until nicely browned on each side. Serve with catsup or curry sauce.

Lentil Hamburgers: Substitute lentils for soybeans and browned ground beef for rice. Omit oil, cheese, and flour.

Quick Soy Burgers: Combine and boil until soft, 1/3 cup crushed soybeans, 2 cups water, 1 bouillon cube, 1 tablespoon chopped onion, and 1 clove garlic, crushed. Add 2 eggs and beat well. Fry in hot oil until light brown.

See page 240 for International Conversion Charts

Meat Hints

When broiling meats or bacon on a rack: Place dry bread in the broiler pan to soak up fat and reduce chances of a fire.

For crisp baked chicken: Rub skin with mayonnaise before baking.

For extra flavor in fried chicken: Add 1/2 teaspoon dry mustard.

Never salt meat before or during cooking since this makes it tough.

To avoid splattering grease: Sprinkle salt in the frying pan while frying foods or invert a metal colander over the skillet.

To make hamburgers: Select a jar lid the proper size for hamburgers. Remove the liner and wash lid well. Fill with meat and smooth top with knife or spatula, turn over and tap. For easier handling, rinse hands in cold water before shaping meat.

For juicier burgers: Add a stiffly beaten egg white to each pound of hamburger or put 1 tablespoon cottage cheese in center of burger.

To coat meat with flour: Place in a bag with seasoned flour and shake.

To wrap meat for barbecue: Wrap in banana or papaya leaves.

To tenderize meats: Wrap meat in crushed or bruised papaya leaves and cook. Or score green papaya and collect the white latex that will flow from the cut. Rub on meat and cook. This contains protein digesting enzyme. Or marinate in vinegar, fresh lemon, or canned pineapple juice for 1–2 hours. If fresh pineapple juice is used, marinate no more than half an hour. Or grind, cube, or pound meat, then marinate. Or add 2–3 tablespoons vinegar to the water the meat is cooked in.

Fresh pork storage: Cut pork into 1–inch cubes or 1/2–inch slices (1 1/2 cm). Cover completely with vinegar. Add several cloves garlic and large amount of salt. Keeps for 1 week without refrigeration or longer if refrigerated. Broil or roast over fire. This is not for use in pork recipes.

To make cracklings: Grind pork fat using the medium grinder blade. Put ground fat in a frying pan or other heavy pan over low flame. Cook approximately 1 hour. Cracklings will be crispy and brown when done.

To render lard: Put ground skin and fat from butchered pork in a large, heavy pan. To each pound of fat, add 1/2 cup of water. Bring to a boil and render slowly, uncovered. As water boils away, any extraneous odors are carried off. When the last sputtering begins and water is all evaporated and lard is nice and clear, remove from heat. Strain into jars.

To keep raw fish fresh and odorless: Rinse in lemon juice and water, dry, wrap, and refrigerate or sprinkle with lemon juice.

When baking whole fish: Wrap in well-oiled cheesecloth. When fish is done, it can be lifted from baking pan without falling to pieces. To remove cloth, slip a spatula under fish and slide cloth out after fish is on platter.

To draw out the salt from salted fish: Add a glass of vinegar to the water in which the salt fish is soaking.

Meat-Cooking Chart

Beef, pork, lamb, young or small game, poultry or wild fowl may be corned, ground, cubed, or made into roasts, loaves, steaks, soups, or stews. Meats may be floured, browned, or stuffed before cooking.

* *Note: For safety at all times, meat should be well-done.*

Poultry can be baked at 325°F until internal temperature reaches 185°F or about 25 minutes per pound. Bake steaks and chops at 350–400°F. Other meats can be baked at 325–350°F until internal temperature reaches 170°F or 30–40 minutes per pound.

Meat	Time	Liquid	Stove Top at 15 Pounds Pressure/ Minutes
Alligator, fish, loaves, and steaks fried 5–10 min.	6–8 min.	2 T	10 min./lb.
Clams, lobster, and shrimp—boiled/ steamed	5 min.	1 C(250 ml)	10–20 min./lb.
Roasts, Swiss steak, corned meats, old wild game, and tough cuts	25 min.	2 C	3–4 hours./lb.
Poultry and young wild fowl	9 min.	2 T	30–60 min./lb.
Ribs and roasts	5–20 min.	1/3 C	45–60 min.
Steaks, chops, ground, or cubed meats—fried 10 min.	10 min.	1/4 C	30 min./lb.
Soups and stews	30–40 min.	2–8 C	1–2 hours

See page 240 for International Conversion Charts

Curried Steaks, Cutlets, or Chops

Brown in pressure cooker:

- 1–2 tablespoons oil
- steaks, cutlets, or pork chops

Add:

- 1–2 cups Curry Sauce, (see page 202)

Pressure 8–10 minutes at 15 pounds, depending on thickness of meat, or cook in a skillet until tender.

Mexican-Style Beefsteak

Trim excess fat from:

- 2 pounds top round steak about 1/2 inch thick

Combine:

- 1/2 cup flour
- 1 teaspoon salt
- 1/8 teaspoon pepper

Pound seasoned flour into both sides of meat and brown meat in:

- 2 tablespoons oil

Add and brown:

- 1 garlic clove, minced
- 1 large onion, chopped
- 1/2 green pepper, thinly sliced

Lower heat and add:

- 2 cups canned, chopped tomatoes
- 1/3 cup stuffed green olives, optional

Cover and cook very slowly until meat is tender, about 1–1 1/2 hours, or bake at 350°F for about 1 hour. If sauce becomes too thick, it may be thinned slightly with a small amount of broth or tomatoes. Serves 6.

Corned Beef

Combine in pan:

- **5 pounds brisket or any cut of fresh beef, tied to keep shape**

Cover with cold water and add:

- **1/2 garlic clove**
- **6 peppercorns**
- **pickling spices, tied in a bag, optional**

Bring to boil, skim off foam, and simmer for 5 hours until tender. Leave in water until lukewarm.

Corned Beef and Cabbage: When beef is almost tender, add cabbage wedges, and if desired, chopped potatoes, carrots, and onions. Cook until vegetables are tender. Drain and serve on a platter.

Corned Beef Hash: Brown in 3 tablespoons margarine, 2 cups cooked, cubed corned beef, 1 cup cooked potatoes or other vegetables, 1/2 cup each chopped onion and celery.

Stir-Fried Greens and Meat

In a lightly-greased skillet, brown:

- **1/2 pound ground beef)**

* *You can substitute chopped fresh meat, canned ham, Spam, or Bacon Bits.*

When meat is nearly all browned, add and brown lightly:

- **1/2 cup chopped raw peanuts, optional**

* *If peanuts are already roasted, add them instead when the greens are almost done.*

To the skillet, add and cook until translucent:

- **1 medium onion, diced**

If desired, add:

- **chopped green or red bell pepper, minced garlic, sliced mushrooms, or other favorite vegetables**

Stir in:

- **3–4 cups mixed chopped greens**

Once greens are coated lightly with fat from the meat (add butter or margarine if more fat is needed), mix in separate container:

- **1 tablespoon soy sauce**
- **1 1/2 cups beef broth or 1–2 beef cubes dissolved in 1 1/2 cups water**

Add the broth to the greens in the skillet. If needed, add more water. Cover and cook over low heat until the greens are tender. Cooking time will vary depending on the type of greens used.

* *Can be served with rice, cornbread, noodles, potatoes, or other breads.*

See page 240 for International Conversion Charts

Easy Jerky

The following recipe is for lean cuts of beef (flank, brisket, or round steak), venison, and the white meat of turkey or chicken. It is important to remove the fat from the meat and cut meat in 1/8-inch to 1/4-inch strips with or across the grain.

Combine in a bowl:

- 1/4 cup soy sauce
- 1 tablespoon Worcestershire sauce
- 1/2 teaspoon salt
- 1/4 teaspoon pepper
- 1/4 teaspoon garlic powder or salt
- 1/2 teaspoon onion powder or salt

Add, cover, and let stand 1 hour or overnight in refrigerator:

- 8–10 cups meat strips

Shake off excess liquid. Lay strips on oven racks. Lay foil on bottom of oven to catch drips. With oven door cracked, roast at lowest possible temperature 8–12 hours. Makes 3/4 pound jerky. Cool and store in airtight containers. Use for Christmas or backpack snack.

* *Use 1 tablespoon garlic or onion juice for powder or salt.*

* *Buffalo, bear, deer, and elk can also be used for making jerky.*

* *Alternate method: Slice meat thin, dip quickly in pot of boiling salt water, season with pepper, and dry in oven or over slow smoky fire for several days until brittle. Store in dry place.*

* *See page 248 for ways to use dried beef.*

Dried Beef: Rub strips with lemon juice and salt. Dry in oven or slow fire.

Smoky Jerky: Add 1 teaspoon hickory-smoke flavored salt.

Spicy Jerky: Add taco sauce, dash of Tabasco, and/or cayenne.

Esther's Liver and Onions

Brown, then remove from pan:

- 1–3 onions, sliced
- 1–2 tablespoons oil or shortening

Place in colander and pour boiling water over:

- 2 cups liver, membranes removed, cut in small pieces

Combine and coat liver with:

- 1/2 cup flour
- 1 teaspoon salt
- 1/4 teaspoon pepper

Fry until brown in very hot oil. Turn heat down to simmer. Add a little water and onions to top of meat. Cover and simmer 15 minutes.

Meatloaf

Combine:

- 1–2 eggs, slightly beaten
- 3/4 teaspoon salt
- 1 1/2 teaspoons soy sauce, optional
- 1/4–1/2 cup catsup or tomato sauce
- 1 small onion, chopped, and fried if desired
- 1 cup bread or cracker crumbs, rice, cereal, or oatmeal
- 2 cups ground beef

Place in a greased loaf pan and top with:

- 2/3 cup tomato sauce or catsup.

Bake at 350°F for 1–1 1/2 hours.

* *Add any or a combination of the following: Chopped celery, green pepper, grated carrots or potatoes, mashed cooked potatoes, celery salt, garlic salt, sage, dry mustard, onion soup mix, Worcestershire sauce.*

* *Add 1/2–1 cup milk for moister meat loaf*

* *Substitute part ground veal, turkey, or sausage for ground beef*

Meatballs: Shape into 24 balls about 1 inch in size and brown on all sides.

Barbecued Meatballs: Combine 1/2 cup each water and catsup, 2 tablespoons vinegar, 1 teaspoon Worcestershire sauce, 2 teaspoons dry or prepared mustard, 1/2 teaspoon each salt and pepper. Pour over browned meatballs. Simmer 15–20 minutes.

Hamburger Balls: Omit all except ground beef. Shape into balls.

Meat Puffs in Sauce: Pour 1–2 cups of tomato or mushroom soup over browned meatballs and simmer for 10–30 minutes.

Mexican Meatballs: Omit soy sauce and catsup. Fry 1 onion and 1 garlic clove, finely chopped, in 2 tablespoons oil. Add 2 cups each tomato sauce and beef broth. Drop uncooked meatballs into sauce. Cover tightly and cook 15–20 minutes. To thicken combine 1/4 cup water and 2 tablespoons cornstarch. Stir into hot sauce. Cook 2 minutes.

Meatball Soup: Increase liquid in Meat Puffs in Sauce recipe.

Oven Meatballs: Place meatballs in a greased 9x13 pan. Cover with 1–2 cups tomato sauce. Bake at 350°F for 30 minutes.

Stuffed Meatballs: Before browning divide meat mixture into 4–6 parts and put in greased baking dish. Make a depression in the center of each ball and spoon in any stuffing you like. Bake at 300°F for 1 hour.

Swedish Meatballs: Add 1/4 teaspoon allspice and 1 cup milk to meat. Omit catsup. Make a gravy of 1 tablespoon flour, 1 bouillon cube, and 1 cup water. Stir until thickened. Add browned meatballs and simmer 15–20 minutes.

See page 240 for International Conversion Charts

Sweet and Sour Meat Sauce

Combine and cook for 3 minutes:

- 2 1/2 cups cubed and drained pineapple, save juice
- 2 tablespoons butter

Add:

- 1/3 cup pineapple juice
- 2 cups green peppers, chopped, optional
- 1 onion, chopped, optional

Add:

- 1–3 tablespoons soy sauce
- 2 tablespoons vinegar
- 1/3 cup white or brown sugar

Mix separately and add:

- 2 tablespoons cornstarch
- 1/3 cup pineapple juice

Dissolve, add to cornstarch mixture, and cook, stirring until thick:

- 1 bouillon cube
- 1 cup boiling water or meat broth and omit bouillon

Simmer 1 hour and pour over cooked meat balls, beef pieces, fish, chicken, pork, turkey, or ham. Serve over rice.

* *Add any of the following: 2 garlic cloves, 1 cup cooked carrots or green beans, 1/2 cup chopped tomatoes, 1 sliced lemon or orange, 1 teaspoon allspice, 1/4 teaspoon ginger, and 2 tablespoons catsup or tomato paste.*

Sweet and Sour Fish: Add 6 whole cloves, 1/2 teaspoon ground cloves, 1 sliced lemon and 1/2 cup raisins. Omit pineapple, butter, juice, green peppers, and cornstarch. Increase vinegar to 1/2 cup. When sauce is cooked, stir in 4 beaten egg yolks. Pour over fish.

Sweet and Sour Soybeans: Simmer 4 cups cooked soybeans with sauce.

Sloppy Joes

Brown in oil or shortening:

- 2 cups ground beef

Add and fry for about 10 minutes:

- 1 green pepper, chopped, optional
- 1 onion, finely chopped

Add, simmer 20–30 minutes, and serve on warm buns:

- 1 tablespoon each sugar, mustard, and vinegar
- 1 teaspoon salt
- 3/4 cup catsup
- 2 cups cooked corn, optional
- 2 cups cooked kidney or other beans, optional

Yeast Pizza Dough

Dissolve until foamy:

- **1 tablespoon dry yeast**
- **1/4 cup warm water**

Combine separately and add:

- **2 tablespoons cooking oil**
- **2–3 tablespoons sugar**
- **1/8 teaspoon salt**
- **1/2 cup warm water**

Add and knead together until no longer sticky:

- **2 1/2–3 1/2 cups flour**

Pat the dough to 1/4-inch thickness on lightly greased baking sheet. Press up around edges to make a slight rim. Bake crust at 425°F for about 12 minutes, then add toppings and bake.

Baking Powder Pizza Dough: Omit all ingredients. Combine 2 cups flour, 1/2 teaspoon salt, and 2 teaspoons baking powder. Cut in 1/3 cup shortening. Add about 3/4 cup milk. Knead on lightly floured board a few strokes.

Deep Dish Pizza: Spread dough in a greased 9x13 pan. Bake crust for 20–25 minutes before adding toppings.

Master Mix Pizza Dough: Omit all ingredients. Combine 3 cups Master Mix (see page 9) and a scant 3/4 cup milk.

Rice Pizza: Omit all ingredients. Combine 4 cups cooked rice, 2 beaten eggs, and 1/2 teaspoon salt. Spread onto well-greased baking sheet. Bake at 400°F for 20 minutes. Add sauce and toppings.

Spaghetti Sauce

Combine and fry:

- **3 tablespoons cooking oil**
- **2 cups ground beef or sausage**
- **1/2 cup chopped onion**
- **1–2 garlic cloves, chopped**

Add:

- **5–6 cups chopped tomatoes or tomato sauce**
- **3/4 cup tomato paste**
- **1 teaspoon basil or thyme**
- **2 tablespoons minced parsley, optional**
- **1 teaspoon salt**
- **1/4 teaspoon pepper**
- **1–2 teaspoons oregano**
- **1 bay leaf**

Simmer over low heat 1–2 hours. Add mushrooms. Pour over cooked pasta and sprinkle with grated cheese, if desired. Serves 6.

See page 240 for International Conversion Charts

Pizza Sauce

Combine and fry:

- **2 tablespoons oil**
- **1 medium onion, chopped**

Add and simmer until thick:

- **3 cups tomato sauce**
- **1 1/2 teaspoons brown sugar**
- **1/2 teaspoon each sugar and salt**
- **1–2 teaspoons bouillon powder**
- **1/8 teaspoon pepper**
- **1/4–1/2 teaspoon oregano, optional**
- **3–4 cloves garlic, minced**
- **1/4 teaspoon each garlic powder and thyme**

Cool. Spread sauce over pizza dough and top with any of the following: cooked hamburger, sausage, ham, bacon, pepperoni, mushrooms, tomatoes, zucchini, onions, green peppers, olives, or pineapple. Top with grated cheese and sprinkle with oregano. Bake at 425°F for 25 minutes.

* *Substitute spaghetti sauce for Pizza Sauce.*

Mini Pizzas: Omit dough. Spread toasted, buttered English muffins, hamburger or hot dog buns, or crackers with sauce and top with toppings.

Quick Pizza: Pour plain tomato sauce over dough. Sprinkle with oregano and garlic salt or powder. Then top with any toppings.

Lasagna

Prepare spaghetti sauce. Combine separately, cook until tender, and drain:

- **16 cups boiling water**
- **1 tablespoon salt**
- **1 tablespoon oil**
- **2–4 cups lasagna noodles or any pasta**

Layer into a greased 9x13 baking pan:

- **1/2 of the prepared spaghetti sauce**
- **1 cup of the cooked noodles**
- **1 cup ricotta or cottage cheese**
- **1 cup grated pizza cheese or sour cream and cream cheese**

Repeat layers with 1/4 of sauce, cooked noodles, ricotta or cottage cheese, and pizza cheese. Top with last 1/4 of the sauce. Bake at 350°F for 30 minutes. Let stand 10 minutes before cutting.

Spinach Butterfly Casserole: Make spaghetti sauce omitting tomato paste and 3–4 cups tomato sauce. Simmer 15 minutes. In a bowl combine 2 cups chopped, cooked spinach, 1/4 cup each grated cheese, bread crumbs, and oil, 2 beaten eggs and 1 teaspoon salt. Use necktie macaroni, if available. Layer macaroni, spinach mixture, and meat sauce. Top with grated cheese. Bake at 350°F for 1 hour.

Stroganoff

Combine and brown:

- **2–4 tablespoons butter or margarine, optional**
- **1 small onion, chopped**
- **1 garlic clove, minced, or 1/2 teaspoon garlic salt**
- **2 cups ground beef or thinly sliced strips of beef**

Add and simmer 15–20 minutes:

- **2 tablespoons flour**
- **1 teaspoon salt**
- **1/2 cup sliced, cooked mushrooms**
- **1 1/4 cups cream of mushroom soup**

Add:

- **1 cup sour cream or yogurt**

Heat until just warmed. Do not boil. Serve over rice or noodles.

* *Roll beef strips in flour, if desired, and fry first. Omit soup. Add 1 tablespoon tomato paste, 1 teaspoon bouillon granules, and 1 cup warm water.*

Macaroni and Meatballs: Combine ground beef, onion, and garlic. Form into meatballs and brown well. Omit flour, mushrooms, and sour cream. Substitute 1 1/4 cups tomato soup and 1 1/2 cups water for mushroom soup. Cover and simmer 20 minutes. Add 2 1/2 cups cooked macaroni and cook 10 minutes.

Macaroni, Tomato, and Beef Casserole: Omit flour, soup, and sour cream. To meat mixture, add 2 cups each uncooked macaroni and stewed tomatoes and 1 cup tomato sauce or water. Bake in a greased casserole at 375°F for 30 minutes. Top with cheese and melt.

Tacos

Fry in hot oil on both sides until slightly crisp, then drain:

- **corn tortillas**

Layer any combination of the following on each tortilla:

- **cooked ground beef, sausage, chopped chicken, or turkey**
- **chopped onion, raw or cooked**
- **mashed beans**
- **shredded lettuce**
- **sliced olives or avocado**
- **sour cream or yogurt**
- **grated cheese**

* *Season meat with tomato, chili or taco sauce, chili powder, garlic, or other seasonings.*

Burritos: Spread fillings on flour tortillas (not fried). Fold bottom 1/3 of tortilla up. Then fold both sides in or roll it up.

See page 240 for International Conversion Charts

Chili

Brown:

- 1 garlic clove, minced, optional
- 1/2 cup chopped onion
- 1/2 cup chopped green pepper, optional
- 2 slices chopped bacon, optional
- 2 cups ground beef

Add:

- 2 cups chopped tomatoes or tomato sauce
- 2 teaspoons sugar
- 1 teaspoon salt
- 1 tablespoon chili powder
- 2 cups cooked beans

Cover and bring to a boil, lower heat, and simmer slowly for 30–45 minutes.

Upside-Down Mexican Dinner: Put chili in greased casserole. Combine 1/2 cup each flour and cornmeal, 2 teaspoons baking powder, and 1/2 teaspoon salt. Add 3/4 cup milk and 1 tablespoon oil. Spoon on top of chili, and bake at 425°F for 25 minutes.

Tamale Pie

Combine and brown:

- 5 tablespoons oil
- 1 cup beef, cut in 1 1/2–inch cubes or ground beef

Add and brown:

- 3 garlic cloves, minced
- 2 medium onions, sliced

Add and simmer 30 minutes:

- 1 1/2 teaspoons salt
- 2 tablespoons chili powder
- 1 teaspoon cumin
- 2 cups cooked, chopped tomatoes, or tomato sauce
- 1 cup raisins or corn, optional
- 1 1/2 cups pitted ripe olives, coarsely cut, optional

Combine separately in a saucepan or add to filling:

- 1 cup cornmeal
- 1 teaspoon salt
- 1 cup water

Add to cornmeal and boil, stirring often, for about 10 minutes:

- 3 cups boiling water

Line greased baking dish with cornmeal mush. Spread with meat filling. Spread remaining mush on top. Bake at 350°F for 1 1/2 hours.

Enchiladas

Have ready:

- **2 cups fried ground beef, sausage or cooked chicken**
- **1 chopped onion, raw or fried**
- **2–3 cups grated cheese**
- **12 corn tortillas**

Combine and simmer 10 minutes:

- **2–3 cups tomato sauce**
- **1 teaspoon salt**
- **1–2 garlic cloves, minced**
- **1–2 teaspoons chili powder, or more to taste**
- **1/2 teaspoon ground cumin, optional**

Cool, then dip tortillas in sauce. Place on each tortilla in layers:

- **cooked meat**
- **onions and grated cheese**

Roll tortillas up and place side by side in a greased 9x13 baking pan. Pour remaining sauce over the tortillas. Top with grated cheese. Bake uncovered at 350°F for 30–35 minutes. Serves 6.

* *Add any of the following to the sauce: 1/2 teaspoon basil or oregano, 1/4 teaspoon hot sauce or cut-up green chilies.*

* *Add any of the following to the fillings for the enchiladas: sour cream or yogurt, cottage cheese, fried mushrooms, mashed beans, or black olives.*

Chicken Enchiladas: Substitute chicken for beef and 1 1/4 cups each cream of chicken and cream of celery soups for tomato sauce.

Chilaquiles: Cut tortillas in eighths. Fry in 2–4 tablespoons oil. Drain. Layer tortillas with cheese in a skillet or greased baking dish. Omit meat, if desired. Pour sauce over all. Bake at 350°F for 20–30 minutes or cook in a covered skillet on low until cheese melts.

Layered Enchilada Pie: Layer in a greased dish, tortillas, meat sauce, and cheese. Cover and bake at 350°F for 20 minutes.

Foil Dinner

In a sheet of aluminum foil (shiny side out) place:

- **1 large, raw ground beef patty, salted**
- **raw sliced carrots, onions, and potatoes**
- **salt and pepper**

Dot with:

- **margarine**

Fold foil to make a sealed package. Place on a baking sheet. Bake at 350°F about 1 hour until tender.

* *Cook directly on coals in double foil, 10 minutes on each side.*

See page 240 for International Conversion Charts

Chicken-Fried Steak

Make patties of:

- **ground beef**

Roll in:

- **beaten egg**

Combine and roll in:

- **cracker crumbs or flour**
- **oregano, onion powder, garlic powder, optional**
- **Worcestershire sauce, optional**
- **salt and pepper, optional**

Fry in pan, until cooked, with:

- **butter or margarine**

* *Use steaks in place of hamburger patties. Brown meat slightly. Pressure cook meat for 20 minutes (if tough). Then roll in egg and flour and fry.*

Shepherd's Pie

Fry:

- **1 onion, diced**
- **2 tablespoons oil**

Add and brown:

- **2 cups ground beef**
- **1 teaspoon salt**
- **dash of pepper**
- **chopped garlic, optional**

Layer in casserole dish:

- **1/2 cup tomato sauce, optional**
- **browned ground beef**
- **2 cups cooked green beans, peas, celery, or carrots**
- **2 cups mashed potatoes**
- **1 cup grated cheese**

Bake at 350°F for 30 minutes.

* *Substitute diced potatoes for cheese and mashed potatoes. Line baking dish with puff pastry, fill, and top with a puff pastry crust, then bake.*

* *Substitute cooked meats for ground beef.*

* *Substitute cream sauce or creamed soups for tomato sauce.*

Hamburger and Cabbage Casserole

Shred:

- 1 small cabbage

Combine in separate bowl, mixture will be quite loose:

- 2 cups ground beef
- 1/2 cup bread crumbs
- 2 cups evaporated milk
- 1/2 cup water
- 1 egg
- 1 tablespoon chopped onion
- 1 teaspoon salt
- pepper

Layer in greased casserole dish:

- half the shredded cabbage
- salt and pepper
- meat mixture
- remaining cabbage
- salt

Cover and bake at 350°F for 45 minutes. Remove cover last few minutes of baking. If desired, dribble a little oil or margarine over cabbage.

Hungarian Cabbage and Noodles

Brown in skillet:

- 2 cups ground beef

Add and stir until tender:

- 1/2 tablespoon shortening, if needed
- small chopped onion
- 3 1/2 cups shredded cabbage
- salt and pepper to taste

Add:

- 1/2 cup parmesan cheese, optional

Combine separately, boil about 10 minutes, then add to beef:

- 8 cups boiling water
- 1–2 teaspoons salt
- 2 cups noodles

Serve hot. Garnish with slices of cheese, if desired.

See page 240 for International Conversion Charts

Texas Hash

Brown in a large, deep skillet:

- 2 chopped onions
- 1 cup diced green pepper
- 3 tablespoons oil
- 2 cups ground beef, canned beef, or pork

Add, cover, and simmer until rice is tender:

- 2 cups whole tomatoes
- 1 1/4 teaspoons chili powder
- 1 tablespoon salt
- 1/8 teaspoon pepper
- 1 cup water
- 1 cup uncooked rice or 2 large cubed potatoes, boiled

Curried Ground Meat

Combine and cook until vegetables are tender:

- 2 1/2 cups ground meat, browned
- 1 1/2 cups water
- 1 teaspoon salt
- 2 onions, chopped
- 10–12 medium carrots, cubed
- 4–5 medium potatoes, cubed, or other vegetable

When vegetables are cooked, mix separately with a little water:

- 1 tablespoon each flour and curry powder

Add to meat and cook for 5 minutes.

Lumpia (Philippines)

Brown:
- **2 cups ground beef or diced meat**
- **1 onion, chopped**

Add and cook until vegetables are tender:
- **1/2 teaspoon salt**
- **1/4 teaspoon pepper**
- **1/4 large cabbage, shredded**
- **1 cup bean sprouts**
- **1 garlic clove, chopped**
- **1 large grated carrot**
- **1–2 tablespoons soy sauce**

Cool and wrap 2 tablespoons mixture in each:
- **20 lumpia or spring roll wrappers**

Cover wrapped lumpia with towel and don't allow them to touch. Fry in deep hot oil until brown. Serve with rice, sauce, or vegetables.

Steak and Kidney Pie

Soak 30 minutes:
- **1 pair beef kidneys with cores, tubes, and membranes removed**
- **4 cups cold water**
- **2 tablespoons vinegar**

Drain, dice, and brown in:
- **2 tablespoons fat**

Add and simmer slowly until tender, about 45 minutes:
- **water to barely cover (add more as needed)**
- **1 teaspoon salt**

Brown separately:
- **2 tablespoons fat**
- **10 small onions, cut up**

Add, cook, and stir about 20 minutes until browned, stirring frequently:
- **2 cups ground steak or chuck**
- **1 teaspoon salt**

Add:
- **3 cups cooked, diced potatoes, chayotes, or vegetable**
- **the kidneys with their cooking water**

Thicken gravy if desired with:
- **2 tablespoons flour and a little water**

Place in an 8–inch casserole. Cover with pastry, cut in several places to let steam out. Bake at 425°F until brown. Serve hot.

See page 240 for International Conversion Charts

Hungarian Goulash

Brown in a large skillet

- 2–4 tablespoons shortening
- 4 cups beef, cubed
- 1 sliced onion and 1–2 cloves, minced garlic

Add, cover, and simmer 1–2 hours, adding water if necessary:

- 3/4 cup catsup
- 2 tablespoons Worcestershire sauce, optional
- 1 tablespoon brown sugar
- 1–2 teaspoons each paprika and salt
- 2 teaspoons paprika
- 1/2 teaspoon mustard
- dash cayenne
- 1 1/2 cups water

Combine separately and add:

- 2 tablespoons flour
- 1/4 cup water

Stir gradually into meat mixture. Boil for 1 minute to thicken. Serves 6 or more. Serve over hot cooked noodles or rice.

Vietnamese Squashed Meat

Brown:

- 2 tablespoons shortening or margarine
- 1 cup finely chopped, or ground meat
- 2 small onions, chopped

Add and simmer for 20 minutes (or more if meat is tough):

- 1 1/2 cups water, more if needed

Add and cook until tender:

- 2–4 cups winter squash, cubed

Add, heat thoroughly, and serve over rice:

- 1 cup roasted peanuts

East Indian Beef Stew

Roll beef in seasoned flour and shake off excess flour:

- 3 cups stewing beef, cubed
- 1/4 cup flour
- salt and pepper to taste
- cayenne pepper, optional

Brown in large skillet with:

- 3 tablespoons oil

Combine and pour over meat:

- 2 onions, diced
- 2 cups beef bouillon or broth
- 1 1/2 teaspoons curry powder, or to taste
- 2 garlic cloves, mashed
- 1/2 teaspoon ground ginger

Cover and cook on low 2 hours or until meat is tender. Or cook in crockpot on low for 6–8 hours. Serve with rice, chutney, grated coconut, grated orange peel, nuts, bananas, raisins, tomatoes, seeds, etc. Serves 4–5.

Curried Corned Beef

Combine and fry until tender:

- 2 tablespoons oil
- 1 medium onion, chopped
- 1 cabbage, chopped

Add and cook until thickened:

- 1–2 teaspoons curry powder
- 1–2 cups each cooked corned beef and coconut cream (250–500 ml)

Spread cooked cabbage mixture on taro leaves. Place taro leaves on top and form the mixture into a round flat shape. Wrap in foil and bake at 350°F for 30–45 minutes.

Chinese Chicken

Marinate for two or more hours:

- 1/2 cup soy sauce
- 1/4 cup lemon juice
- 1 chicken, cut up

Bake chicken in greased pan at 350°F for 30 minutes, skin side down. Turn and bake for 15 minutes more.

See page 240 for International Conversion Charts

Fried Chicken

Combine in sack and shake to coat:

- **1/2 cup flour or crushed corn flakes**
- **1 1/2 teaspoons salt**
- **1/4 teaspoon pepper**
- **1 teaspoon paprika**
- **1/2 teaspoon oregano, optional**
- **1/8 teaspoon curry powder, optional**
- **1 chicken, cut in serving-size pieces**

Brown in large skillet

- **coated chicken pieces**
- **1 cup hot oil or shortening**

Cover and simmer about 30 minutes until tender. Uncover last 10 minutes.

Dijon Chicken: Omit flour, salt, and pepper. Combine and coat chicken with 1/2 cup each sour cream and Dijon mustard and 1/8 teaspoon garlic powder. Then roll in seasoned bread crumbs. Follow remaining directions for Oven-Fried Chicken (recipe below).

Farm-Style Fried Chicken: Simmer chicken until tender. Cool and coat chicken with flour mixture. Fry and serve.

Oven-Fried Chicken: Remove skin if desired. Coat chicken with flour mixture. Place in greased 9x13 pan. Bake chicken at 400°F for 45–60 minutes.

Vasa (West Africa)

Fry until crispy, then remove from skillet:

- **1/2 cup hot oil**
- **1 chicken, cut in pieces**

Combine separately and cook 10 minutes:

- **2 large bouillon cubes or 2 tablespoons bouillon**
- **2 medium onions, grated**
- **2 medium onions, sliced thin**
- **4 heaping teaspoons mustard**
- **juice of 2 large lemons**
- **2 garlic cloves, crushed**
- **salt and pepper to taste**

Add:

- **cooked chicken pieces**
- **1 bouillon cube, crushed**
- **water to make plenty of sauce**
- **salt and pepper to taste**

Simmer 1–1 1/2 hours. Serve over hot rice.

Chicken or Meat Curry (Nepal)

Fry until golden:

- **2 cups onions, sliced fine**
- **1/2 cup oil or ghi**

Lower heat, add, and fry 3–4 minutes, stirring constantly:

- **4 garlic cloves, ground into a paste**
- **1 teaspoon water**
- **1 teaspoon turmeric**
- **1 teaspoon cumin**
- **2 teaspoons coriander**
- **1 teaspoon ginger**
- **2 teaspoons chili**
- **salt to taste**

Increase heat, add, and fry for 5 minutes:

- **4 cups lean meat or chicken, or cubed or ground beef**

Add and mix thoroughly:

- **1/2 cup yogurt or 1 cup chopped tomatoes**
- **2 bay leaves**

Add, cover, and simmer until meat is tender:

- **1 teaspoon garam masala (recipe below), optional**

* *Add any chopped, cooked vegetables.*

Garam Masala: Combine 1/4 teaspoon each cloves, cinnamon, and nutmeg, 1/2 teaspoon each cardamom and black pepper, and 1 teaspoon each coriander and cumin.

Japanese-Style Chicken

Combine in a shallow dish:

- **3/4 cup flour**
- **1/2 teaspoon salt**

Combine separately and add, stirring until just moistened:

- **1/2 cup very cold water**
- **1 beaten egg**

Dip in batter and brown in deep hot oil for about 5 minutes:

- **3 chicken breasts, skinned, boned, and cut in 1-inch cubes**

Drain on paper towels, combine, and dip chicken in:

- **2 tablespoons prepared mustard**
- **1 tablespoon soy sauce**

Serve with rice. Serves 6–8.

* *Skewer pieces of chicken and green onion, dip in batter, and fry.*

* *Use wheat flour for white and add 1 teaspoon baking soda.*

Hawaiian Chicken

Combine in sack and shake to coat:

- 1/2 cup flour
- 1–3 teaspoons salt
- 1/4 teaspoon pepper
- 1 chicken, cut up

Fry in:

- 2–4 tablespoons hot shortening

Combine and pour over chicken:

- 3 1/2 cups of half-strength pineapple or orange juice
  6 tablespoons each vinegar and brown sugar
- 3/4 cup catsup
- 2 onions, chopped

Bring to a boil, cover, and simmer 1 1/4 hours until chicken is tender and sauce is thickened. Add, simmer 5 minutes, and serve over rice:

- 2 cups pineapple chunks, optional
- 1 medium bell pepper, cut up, optional

Turkey or Chicken Pot Pie

Combine and simmer for 10 minutes:

- 3–4 cups chicken or turkey broth
- 3 medium carrots, sliced
- 2 medium potatoes, chopped

Cook for another 10 minutes, then add:

- 1 chopped onion, fried, optional
- 1 cup peas, frozen or cooked
- 3 tablespoons cornstarch, added to 1/4 cup water
- 2 cups turkey or chicken, cooked and chopped

Season to taste with salt, garlic, thyme, and poultry seasoning. Put in 9-inch pie crust and top with crust. Bake at 450°F for 10 minutes, then reduce to 350°F for 1 hour. Cool and cut.

* *Use any leftover cooked vegetables and meat in place of turkey and vegetables. Use 1–2 cups of broth or creamed soups.*

Scalloped Chicken

Layer in a greased 9x9 pan:

- 1 chicken or turkey, boiled and deboned
- 6–8 cups stuffing

Melt in skillet:

- 1 cup butter

Stir in until bubbly:

- 1 cup flour
- 1–3 teaspoons salt
- 1/4 teaspoon pepper

Slowly add and continue stirring until thickened:

- 4 1/2 cups chicken broth or milk
- 2 cups evaporated milk or substitute

When thickened, add:

- 4 egg yolks, optional

Pour gravy over chicken. Bake at 350°F for 45 minutes.

Chicken-Broccoli Bake

Melt in a 9x9 pan in a 400°F oven:

- 2 tablespoons butter

Place in pan and turn to coat with butter:

- 1 chicken, cut up

Arrange skin sides up and sprinkle with:

- 1/2 teaspoon garlic salt

Bake uncovered at 400°F for 1 hour. Mix separately:

- 1 1/4 cups cream of chicken soup
- 1/2 cup mushroom pieces, cooked
- 1/4 cup water
- 1 teaspoon Worcestershire sauce, optional
- 1/2 teaspoon dried thyme leaves

Peel and cook until tender:

- 3 cups broccoli

Remove chicken from oven. Drain fat from dish. Arrange broccoli along sides of chicken. Spoon soup mixture over broccoli. Bake uncovered at 350°F about 20 minutes. Garnish with paprika.

* *Use cubed, deboned cooked chicken, cooked chopped broccoli, and soup mixture. Bake at 350°F for 20 minutes. Top with grated cheese if desired.*

See page 240 for International Conversion Charts

Chicken Strata

Spread in an ungreased 9x13 pan:

- **8 slices bread, buttered and cubed**

Combine and spread over bread cubes:

- **2 cups cooked chicken or turkey meat, chopped**
- **1/2 cup celery and/or onion, chopped, optional**
- **1/2 cup mayonnaise**
- **1/4 cup milk**
- **1/2 teaspoon salt**
- **1/4 teaspoon pepper**

Beat together and pour over chicken mixture:

- **2 eggs**
- **1 1/2 cups milk**

Refrigerate 4 hours or overnight. Just before baking, pour over mixture:

- **1 1/4 cups cream of mushroom soup or cheese soup**

Bake at 350°F for 1 hour.

Egg and Cheese Strata: Omit chicken mixture and mushroom soup. Spread 2 cups grated cheese over bread. Increase eggs to 6. Add 1/2 teaspoon salt. Sprinkle with parsley flakes, bacon, or sausage.

Stuffing

Fry:

- **1/2 cup chicken fat, butter, or oil**
- **1/2 cup onion, chopped**
- **1/2–1 cup celery, chopped**

Remove from heat and add:

- **1/2 teaspoon salt**
- **1 teaspoon poultry seasoning or sage**
- **dash of pepper**
- **1 egg, beaten, optional**
- **3/4–1 cup chicken stock or milk**

Pour over and toss lightly:

- **6–8 cups dry bread cubes**

Stuff meat, and bake in greased pan at 350°F for 1/2–1 hour. If stuffing a chicken or turkey, do not leave stuffing in bird before or after cooking because it can cause food poisoning.

* *Add any or a combination of the following: 1 peeled and chopped apple, 1/2–1 cup sliced water chestnuts, chestnuts, or other nuts, 3/4 cup raisins, 1/2 cup sliced, cooked mushrooms.*

Corn Bread Stuffing: Use half cornbread crumbs and dry bread crumbs.

Fish Stuffing: Add 3–4 tablespoons lemon juice. Omit egg and poultry seasoning. Reduce chicken stock to 1/3 cup. Combine everything together. Do not fry onions or celery.

Hungarian Chicken Paprikash

Combine in large pan and brown:

- **2 tablespoons shortening or butter**
- **2 onions, chopped**
- **1 garlic clove, chopped**

Stir in:

- **1 tablespoon paprika or other mild red pepper**

Add and brown in mixture:

- **2 chickens, cut up**

Add:

- **2 chicken bouillon cubes**
- **salt and pepper to taste**
- **4 cups water**

Bring to a boil, then simmer for 1 hour. Combine separately and add:

- **2 tablespoons flour or cornstarch**
- **1/2 cup sour cream, optional**
- **1/4 cup water**

Serve over fried rice or noodles. Serves 8–10.

Yellow Braised Chicken (Indonesia)

Stir-fry in saucepan:

- **2–inch green ginger, finely chopped**
- **3 onions, chopped**
- **3 cloves garlic, chopped**
- **1 tablespoon ground coriander**
- **1/2 teaspoon ground cumin**
- **1 teaspoon turmeric**
- **2 tablespoons oil**

Add and coat well:

- **1 chicken, cut in serving-sized pieces**

Add and simmer until chicken is tender:

- **2 cups Coconut Milk or Coconut Cream (see page 102)**
- **juice of 1/2 lemon**
- **salt and pepper**

Serve over rice with slices of lemon.

Aji de Gallina (Peru)

Boil until tender, then remove bones and shred:

- **1 chicken**
- **4 cups water**
- **1 leek, chopped**
- **2 onions, chopped**
- **1 carrot, chopped**
- **1 tomato, chopped**
- **3/4 cup olive or other oil**

Combine separately and brown:

- **1/2 cup olive oil or other oil**
- **1/2 teaspoon cumin**
- **1 onion, chopped**
- **1 garlic clove, mashed**
- **3 tablespoons mashed hot pepper or chili powder to taste**

Combine, add to above, simmer 15 minutes, and blend:

- **2 cups bread crumbs**
- **1 cup evaporated milk**

Add and simmer 15 minutes:

- **1 cup cheese, grated**
- **chicken mixture**
- **salt to taste**
- **chicken stock, optional**

Garnish with potatoes, if desired, and serve with rice. Serves 6–8.

Lemon Chicken and Zucchini

Heat large skillet over high heat. Stir-fry for 3–5 minutes:

- **2 tablespoons oil**
- **3 1/2 cups sliced zucchini or chayote**
- **1 teaspoon fresh ginger or 1/2 teaspoon ginger powder**

Stir-fry separately in hot skillet:

- **1 tablespoon oil**
- **3 cups chicken breasts or thighs, skinned, boned, and cubed**

Combine separately, add to chicken, and cook until thick:

- **1/4 cup hot water**
- **1 chicken bouillon cube**
- **2 tablespoons cornstarch**
- **1 tablespoon soy sauce**
- **1 teaspoon sugar**
- **1 teaspoon salt or to taste**

Add, cover, and cook 1 minute:

- **prepared zucchini**
- **2 tablespoons lemon juice, or more to taste**

Serve with rice. Garnish with lemon slices or tomato slices. Serves 4–6.

Taco Chip Main Dish

Crush:

- **1 medium-sized bag nacho chips**

Spread two-thirds of the crushed chips over the bottom of an 8x10-inch casserole dish. Reserve the remaining chips.

In a bowl combine:

- **1 cup sour cream or 1 cup regular cream mixed with 1 tablespoon vinegar**
- **1 15–oz can condensed cream of chicken soup**
- **3/4 cup shredded cheddar or Monterey Jack cheese**
- **1 1/2–2 cups cooked chicken, chopped**
- **2 tablespoons dry taco seasoning mix (see page 254)**
- **a few drops of hot sauce, if desired**

Spread the chicken mixture over the nacho chips in the casserole dish. Sprinkle the remaining nacho chips over that, and then top all with 1/4 cup cheese. Bake at 375°F for 30 minutes. Serves 4–6.

* *Add chopped onions, black olives, tomatoes, or bell peppers if desired.*

Pork and Yams

Peel and slice into half-inch rounds and set aside:

- **3 yams (sweet potatoes)**

In a frying pan add:

- **1 tablespoon oil**

Stir-fry in the oil over medium-high heat until browned:

- **1 large onion, peeled and sliced**
- **2 cups pork, trimmed of fat and cut into 1-inch cubes**

Add the yam slices and stir-fry for an additional 1–2 minutes. Reduce heat.

Add:

- **4 tomatoes, chopped**
- **1 bay leaf**

Cover and cook over medium heat until the yams are soft and the pork is cooked through.

Add to taste:

- **1 tablespoon or more soy sauce**
- **salt and pepper**

Before serving, remove the bay leaf from the pan and discard. Serve with rice. Serves 6.

See page 240 for International Conversion Charts

Fried Pork

Dip in water or milk:

- 8 slices of pork

Combine and dip pork in the following mixture:

- 2 tablespoons each cornmeal and flour
- 1 teaspoon each salt and sage
- 1/2 teaspoon each onion powder, sugar, and paprika
- 1/2 teaspoon each MSG, garlic powder, and chili powder

Fry in hot oil until well cooked, about 40 minutes.

Sausage

Combine:

- 8 cups ground pork, beef, turkey, or a combination
- 5 teaspoons salt
- 4 teaspoons ground sage, poultry seasoning, or celery seed
- 1 teaspoon pepper
- 1/2 teaspoon cloves, optional
- 4 garlic cloves, minced
- 1 teaspoon sugar
- 1 teaspoon chili powder, optional
- 1/2 cup water, optional

Add:

- 2 cups finely chopped bacon, optional

Shape into patties, coat with flour, and brown in oil. Cover and continue to cook over low heat until well done. Refrigerate sausage overnight or freeze.

* *Omit coating with flour and combine as meatloaf.*

* *Crumble sausage before cooking and use on pizza or in eggs or quiches.*

Chorizo: Omit sage and cloves. Add 1/2 cup each chili powder and vinegar, 1 tablespoon each ground cumin and oregano, 2 teaspoons liquid hot pepper sauce. Refrigerate 24 hours, then fry.

Cuban Pork or Lamb Roast

Insert slivers of peeled garlic into a pork or lamb roast. Rub meat with salt and 1 teaspoon cumin. Squeeze lemon juice over all surfaces. Let set at least 1 hour. Bake at 350°F for 2 hours or until well cooked.

Pork Adobo (Philippines)

Brown:

- 2–4 tablespoons oil or shortening
- 3–4 cups pork cubes, chicken pieces, or a combination
- 4 large garlic cloves, cut in fourths

Add and simmer in a covered heavy pot until tender:

- 1/2 cup vinegar, or more for a more tart flavor
- 2 large bay leaves
- 2 whole peppercorns, crushed
- 1 teaspoon salt
- 1/4–1/3 cup soy sauce
- 2 teaspoons brown sugar or more for a less tart flavor
- 3 cups water

To make gravy, add a little cornstarch and water. Serve over rice.

* *Use alligator, chicken, or any combination of meats for pork.*

Pigs in Blankets

Combine and knead 20 times:

- 2 cups Master Mix (see page 9)
- 1/2 cup water

Roll into a 13-inch circle (32 1/3 cm) and divide into 8 wedges.

Place on wide edges of dough:

- 8 hot dogs

Roll and seal. Bake at 450°F for 15 minutes.

Chinese Pork

Combine and let stand 15 minutes:

- 1 cup boneless pork, cut in thin strips
- 1 tablespoon cornstarch
- 1 tablespoon soy sauce
- 1 tablespoon vinegar
- 1 garlic clove, minced
- 1/4 teaspoon powdered ginger
- 1/2 teaspoon sugar

Stir-fry meat until golden brown in:

- 1 teaspoon oil, or more

Combine separately and fry:

- 1 tablespoon oil
- 2 medium onions, cut in thin crescents
- mushrooms, sliced

See page 240 for International Conversion Charts

Combine separately, add to onions, and let bubble 1 minute:

- 1 tablespoon cornstarch
- 2 tablespoons soy sauce
- 1 cup water

Add and cook until tomatoes are heated:

- cooked pork
- 2 peeled tomatoes, cut in wedges, optional
- cooked, chopped celery, green beans, bean sprouts, or snow peas

Serve over rice with fish or hot sauce, optional. Pressure cook meat, if desired.

Wild Meat

Wild meat can be baked, roasted, fried, barbecued, and stewed like any other meat. As in domesticated meat, the younger the animal or bird, the more tender it is and the less cooking it requires. Use younger meat for pan frying, barbecuing, and baking; use tougher meat in casseroles, pies, and stews. Wild meat is leaner than domesticated meat, so to keep moisture in, wrap or cover with foil when cooking and add butter, margarine, oil, or bacon fat.

Fried pig, deer (venison), turtle, caribou, or alligator: Cut the meat into small cubes or steaks and fry in a hot skillet. When juices start to gather, add a little water, a bay leaf, several whole black peppers, and a piece of papaya leaf. Turn heat down and simmer until all juices disappear and meat is tender. Fry lightly to bring out the flavor. Serve with rice.

To remove strong taste from wild game: After tenderizing, simmer for 6 hours in 1–2 cups each strong coffee and water. Add seasonings and onions the last 20 minutes. Thicken liquid for gravy.

The following recipes use any type of fish.

Sautéed Fish

Heat oil in pan and add small amount of water, chopped mushrooms, green onions, lemon juice, and fish. Stir over medium heat until done.

Pan-Fried Fish

In a bowl, place enough flour to coat the fish and add a little rosemary, cumin, salt and pepper, or other seasonings, and mix well. Dip washed fish first in beaten egg, then flour or crumbs. Fry both sides in hot oil until tender.

Deep-Fried Fish

Make a batter of 1/2 cup oil, 1 1/4 cups flour, 1 1/2 cups milk, and 1 egg. Dip fish in batter and fry in deep fat until browned on both sides. Drain and serve.

Broiled Fish

Dip fish in cold milk, roll in crumbs (bread, cracker, or cornmeal), and brown in pan or broiler. Or brush fish with small amount of margarine or oil and lemon juice. Flavor with your favorite herbs and spices and broil 4–5 inches (10–13 cm) from heat source.

Poached Fish

Estimate amount of liquid needed to barely cover your fish in a saucepan or frying pan. Liquid may be milk, water, or juice seasoned with chopped carrots, celery, onions, and peppercorns or pepper. Simmer about 10 minutes and add fish. Poach until done.

Boiled Fish

Tie fish servings in cheesecloth. Lower into kettle containing hot liquid to cover fish. Add water to reduce temperature just below boiling. Add 1 teaspoon each salt and vinegar or lemon juice, one onion, one bay leaf, and one clove. These make flesh firm and white. Simmer 6–10 minutes. Remove, drain, and place on hot platter. May serve with any sauce or can be used for fish salad.

Coconut Boiled Fish: Omit all ingredients above. Combine 1 cup each grated coconut and water, 1 1/2 teaspoons lemon juice. Strain and add 1 small chopped onion, 1 cup water, 1 small chopped tomato, and pepper, optional. Add fish that has been cut and salted and cook until it flakes.

Lemon Boiled Fish: Omit bay leaf and clove. Add 2 teaspoons vinegar, 1 onion, 6 whole peppercorns, and 1 stick cinnamon. Cook until fish flakes, remove, then drain fish. Cover with a hot lemon sauce.

Philippine Boiled Fish: Combine 2–4 tablespoons oil, 1 cup water, 1/2 teaspoon Worcestershire sauce, 1 medium chopped onion, 2 cloves of chopped garlic, and fish. Boil just until it flakes.

Steamed Fish

Place seasoned seafood on a rack set 2 inches above a boiling liquid and cover tightly. Reduce heat and steam until cooked. Shellfish are excellent when steamed.

Baked Fish

Layer in greased baking dish:

- **2 slices onion, optional**
- **fish, whole or fillets**
- **2 more slices onion, optional**
- **1 cup tomato sauce (any meat or cream sauce)**
- **herb seasonings to taste**
- **salt and pepper to taste**

Bake at 350°F for 1 hour or until done.

* *Wrap fish in well-oiled cheesecloth to make it easy to remove whole from pan.*

See page 240 for International Conversion Charts

* *Omit sauce and onions. Pour over fish 2–4 tablespoons each butter or margarine and lemon juice. Sprinkle with Parmesan cheese, if desired.*

Baked Stuffed Fish: Slit fish, put stuffing in cavity, and bake as above.

Abalone

To clean a fresh abalone that is still in the shell: Take a strong wooden spoon and shuck the abalone from the shell. Place the abalone on a firm surface and strike hard with a wooden mallet or board and allow the abalone to relax for 1–3 hours or overnight in the refrigerator. Trim off the wavy edge around the bottom of the foot. Remove a thin slice of yellow-brown from the bottom of the foot and discard. The abalone is now ready to be sliced and prepared in one of the following ways:

Fried Abalone: Pound abalone slices thin. Dip pounded abalone "steaks" in beaten egg, then in cracker crumbs and fry for a short time.

Boiled Abalone: First cut abalone in slices, then slice in strips like shoestring potatoes. Drop strips in rapidly boiling water for 10 minutes. Drain and serve hot with butter, pepper, and salt, or dip in a sauce or hot butter, or place in a cream sauce alone or with vegetables. Cool and use in salads or crumble strips and use them in a fish loaf.

Fish Patties

Combine and form into patties:

- **2 cups fresh, smoked, or canned fish, cooked**
- **1/2 onion, grated or chopped fine**
- **1 egg**
- **1/2 cup bread or cracker crumbs, oatmeal, or cooked rice**
- **salt and pepper to taste**
- **parsley, optional**

Roll patties in:

- **flour and salt**

Fry in small amount of oil.

* *Add any or a combination of the following for patties, loaf, or cakes: 1/2–1 teaspoon sage, thyme, or other fish seasoning, 1–2 tablespoons each chopped parsley and celery, 1/2 teaspoon celery salt, and 1 teaspoon lemon juice. Sprinkle with curry powder or nutmeg. Moisten mixture with tomato sauce, if desired.*

Fish Cakes: Dip into beaten egg, then bread crumbs, and fry in hot skillet.

Fish Loaf: Add 1/4 cup melted margarine or oil and 1 cup milk. Bake in greased loaf pan at 350°F for 40 minutes.

Tunaburgers

Combine and stir lightly until well mixed:

- 1 cup drained and flaked tuna or any cooked fish
- 1/2 cup cubed cooked potatoes
- 2 radishes, thinly sliced
- 1 teaspoon grated onion
- 1/3 cup each chopped celery and salad dressing
- 1 cup cheese, cubed
- 1 tablespoon chopped parsley
- 1/8 teaspoon curry powder, optional

Place filling in:

- 4 rolls, split and buttered

Wrap filled rolls in foil and bake at 375°F for 15 minutes.

Cuban Fish

Fry:

- 2 tablespoons shortening or oil
- 4 garlic cloves, minced
- 1 large onion, sliced
- 1/2 medium bell pepper, thinly sliced

Add and simmer 20 minutes and serve over rice:

- 1 lobster, shrimp, or any cooked fish, cut in pieces
- 3 pimentos, thinly sliced, optional
- salt and pepper to taste
- 1/4 cup vinegar or lemon juice
- 2 cups any cooked vegetables, optional

Fish from Cameroon

Cut fish in sections. Brown in hot oil. Remove fish and brown until soft:

- 2 tomatoes, chopped fine
- 2 tablespoons oil
- thin carrot and celery sticks, optional

Add:

- 1 onion, sliced and fried
- 3 garlic cloves, chopped fine
- 2 celery stalks, chopped fine
- 2 beef bouillon cubes or 2 teaspoons consommé powder
- 1 stalk of fresh basil, chopped, or 1/2–1 teaspoon dry basil
- browned fish
- 1 cup water

Cover and cook until done.

See page 240 for International Conversion Charts

Creamed Tuna and Vegetables

Drain and combine, reserving all liquids:

- 1 cup tuna or any cooked fish
- 1 1/2 cups cooked, diced carrots
- 1 1/2 cups cooked, diced potatoes
- 1 cup cooked peas
- 3 tablespoons chopped onion

Combine separately in skillet and cook until bubbly:

- 1/4 cup cooking oil or shortening
- 1/4 cup flour
- salt and pepper to taste

Add slowly, stirring until it thickens:

- 2 cups liquid, reserved liquids, and milk

Combine vegetables with sauce and put in a greased baking pan. Cover with pie crust or buttered crumbs. Bake at 350°F for 20–30 minutes.

Tuna Noodle Casserole

Combine and heat through:

- 1 1/4 cups creamed soup or white sauce
- 1/2 cup milk

Add and heat until melted, stirring constantly:

- 1 cup grated cheese

Combine separately and add:

- 3 cups medium noodles, cooked and drained
- 1 cup tuna or mackerel, drained
- 1/2 cup mayonnaise
- 1 cup chopped celery
- 1 cup peas, optional
- 1/3 cup chopped onion, optional
- 1/2 teaspoon salt

Place in a greased pan and top with:

- slivered almonds, optional

Bake uncovered at 425°F for 20 minutes.

Tuna Ginataan
(Tuna in Coconut Milk)

Prepare coconut milk from:

- **1 fresh coconut**

Grate the white flesh of the coconut into a large bowl and pour in:

- **1 cup very hot water**

When water is cool enough, squeeze the soaked, grated coconut into the water with your hands about 20 times to extract "milk." Put the coconut milk through a strainer and set aside. Pour over the already-squeezed, grated coconut left in the bowl:

- **1 1/2 cups of hot water**

When cool enough, repeat the squeezing process to make a second batch of coconut milk. Strain as before and set aside. This batch will be thinner and less rich than the first batch of coconut milk.

Put the second batch of coconut milk in a large saucepan and then add:

- **1 pound fresh tuna steak, cut into large chunks**

The coconut milk should be level with the tuna, but not cover it. Bring to a boil, then reduce heat and simmer the tuna in the coconut milk for 6 minutes.

Add and simmer for 3 more minutes:

- **1 small onion, sliced thinly into rings**
- **2 tablespoons soy sauce**
- **salt and white pepper to taste**

Add and simmer for an additional 8 minutes:

- **1/2 pound trimmed green beans, left whole**
- **1/2 cup sweet red bell peppers, chopped**

Stir in:

- **1 cup kamote tops (leaves only) or other quick-cooking greens such as spinach**

Pour the first batch of coconut milk over the fish and vegetables in the pan. Bring to a quick boil, allowing it to cook for 30 seconds only. Immediately remove the pan from the heat. It is preferable if there is only a small amount of coconut milk left in the pan at the end. Can be served over rice or with cornbread if desired. Serves 4–6.

* If available, you may use 1–1 1/2 cups canned coconut milk in this recipe instead of preparing your own.

See page 240 for International Conversion Charts

Sides

*See page 176 for this
Yam Chip recipe.*

Fried Snacks

When we first arrived in Mexico, our boys were one, two, and six-years-old. One day we visited the home of a Mixtec pastor. His wife wanted to be hospitable but didn't have much to offer us. She went into her cook house and came out with a small bag of something she had cooked herself. Our boys accepted them and ate readily. We thought that the boys didn't recognize their snack as fried grasshoppers, so we didn't say much since we thought it would disturb them. It was then that our two-year-old exclaimed, "Look, I can see his eyes!" and popped it into his mouth!

—Candice Beatham

From the kitchen of:

Beverage Hints

Tea makes a good punch base.

To grind coffee: Put coffee beans through a corn grinder with burrs set very loose. Blow and shake to separate the hull from the bean. Grind according to method of making coffee: for kettle, coarse; for percolator, medium; for drip, fine.

To roast coffee beans: Put coffee beans in a heavy skillet over medium heat; stir constantly to keep them from burning. The beans will turn from green to yellow, then to brown. The color when roasted should be a rich, deep brown, not black. To save time, roast more than one batch. Skillet is very hot after the first batch is done and will roast the second batch more quickly.

Black Tea

Add boiling water to tea leaves. Cover and set for 3–5 minutes in a warm place. Strain.

Spiced Tea Mix

Combine and store in tightly covered container:

- 1 cup instant tea
- 1 cup orange flavored drink mix
- 1/3 cup sweetened lemonade mix
- 1 teaspoon cloves
- 1/2 teaspoon cinnamon
- 1/2 teaspoon nutmeg

To make spiced tea: Combine 2 teaspoons mix to 1 cup hot or cold water.

- *If desired, add 1 cup red hots to mix and use hot water.*

Spiced Tea

Combine:

- 3–4 cracked sticks of cinnamon
- 1 tablespoon dried, grated orange or lemon peel
- 8–16 crushed whole cloves
- 1/2 cup black tea leaves

Use 1 rounded teaspoon for each cup of tea. Brew 5–6 minutes.

Cinnamon Stick Tea

Boil until tea becomes as dark as desired:

- 4 cups water
- 1–2 cinnamon sticks

Tea Punch

Let stand 6 minutes, then strain:

- 4 cups boiling water
- 1/2 cup loose tea

Add and chill:

- 4 cups sugar
- 16 cups cold water
- 10 cups pineapple juice
- 2 cups lemon juice

Makes 32 cups.

Gelatin Beverage

Dissolve:

- 1–2 tablespoons flavored gelatin dissolved in hot water or juices added to taste

Cocoa Mix

Sift into a large bowl:

- 2 cups powdered whole milk
- 2 cups powdered non-fat milk
- 1 cup powdered creamer, optional
- 3/4 cup cocoa
- 1/8 teaspoon salt

Add:

- 1–2 cups sugar

Mix well. Store in airtight container.

* *To make hot cocoa: Fill container 1/4 full with Cocoa Mix. Add a small amount of water and stir until well blended. Fill container to top with hot water, stir only to blend.*

* *For a richer mix: Use 4 cups powdered whole milk and omit non-fat milk.*

* *To use only non-fat milk: Omit whole milk and creamer. Use 5 cups of non-fat milk and 2 cups sugar.*

* *To use sweetened chocolate powder: Decrease sugar to 1/4 cup.*

See page 240 for International Conversion Charts

Hot Cocoa

Combine:

- 2 tablespoons cocoa
- 3–4 tablespoons sugar or 1 teaspoon sweetener
- 1/8 teaspoon salt
- 1 cup milk powder

Add and stir well:

- 1/2 cup water

Add:

- 3 1/2 cups boiling water
- 1 teaspoon vanilla

Serve. Makes 4 cups.

Café con Leche

Pour very hot milk over desired amount of instant coffee in cup.

Tomato Juice

Simmer:

- fresh tomatoes until soft

Strain and add:

- 1 teaspoon salt for each 4 cups of juice

Season to taste with lemon juice, sugar, or a few drops of onion juice.

Vegetable Juice Cocktail

Combine:

- 4 cups potato or vegetable water
- 3/4 cup tomato paste
- grated onion, garlic salt, salt, and pepper to taste

Bring to a boil. Chill and serve.

Brazilian Fruit Shake

Combine in blender until thoroughly blended:

- 1 cup orange juice, milk, or yogurt
- 2–3 cups cut-up fruit, any combination

Add a few ice cubes and blend until thoroughly mixed. Serves 3–4.

Banana Milkade

Mash thoroughly:

- **3–4 large ripe bananas or other fruit**

Add and beat together with beater or blender:

- **4 cups milk**
- **2 tablespoons sugar**
- **1/4 cup pineapple juice, optional**
- **1/2 teaspoon vanilla, optional**
- **a dash of nutmeg on each glassful, optional**

Flavored Gelatin Milkade: Omit bananas and sugar. Dissolve 1/3 cup flavored gelatin in 1/2 cup boiling water.
Add to milk mixture.

Diet Root Beer

Combine:

- **1 tablespoon dry yeast**
- **1/2 cup warm water**

Add:

- **7 1/2 cups water**
- **1 1/2 tablespoons root beer extract**
- **2 tablespoons sugar or sweetener to taste**

Place in sterilized jars with tight lids and allow to stand overnight out of refrigerator. Then refrigerate one day before drinking.

Ginger Ale: Substitute for the root beer extract, one 2–inch piece of fresh ginger root which has been pulverized in the blender or chopped and mashed.

See page 240 for International Conversion Charts

Layered Mexican Dip

Layer in medium-size casserole dish or pan in the order given:

- refried beans
- browned hamburger with or without onion
- grated cheese
- diced tomatoes or Mexican salsa
- guacamole
- sour cream

Garnish with:

- olives, chopped green onions, and/or grated cheese

Serve with chips.

Guacamole

Combine:

- 2–3 ripe avocados, mashed until smooth
- 1 tablespoon lemon juice or vinegar
- juice of a small lime or lemon
- 1/2–3/4 teaspoon salt
- 1 small onion, diced fine
- snipped parsley or cilantro, optional
- 1 ripe tomato, finely chopped, optional
- 1 green chili, chopped, optional

Serve immediately as a dip or a side dish. Serves 3–4.

Hot Cheese Dip

Fry:

- 1 tablespoon margarine or butter
- 1/3 cup chopped onion

Stir in:

- 1 tablespoon flour

Add and heat until melted:

- 2 cups shredded cheddar cheese or other cheese
- 1 cup tomatoes, finely chopped
- 1 tablespoon finely chopped hot chili pepper, or to taste

Serve hot with tortilla chips or potato chips. This dip is good hot or cold.

If using hot, keep it warm. Do not try to reheat.

Powdered Milk Dip

Put in a small bowl:

- **1/2 cup powdered whole milk**

Add slowly and stir until of dip consistency:

- **2–3 tablespoons water, onion, pickle, or pimento juice**

Add and stir until well blended:

- **1/8 teaspoon or more garlic, onion, or celery salt**
- **1–2 tablespoons dry onion flakes or chopped onion**
- **2 tablespoons melted cheese or sour cream, optional**

Serve with tostadas or tortilla chips.

Onion juice: Cook onion until tender in a little water. Add liquid to dip.

Gingered Fruit Dip

Combine and blend:

- **1 cup low-fat cottage cheese, sour cream, or yogurt**
- **1 small banana, cut up**
- **1/8 teaspoon ground ginger**
- **1 tablespoon milk**

Store in an airtight container. Chill. Garnish dip with orange peel, if desired. Serve with fresh fruit sliced to dip. Makes 1 1/4 cups.

Taco Appetizer

Cut into 6–8 triangles and fry until crisp:

- **tortillas**

Spread on each tortilla and broil until cheese melts:

- **refried beans**
- **grated cheese**

* *Top with chopped cooked chicken or ground beef and chopped chilies.*

Main Dish Tostadas: Fry whole tortillas. Top with beans, cheese, meat, lettuce, and tomatoes, if desired.

Ham and Cheese Rolls

Combine:

- **2 cups each cooked ground ham and grated cheese**
- **3/4 cup tomato sauce**
- **4 teaspoons green pepper, chopped**
- **1 teaspoon celery seed, optional**
- **1 onion, minced**
- **3 drops Tabasco or other hot sauce, optional**

Spread mixture on hard rolls or French bread and place under the broiler until the cheese melts.

Tortilla Egg Sandwich

Fry in a little cooking oil:

- **whole tortillas**

Spread on fried tortillas:

- **scrambled eggs**
- **fresh tomatoes and onions, chopped**
- **grated cheese**

Put tortillas on cookie sheet and broil until cheese melts.

Tuna Salad Sandwich

Combine:

- **1 cup tuna, drained**
- **1/2 teaspoon salt, optional**
- **1/4 cup mayonnaise**

Toss together lightly. Use as sandwich filling or serve with lettuce and garnish with slices of hard-cooked eggs.

* *Add any combination: Hot sauce. 1 tablespoon lemon juice, 1/4–1/2 cup pickle relish, 1–2 teaspoons mustard, 1/2–1 cup chopped celery, cucumber, carrots, or peas.*

Egg Salad Sandwich

Combine:

- **4 hard-cooked eggs, finely chopped**
- **1/4 cup or more crumbled, crisp bacon, optional**
- **2 tablespoons pickle relish or chopped pickle**
- **1/4 teaspoon salt**
- **2–3 tablespoons mayonnaise**
- **1/2–1 teaspoon mustard, optional**

Use as sandwich filling or serve on lettuce as salad. Makes 1 1/2 cups.

Chicken Salad Filling: Use 1 cup cooked chicken for eggs.

Tuna Salad Filling: Substitute 1 cup tuna for eggs.

Bean Cakes

Soak for 8 hours, then cook until tender:

- 1 cup white beans, pea beans, or black-eyed peas
- water to cover beans

Mash beans and add:

- 1-inch fresh ginger, shredded finely, optional
- 3 garlic cloves ground to a paste
- 1 teaspoon salt
- 1/8 teaspoon black pepper
- 1/2 teaspoon coriander seed, optional
- 1/4 cup chopped onion

Make balls 1–2 teaspoons each or flatten into cakes so they cook faster.

Fry a few at a time until uniformly golden. Serve with a hot taco-like sauce, guacamole, mint sauce, or chutney. Makes 60–70 balls. Serve with cheese and rice for a complete protein main dish.

Yam Chips

Peel and slice into thin pieces (about 1/8 inch):

- fresh yams (sweet potatoes)

Fry a few at a time in:

- 1-inch oil

Remove with a slotted spoon when they puff up. Sprinkle lightly with:

- salt, optional

* *Can also be seasoned with sugar, cinnamon, and cayenne pepper.*

See page 240 for International Conversion Charts

Jam and Jelly Hints and Definitions

Jelly: Made from fruit juice.

Jam: Made from crushed or ground fruit.

Conserves: Jams with a mixture of fruits and usually nuts and raisins.

Preserves: Jams made with whole fruits or large pieces of fruit in a thick, often jellied syrup.

Marmalade: A soft jelly containing small pieces of citrus fruit and rind.

Fruit Butter: A spiced fruit pureed in a blender.

Pectin: A natural carbohydrate that causes food to jell. All fruits contain it but in differing amounts. All fruits have more pectin when underripe.

Acid: Adds to the flavor and also to the jelling process. Ripe fruits have less acid than underripe fruits.

If pectin is low: Use some underripe fruit and reduce the sugar to 3/4 cup per cup of fruit. One fourth of the fruit should be slightly underripe, unless you are adding pectin.

To test if fruit has enough pectin to jell properly: Add 1 teaspoon cooked fruit juice to 1 tablespoon rubbing alcohol and mix. If a jellylike mass forms that can be picked up with a fork, there is enough pectin. (**Warning**: do not eat tested fruit juice. Discard.) If there is not enough pectin, add 1 tablespoon pectin for each cup fruit juice. Test again. Continue adding 1 tablespoon pectin at a time and testing.

Fruits with sufficient acid and pectin to gel: Sour apples, sour blackberries, crabapples, cranberries, currants, gooseberries, lemons, loganberries, plums, quinces, and sour prunes.

Fruits that may need acid or pectin added: Ripe apples, ripe blackberries, sour cherries, chokecherries, elderberries, grapefruit, grapes (California), loquats, and oranges.

Fruits that always need additional acid or pectin: Apricots, figs, grapes (Western Concord), guavas, peaches, pears, pomegranates, prunes, raspberries, and strawberries.

For fruit with a high pectin content: For each cup of juice use 3/4–1 cup sugar.

For fruit with a low pectin content: Use 2/3–3/4 cup sugar.

To make pectin or apple jelly: Save apple peelings, cover with water, boil, strain through jelly bag, and freeze until needed. When cooking a low pectin fruit, throw in a block of frozen pectin.

To remove mold on homemade jelly: Skim and throw away the mold.

For variety in jams or jellies: Add cinnamon, allspice, nutmeg, or ginger to some batches. In fruit without enough acid, add 1 tablespoon lemon juice to each cup of fruit

For jellies, pickles, mustard, and vinegar: Refrigeration is not needed.

If jelly is too soft: Too much juice, acid, or too little sugar was used, or it was not cooked long enough.

If too syrupy: Too little pectin used, or too much or too little sugar.

If too stiff: Too much pectin, fruit not ripe enough, or it was overcooked.

If too cloudy: Stood too long before being poured into jars, not strained well enough, or the fruit was under-ripe or cooked too long.

Canning Jams, Jellies, or Preserves

1. Wash, prepare, and cook fruit according to recipe.

2. Do one of the following jelly tests:

   a. Insert a thermometer into center of jam or jelly. When 9 degrees above boiling point, it is done. (see chart on page 235 in Health Precautions for boiling point.)

   b. Pour a little syrup onto a cold plate and place it in the refrigerator for 1 minute. If mixture jells, it is done.

   c. Dip a cool metal spoon into the boiling juice. Lift it out and let the syrup drop slowly. It is ready when 2 drops barely leave the spoon.

3. Pour into hot jars, skimming off any foam. Fill to 1/8 inch from top. Wipe rims clean.

4. Place hot lids and rings on jars and hand tighten.

5. Cool on a padded surface. Check seal by tapping with fork. High sound equals seal. Low sound equals no seal. If not sealed, refrigerate or process again with new lids.

6. Label and store in a cool, dark place.

To seal with paraffin:

1. Heat paraffin in a clean can set in a pan of water over a fire. White candles may be used if paraffin is not available.

2. Pour hot paraffin over jelly about 1/8 inch thick. Tip jar slightly and rotate to make a good seal around the edge. Be sure the edge is clean.

3. Let glasses stand until wax hardens. While wax is still hot, prick any bubbles that form on the surface. Place tops on jars.

To remove paraffin easily: When making jelly lay a piece of string, long enough to hang over the edges, across the top of the jelly glass. Pour hot paraffin over string. To remove paraffin, lift the string.

Making Jelly

Make jelly from apples, guavas, mangos, plums, berries, or other fruit.

1. Prepare juice.

   a. Wash fruit and remove stems. Do not core or peel apples or other firm fruits. If fruit is soft, cut into small pieces or crush.

   b. Place fruit in pan. Add about 1/4 cup of water to each 2 cups of fruit, unless firm, such as apples, then add about 1 cup.

See page 240 for International Conversion Charts

c. Bring to a boil. Cook at medium heat 5–10 minutes or until tender. Do not overboil as it reduces the jelling strength.

d. Strain through a cloth bag (a pillow case works well). Hang bag over a bowl until all juice has dripped through. Or put in a colander lined with several layers of cheese cloth, a dish towel, or a piece of sheet.

e. Place juice in a large saucepan. Refrigerate pulp and use later for making fruit leather or butter.

2. Test juice for pectin (see page 177). Add pectin if necessary.

3. Combine and boil:
- 2 cups fruit juice
- 1 1/2–2 cups sugar
- 2 teaspoons lemon juice
- 1 teaspoon butter to keep from boiling over, optional

4. Do jelly test. (see page 178).

5. Place in jars and seal (see page 178).

Quick Strawberry Jam

Cook together until consistency of jam:
- 2 cups crushed strawberries
- 2 cups sugar
- 1–2 tablespoons juice, optional,

* *Use any type of fruit or combination of fruits.*

* *Use 1 1/2 cups sugar and 1/2 cup strawberry gelatin.*

Peach Jam: Use peaches with peach, lemon, or pineapple gelatin.

Squash Jam: Use cooked, mashed squash. Add cinnamon and ginger.

Berry Jam: Use any type of berries and any berry gelatin.

Rhubarb Jam: Use 4 cups chopped rhubarb and berry gelatin.

Rhubarb-Pineapple Jam: Use 2 cups each chopped raw rhubarb, crushed pineapple, and sugar. Add strawberry gelatin, if desired.

Green Tomato Jam: Use green tomatoes. Add water to just cover. Cook until tender. Add lime juice and sugar. Continue cooking.

Fruit Preserves

Combine and make heavy syrup by boiling:
- 3 cups sugar
- 1 cup water

Add:
- 6 cups fruit (whole small fruit or larger fruit cut)
- juice of 1 large lemon

Bring to boiling, then cook over low heat until clear. Do jelly test. Pour into prepared jars and seal (see page 178).

* *Use any fresh fruit available: cherries, berries, prunes, kumquats, etc.*

Pickled Fruit: Follow same directions, but add 1–2 sticks of cinnamon, 1/2 teaspoon whole cloves, and a few allspice berries. Replace 1/2 cup water with 1/2 cup vinegar.

Conserves

Combine and heat to boiling:

- 7 cups sliced, peeled fruit
- 4 cups sugar
- 3 cups raisins
- 1 orange, quartered and thinly sliced
- 1 lemon, quartered and thinly sliced

Boil and stir 25 minutes until mixture begins to thicken and add:

- 1 cup chopped nuts

Put into jars and seal (see page 178).

Orange Marmalade

Boil until tender:

- 6 medium oranges (discard white membrane if desired)
- 1 large lemon

Quarter, remove seeds, core, slice, measure fruit and juice, and add:

- double amount water
- equal amount of sugar (cup for cup)

Cook rapidly, stirring occasionally until foam can't be stirred down and syrup won't run on saucer. Do jelly test. Pour into sterilized jars and seal (see page 178).

* *Before ready to jell, add 2 packages orange gelatin. Reduce sugar to taste.*

* *For a darker, stronger marmalade: After adding water, let stand 24*

hours, then bring to a boil. Cook until fruit is tender; measure and add 3/4 cup sugar to each cup fruit and juice. Let stand overnight again. Third day, bring to boil and cook rapidly until jelly test; bottle and seal. If available, add juice from 2 sour oranges.

Papaya Marmalade: Use 6 cups grated papaya. Cook until mixture thickens and fruit begins to appear translucent. Add 5 cups sugar and 1/2 cup lemon juice and continue cooking.

Apple Butter

Boil until tender and mash:

- 6 cups apples, quartered (save peelings for Apple Jelly)
- 1–2 cups of white or brown sugar
- 2 teaspoons cinnamon
- 1 teaspoon cloves
- 1 tablespoon lemon juice
- 1/4 cup cider vinegar or vinegar

Stir together and bring to boil. Cook on low heat until thick and shiny, stirring frequently (at least 1/2 hour). Long slow cooking gives the rich buttery flavor and blends spices. Seal (see page 178).

* *This recipe can be used with any tropical fruits such as papaya, cooking bananas, tecojotes, etc.*

Apple Jelly: Save peelings and cores from apples used for apple butter or apple pies. Cover with water and boil until tender. Do not cook more than 8 cups of juice at one time. Use a pan 4 times the volume of juice and sugar.

See page 240 for International Conversion Charts

Mango Butter: Substitute cooked mangos for apples. Strain mangos.

Coconut Butter (Vanuatu): Combine 6 coconuts, finely grated, and 6 cups boiling water. Squeeze through muslin or strong net. Strain again and allow to set overnight. Then put in jar and churn as butter. Wash and salt to taste. Use to make pastry biscuits or in place of margarine or butter.

Pickle Hints

* *Pickling salt or non-iodized salt are preferable as they will not discolor or affect the taste of your pickles, but any salt will work.*

* *Distilled water will not affect the color or taste of your pickles, but tap water will also work.*

To Seal Pickles:

1. Prepare a water bath that will cover jars to the neck.

2. Scald jars to sterilize. Be sure that the rim of the jar has no chips and is clean.

3. Put lids into hot water to soften seal.

4. After filling jars, wipe rim with a clean cloth, seal, apply screw bands, and hand tighten, so as not to injure seal.

5. Place jars into water. Boil 10–15 minutes, then place on a padded surface.

6. As they cool, jars should seal themselves. Test by tapping lids with spoon. They should "ping." A "clunk" indicates an unsealed lid. Unsealed jars should be refrigerated. Sealed jars will keep indefinitely.

Indonesian Cucumber Relish

Combine:

- **4 medium cucumbers, peeled, de-seeded, and diced**
- **1/2 cup onion, chopped**
- **1 teaspoon salt**
- **1/4 cup sugar**
- **1/2 cup vinegar**
- **water to barely cover**

Keeps well in the refrigerator for about a week.

Refrigerator Pickles: Slice cucumbers instead of de-seeding and dicing. Add 1/2 cup chopped green pepper, 1 teaspoon celery seed, 1/2 teaspoon mustard or mustard seed, and sugar to taste.

Pico de Gallo (Mexico)

Combine:

- 1/2 cup chopped onion
- 1 1/2 cups chopped tomato
- 3 tablespoons chopped fresh cilantro
- 1–2 tablespoons lemon or lime juice
- 1 garlic clove, minced, or a sprinkle of garlic powder
- 1 small green hot pepper, chopped fine, optional
- salt and hot peppers to taste

Serve with Mexican food, eggs, or casseroles.

Banana Medley (Tanzania)

Combine in saucepan:

- 4 ripe eating bananas, peeled and sliced
- 1/2 cup chopped onion
- 1 medium tomato, peeled and chopped
- 1/2 cup coconut milk (see page 102)
- 1/2 tablespoon butter
- 1/8 teaspoon turmeric
- 1/4 teaspoon salt

Bring to a boil, reduce heat, and simmer for 15 minutes. Serve warm or cold as an accompaniment to meat. Serves 34.

Pickled Beets

Layer alternately:

- 6–8 beets, cooked, peeled, and sliced
- 3 sliced onions, optional

Bring to boil:

- 1/4 cup vinegar
- 3/4 cup water or beet juice
- 3 tablespoons sugar
- 2 whole cloves or 1/8 teaspoon ground cloves, optional (1/2 ml)
- 1/4 teaspoon salt
- 1/4 bay leaf, optional
- 1/4 teaspoon cinnamon or cinnamon stick, optional
- 1/8 teaspoon pepper

Pour over beets and chill or place in sterile jars and seal with water bath.

See page 240 for International Conversion Charts

Banana Chutney

Boil for 2–3 minutes:

- **4 cups mashed, ripe eating bananas**
- **1 cup sugar**
- **1 cup vinegar**

Add and let stand to cool:

- **2 teaspoons curry, optional**
- **2 teaspoons cinnamon**

Add:

- **1 cup diced onions, may be added during cooking**

Keeps in the tropics without refrigeration about 10 days.

Refrigerator Dill Pickles

Combine and leave covered 3 hours or overnight in refrigerator:

- **4 cups sliced cucumbers**
- **2 tablespoons salt**
- **water to cover**

Drain, rinse, and place in a large saucepan and add:

- **1 1/2 cups vinegar**
- **1 heaping tablespoon dill seed**
- **1 tablespoon sugar**
- **garlic cloves, chopped**

Bring to a boil, stirring from time to time. When cucumbers turn a pale yellow, place in jars. Store in refrigerator. If cucumbers have tough skins, peel and seed them before slicing.

Dilled Onions: Omit cucumbers and use about 12 sliced white onions. Decrease dill to 1 teaspoon. Add 1 teaspoon caraway seed and increase sugar 1 cup. Bring to rolling boil and pour over onions.

No-Dill Pickles

Combine in quart jar and leave uncovered 4–5 days, then refrigerate:

- **small cucumbers**
- **10 bay leaves**
- **5 fresh garlic cloves**
- **3–4 celery tops**
- **boiling water to cover with 1 teaspoon salt added for each**
- **cup of water**

Dill Pickles or Okra

Put into sterilized quart jar:

- 4–6 small to medium cucumbers or okra, whole or cut

Add to jar:

- 1 garlic clove
- 1–3 teaspoons dill seed
- 1/2 bay leaf, optional
- 1 slice raw carrot, optional
- 1 dry or fresh red pepper, optional

Boil and pour on cucumbers.

- 1 1/4 cups vinegar
- 2 1/2 cups water
- 2–3 teaspoons salt

Seal in water bath and let stand 3 days before use.

Bread and Butter Pickles

Slice into a large bowl:

- 20–25 medium or large cucumbers or other vegetables
- 6–12 large onions, optional
- 2 green or red peppers, optional

Pour over and let stand 3 hours:

- 1/2 cup salt
- water to cover

Drain, rinse, and drain. Combine separately and bring to a boil:

- 5 cups vinegar
- 5 cups white or brown sugar
- 1 1/2 teaspoons turmeric or allspice
- 2 tablespoons mustard seed
- 1/2 teaspoon ground cloves or 1 stick cinnamon, optional
- 1 1/2 teaspoons celery seed, optional

Add the vegetables gradually with very little stirring. Allow to boil for 5 seconds. Pack in hot sterilized jars. Seal with water bath.

See page 240 for International Conversion Charts

Salad Hints

Crisp salad: To keep a vegetable salad fresh while standing, place an inverted saucer in bottom of bowl before filling with salad.

Fresh fruits that will prevent gelatin from firming up: Pineapple, figs, papaya, and kiwi fruit.

Source of gelatin: Boil a chicken or clean pig's feet. Cool and skim off fat that rises to the top. Use the gelatin in tomato aspic salad, etc.

How much to use: One tablespoon of plain gelatin thickens two cups liquid.

To set gelatin without refrigeration: Set at night. In the morning wrap a wet cloth around it and set in a cool place. Usually keeps until noon.

To use flavored gelatin powder in a fruit salad: Sprinkle over top or stir into fruit.

To add ingredients after gelatin is already set: Warm it for a few minutes and let it set again to the right consistency.

To measure flavored gelatin: 1 small package of flavored gelatin equals about 1/3 cup.

Potato Salad

Combine and refrigerate:

- 10 medium potatoes or chayotes, cooked and diced
- 1 cup celery, chopped
- 1 cup pickles, chopped
- 2 onions, chopped, raw or browned
- 1/4 cup cooked, chopped bacon, optional
- 2 tablespoons mustard
- 1 cup mayonnaise
- salt to taste
- 2 tablespoons pickle juice or vinegar
- 5–7 hard-boiled eggs, chopped, optional

Pasta Salad

Cook until tender, drain, and rinse:

- 4–6 cups boiling water
- 1–3 teaspoons salt, optional
- 1 cup macaroni or other pasta

Combine separately and add:

- 1/4–1/2 cup mayonnaise or salad dressing
- 1–2 tablespoons sugar
- 1 tablespoon vinegar
- 1/4 cup finely chopped onions, optional
- 1/4 cup finely chopped green pepper, optional
- 1 cup finely chopped celery, optional

* *Omit sugar and vinegar. Add 1/4 cup pickle relish.*

* *Add raw, chopped broccoli, carrots, cucumbers, or zucchini.*

* *Add 1/2–1 cup, cooked, cut-up meat, cheese, nuts, or seeds.*

Sprouts

Combine in a jar, cover with warm water, and soak overnight:

- 1–2 tablespoons seeds

In the morning, cover jar with a nylon mesh or cheese cloth and drain. Rinse and drain 2–4 times a day for the next 2–5 days, until sprouted. Each time after draining, place jar on its side in a dark area until sprouts are about 1-inch long, then place in a sunny area for a day to green the sprouts.

Seeds that work well for sprouting: Alfalfa, almond, bean, chickpea, corn, lentil, mung bean, pea, pumpkin seed, radish, rice, sesame, sunflower, vegetable, soybean, and wheat. Sunflower seeds mature in 1–2 days.

Cuban Salad

Cook until tender, 3 or more vegetables:

- carrots, sliced or sticks
- cabbage slices
- peas
- green beans
- corn

Chill and layer cooked, drained vegetables with the following:

- fresh tomatoes, avocados, cucumbers, onions, and lettuce

Pour your choice of salad dressing over all.

See page 240 for International Conversion Charts

Coleslaw

Combine and let stand:

- 1 medium head cabbage, finely shredded
- 1/2 onion, finely chopped, optional
- 1 cup sugar

Combine separately, bring to boil, pour over cabbage, drain, and serve:

- 1 cup vinegar
- 3/4 cup oil
- 1/2–1 teaspoon salt
- 1 teaspoon dry, or 3 teaspoons prepared, mustard
- 1 teaspoon celery salt, optional

* *To reduce calories, cut amount of oil, vinegar, and sugar in half and add 1/2 cup water to boiling mixture.*

* *To vary, add any of the following: 1–2 cups grated carrots and 1/2–1 cup chopped apple or crushed pineapple.*

Creamy Coleslaw: Omit vinegar, oil, mustard, celery salt, and sugar. Combine and pour over cabbage, 1/2–1 cup mayonnaise, 1–2 tablespoons vinegar, 2 teaspoons sugar, and celery seed.

Hot Cabbage Slaw: Omit sugar, vinegar, oil, salt, mustard, and celery salt. Combine and cook until thick, 1 beaten egg, 1/2 cup sugar, 3 scant tablespoons each vinegar and water, and 2 tablespoons butter. Pour over cabbage. Serve immediately or chill first.

Three Bean Salad

Combine in a bowl:

- 2 cups cooked green beans or wax beans, chopped
- 2 cups cooked garbanzo beans
- 2 cups cooked kidney beans, black beans, or similar beans
- 1 onion, chopped
- 1/2 cup chopped green pepper

Combine separately, then pour over beans and marinate overnight:

- 3/4 cup sugar
- 2/3 cup vinegar
- 1/3 cup oil
- 1 teaspoon salt and a dash of pepper

* *Use dressing for any lettuce salad or use to marinate vegetables.*

* *Use just one type bean.*

* *Add diced tomatoes.*

Bacon-Lettuce Bowl

Combine in salad bowl:

- 1 head lettuce or spinach, shredded
- 4 slices bacon, cooked and cut in pieces

Combine in pan and heat just to boiling:

- 2 tablespoons bacon drippings
- 2 tablespoons sugar
- 1 tablespoon water
- 2 tablespoons vinegar
- 1/2 teaspoon salt

Drizzle over lettuce and toss to mix well.

Taco Salad

Combine:

- 1 head lettuce, shredded
- 1–2 cups grated cheese
- 1–2 cups chopped tomatoes
- 1/2 cup sliced olives, optional

Combine separately and heat:

- 4 cups ground beef, browned
- 1 onion, chopped
- 2 cups cooked kidney beans
- 1–2 cups tomato sauce
- 1–2 teaspoons chili powder

Pour over salad and toss. Mix in just before serving:

- 2 cups broken corn or tortilla chips

* *Substitute French or Russian dressing for tomato sauce and chili powder.*

* *Layer salad onto individual plates in the following order: chips, lettuce, meat sauce, cheese, and tomatoes.*

Gelatin

Combine and let stand a few minutes:

- 1 tablespoon plain gelatin

Add, stir, and refrigerate or let stand until set

- 1 1/2 cups boiling water
- 1 or more tablespoons sugar, optional

Flavored Gelatin: Use 3/4 cup sugar with 2 tablespoons gelatin and 1 package flavored drink mix, or 2 tablespoons drink mix. Add 2 cups boiling water, stir. Use 2 cups cold water or fruit juice, except fresh pineapple, in place of water, and chill. Place sliced fruits in gelatin.

See page 240 for International Conversion Charts

Tomato Aspic Salad

Dissolve and set aside:

- 1 tablespoon plain gelatin
- 1/4 cup cold water

Combine separately in a saucepan and cook for 10 minutes:

- 2 cups tomato juice
- 1/2 medium onion, sliced
- 12 whole cloves
- 1/2 teaspoon salt
- 1/2 teaspoon sugar

Add the dissolved gelatin and cook 1 more minute. Strain into mold or serving dish and chill. May serve with either mayonnaise or cottage cheese, mixed with a little celery seed and garlic salt, or a little dry onion soup mix.

Papaya Peanut Salad

Combine:

- 1 small ripe papaya or other fruits, cut up
- 2–3 bananas or other fruits, cut up
- 1/2 cup chopped peanuts or other nuts

Pour over and toss lightly until blended:

- 1/4 cup flavored gelatin powder
- juice from 1 lemon

Frozen Fruit Salad

Combine and blend well:

- 1 cup cream cheese, softened
- 1 teaspoon mayonnaise
- 1 tablespoon cherry juice, optional for color
- 2 1/2 cups fruit cocktail, drained, or fresh fruit cut up
- 1/2 cup maraschino cherries, drained and cut up, optional
- 1 1/2 cups peaches, pears, or any other fruit, cut up
- 2 1/2 cups marshmallows, cut up

Fold in:

- 1 cup cream or chilled evaporated milk, whipped

Freeze in tray lined with waxed paper, so it may be lifted out and sliced easily, or it may be frozen in milk cartons. This salad is creamy because the juice of the fruit is not used.

Pineapple Carrot Salad

Dissolve:

- 1/3 cup lemon or other flavored gelatin powder
- 1 cup boiling water

Add and chill until slightly jelled:

- 1/4 teaspoon salt
- 1 tablespoon vinegar or lemon juice, optional
- 1 cup pineapple juice or water

Fold in:

- 1 cup drained, crushed pineapple
- 1 cup shredded, raw carrots

Chill until set. Top with whipped cream or mayonnaise.

* *Do not use fresh pineapple as it will not set.*

* *Substitute other fruits for pineapple: peaches, apples, berries, or bananas.*

Cucumber Cream Salad: Omit pineapple juice, pineapple, and carrots. Add 3/4 cup cold water and 1 teaspoon grated onion. After chilling add 1/2 cup mayonnaise, 2 cups minced cucumbers without seeds, and 1 cup cottage cheese or sour cream.

Pineapple Cheese Salad: Omit carrots. Add 1 cup grated cheese.

Pineapple Cream Salad: Omit carrots. Add 1/2 cup finely chopped celery. Add and whip together, 1/3 cup cream cheese and 2 cups whipping cream.

Apple Gelatin Salad

Dissolve:

- 1/3 cup red flavored gelatin
- 1 cup boiling water

Add:

- 1/2 cup applesauce or cooked banana sauce

Add and chill until firmly set:

- 1/2 cup cold water

Apple-Cheese Salad: Omit applesauce. Add 1/2 cup cold water, 1 cup each grated cheese and chopped apples, and 1 tablespoon diced pimentos.

Apple-Nut Salad: Omit red gelatin and applesauce. Use apple gelatin and add 1/2 cup fruit juice or water, 1 cup chopped apple, and 1/4 cup chopped nuts.

Cinnamoned-Apple Gelatin: Add 1/4 teaspoon cinnamon.

Cranberry Salad: Substitute 2 cups cranberry sauce for water and applesauce. When partially firm, beat in 1/2 cup mayonnaise. Fold in 1/2 cup chopped nuts and 1 apple, diced.

Festive Cranberry Salad: Substitute 1 cup whole cranberry sauce for cold water and applesauce. Pour salad into a greased casserole. When set, top with 1 cup sour cream. Garnish with cranberries and mint.

See page 240 for International Conversion Charts

Flavored Gelatin Dessert Salad

Combine:

- 1/3 cup flavored gelatin powder
- 3/4 cup boiling water

Add, then refrigerate until partially firm:

- 1/3 cup lemon juice
- 1/2 cup sugar

When partially firm, add:

- 1 2/3 cup evaporated milk, well chilled and whipped

Chill. Add any chopped fruit, if desired.

Cheese Pineapple Mold: Dissolve gelatin in 2 cups boiling pineapple juice and water. Pour 1/4 of this mixture into an oiled mold or loaf pan and refrigerate. Combine separately and beat 1/3 cup cream or cottage cheese, 1 cup sour cream or yogurt, and the lemon juice and sugar. Add remaining gelatin mixture gradually, then stir in 1–2 cups each crushed pineapple and grated cheddar cheese. Pour over plain gelatin in mold and refrigerate. When set, invert and top with grated cheese.

Gelatin Yogurt Salad: Omit lemon juice, evaporated milk, and sugar. Increase water to 1 cup. Add 1 cup plain yogurt.

Cucumber and Tomato Salad

To make the dressing, whisk the following together in a large bowl:

- 1/4 cup cider vinegar
- 1 teaspoon white sugar
- 1/2 teaspoon salt
- 1/2 teaspoon chopped fresh dill
- 1/4 teaspoon ground black pepper
- 1 tablespoon vegetable oil

To make the salad, prepare:

- 2 cucumbers, sliced thinly
- 1 cup sliced red onion
- 2 ripe tomatoes cut into wedges

Add the vegetables to the dressing in the bowl. Toss to coat. Let stand at least 15 minutes before serving. Serves 6.

Lou's Broccoli Salad

Chop by hand, or use a food processor to chop:

- 4 cups fresh broccoli florets and stems, chopped
- 1/2–3/4 cup red onion, chopped
- 1 cup chopped celery
- 2/3 cup chopped walnuts or other nuts, optional
- 1/2 cup ready-made bacon bits, or 8 slices crisply fried bacon, crumbled

Add whichever of the following that you have available:

- 1 apple, chopped
- 1 cup raisins
- 1 cup grapes, each cut in half

For the salad dressing, mix by hand or in a food processor:

- 1 cup light mayonnaise
- 1/3 cup sugar
- 2 tablespoons vinegar

Pour dressing over the salad and toss gently. Serves 8–10.

Mon's Thai Salad

Blend until creamy:

- 1/2 teaspoon peeled, fresh ginger, finely chopped, optional
- 1/3 cup crushed peanuts or 1/4 cup peanut butter
- 1/4 cup soy sauce
- 1 garlic clove, minced
- 1/4 cup sesame oil
- 1/4 cup water
- 1 tablespoon honey or agave nectar
- 1/4 cup chopped scallions (green onions)
- 2 tablespoons chopped cilantro leaves

Chill for 20 minutes while you make the following.

Combine:

- 1 head of romaine or other lettuce, torn in pieces
- 1/2 medium cucumber, chopped
- 1 small carrot, shredded
- 1 cup fresh broccoli florets and stems, chopped
- 1 cup of fresh cauliflower, chopped
- 1 large tomato, chopped
- 3/4 cup mandarin orange segments, chopped
- 6–8 canned baby corn, each cut in half
- 3 water chestnuts, chopped fine

* *If you don't have all the veggies, just substitute what you have.*

Pour the chilled dressing over the salad, toss, and serve. Serves 6.

See page 240 for International Conversion Charts

Honey-Pineapple Dressing

Mix, shake well, and chill. Good for fruit salads:

- 1/2 cup honey
- 1/4 cup lemon juice
- 1/4 teaspoon salt
- 3 tablespoons crushed pineapple

French Dressing

Combine in a jar and shake well:

- 1/2 teaspoon each, dry mustard and salt
- 1/8 teaspoon pepper
- 1 teaspoon paprika
- 1/4 cup vinegar or lemon juice
- 1/2 cup oil

Use spices, onions, eggs, sauces, garlic, and catsup to vary flavor.

Italian Dressing

Shake in covered jar and refrigerate:

- 1/2 cup oil
- 2 tablespoons vinegar
- 1 tablespoon finely chopped onion
- 1 teaspoon each sugar and salt
- 1 teaspoon dry mustard

- 1 teaspoon dried basil leaves
- 1 teaspoon oregano
- 1/4 teaspoon pepper
- 1–2 garlic cloves, crushed, to taste
- 1–2 tablespoons lemon juice
- 1 teaspoon dried bell peppers, optional

* *Add poppy seed, celery seed, paprika, chili, catsup, pickles, or parsley.*

Uncooked Mayonnaise

Blend well:

- 2 eggs
- 1 1/2 teaspoons salt
- 1 1/4 teaspoons mustard
- 1/2 teaspoon paprika, optional

Continue blending and slowly add:

- 1 cup oil

Add:

- 1/4 cup lemon juice or vinegar

Add slowly while blending at high speed:

- 1 cup oil

* *Add onion, garlic, tomato juice, or other seasonings, if desired.*

Uncooked Eggless Mayonnaise: Omit mustard, paprika, eggs, and 1 cup oil. Add 2/3 cup evaporated milk and slowly add oil, 1 teaspoon salt, 1–2 teaspoons honey, and lemon juice while blending.

Cooked Mayonnaise

Combine in saucepan:

- 1/3 cup flour or 2 1/2 tablespoons cornstarch
- 1–2 tablespoons sugar
- 1 teaspoon salt
- 1 teaspoon dry or 2 teaspoons prepared mustard

Mix together, add, and cook until thick, stirring constantly:

- 3/4 cup water
- 4 egg yolks or 2 whole eggs, beaten

Add a little at a time while beating or blending:

- 1/4 cup mild vinegar or lemon juice
- a few drops garlic juice or garlic powder
- 1 cup salad oil

Cool. Makes 2 cups.

* *To prevent cooked salad dressing from curdling: Stir the beaten eggs into the cold vinegar before cooking and cook slowly in a double boiler.*

Eggless Cooked Mayonnaise: Omit eggs and oil. Decrease flour to 2 tablespoons and salt and mustard to 1/2 teaspoon. Use milk for water. Add 1 teaspoon butter with vinegar. Will thicken as it cools.

Fruit Salad Dressing: Omit mustard and use lemon juice. After adding oil, add a little milk or cream, vanilla, and sugar, if desired.

Mayonnaise Options: Use 1/2 cup cooked or uncooked mayonnaise per recipe.

Creamy Russian Dressing: Add 2 tablespoons chili sauce and 1/8 teaspoon each minced garlic and onion powder.

Green Goddess Dressing: Add 1/2 cup sour cream, 2 tablespoons each minced parsley and green onion, 1/2 teaspoon salt, 1/8 teaspoon each minced garlic and pepper, 1 tablespoon vinegar, and 3 drops green food coloring.

Ranch Dressing: Add 1 cup buttermilk, yogurt, or sour cream, 1/4 teaspoon each onion powder and salt, 1/8 teaspoon each garlic powder, pepper, celery salt, thyme, and sugar and 1/2 teaspoon basil. Refrigerate several hours before serving.

Sour Cream-Mayonnaise Dressing: Add 1/2 cup sour cream or yogurt. Use for coleslaw, potato, or macaroni salads.

Thousand Island Dressing: Add 2 tablespoons each catsup or chili sauce and pickle relish, and 1 hard-cooked egg, chopped fine, optional.

See page 240 for International Conversion Charts

Soup and Sauce Hints

To prevent potatoes from getting mushy when making stew: Cook them separately and add to stew just before serving.

To add more iron to your diet: Cook soup or stew in a cast iron pot.

To prevent milk or cream from curdling when used in combination with tomato juice or sauce: Add baking soda to each before they are mixed.

To prevent soup from lumping when adding flour to thicken: Remove pan from the fire before adding flour. Mix the flour or cornstarch with a little cold water first. Flour is the best thickener for hot soup; cornstarch is best for soups to be served cold.

If you put in too much salt: Add a small quantity of sugar or vinegar, then simmer a little longer. In soup or gravy, add a cut-up raw potato to absorb the excess salt or increase the quantity of liquid.

To improve flavor and richness of any soup: Add bouillon cubes or consommé powder, to taste. Since bouillon cubes and consommé powder are salty, they should be used as part of the salt required in recipes.

To make 1 cup bouillon or consommé: Add to each cup of hot water, 1 standard bouillon cube or 1 teaspoon consommé powder.

To remove excess fat from soup: Add lettuce leaves for a few minutes and remove before serving or add ice cubes and remove them immediately.

For too much garlic: Add a small bunch of parsley for 10 minutes.

To thicken gravy or sauce: Measure flour into cold water or milk in a glass jar with a tight-fitting lid. Cover and shake well to blend before stirring into hot liquid.

To reduce tomato taste in sauce: Add a little brown or white sugar (or both) and grate a raw carrot into the sauce.

To prevent cheese sauce from becoming stringy and leathery: Stir cheese in toward the end of the cooking time.

To make instant white sauce: Blend 1 cup each butter and flour. Spread in ice cube tray, chill, and cut into 16 cubes. Store in freezer. For medium white sauce add 1 cube to 1 cup milk and heat slowly.

Cream of Tomato Soup

Fry:

- 1–2 tablespoons finely-chopped onion
- 2 tablespoons oil

Stir in and cook until smooth and bubbly, stirring constantly:

- 3 tablespoons flour
- 2 teaspoons sugar, optional
- 1 teaspoon salt
- 1/8 teaspoon pepper
- 1 tablespoon parsley, optional

Remove from heat and gradually stir in:

- 2 cups tomato juice

Bring to a boil, stirring constantly. Boil 1 minute. Gradually add:

- 2 cups milk

Heat rapidly to serving temperature. Serve immediately. Serves 4.

* *Prepare biscuit or dumpling dough. Drop into boiling soup and steam until fluffy. Tuck a cheese cube into dough before boiling, if desired.*

Cheese Soup: Substitute chicken broth for cold milk. Fry 3/4 cup chopped celery or carrot with onion. Add 2 1/2 cups shredded cheese after boiling. Heat, but do not boil.

Manhattan Clam Chowder: Add 2 cups diced cooked potatoes and 1/2–1 cup tuna, clams, or any cooked fish (120–250 ml).

Boston Clam Chowder: Use milk for tomato juice in above chowder.

Potato Soup: Substitute milk for tomato juice. Add 2 cups cooked, diced potatoes. Add fried bacon, if desired.

Potato-Cheese Soup: Combine options for potato and cheese soups.

Squash Soup: Use milk for tomato juice and add 4 cups cooked, mashed squash.

Nail Soup

Combine in pan:

- any cooked, chopped meat or stock
- any cooked vegetables
- cooked rice, split peas, noodles, etc.
- seasoning to taste
- water or broth

See page 240 for International Conversion Charts

Bean Soup

Combine, bring to a boil, cover, and let stand 1–2 hours:

- 2 cups beans
- 1–2 teaspoons baking soda
- water to cover

Drain and add:

- 8 cups bean broth, bouillon, or water
- 1–3 bay leaves
- 1 cup chopped onions
- 1 1/4 cups chopped tomatoes, optional
- 2 teaspoons sugar, optional
- 1 garlic clove, minced
- salt and pepper to taste

Cook until beans are tender.

* If a creamier soup is desired, strain or mash the beans.

* Add any or a combination of the following: 1 teaspoon each oregano or ground cumin, 2 teaspoons chili powder, 1/2 cup chopped green pepper, 1 cup cooked, chopped pork, with broth, 1 cup diced carrots, 3 whole cloves or 2 stalks chopped celery.

Peanut Soup: Substitute peanuts for beans. Boil 20 minutes and drain. Rinse with cold water and return peanuts to rinsed kettle. Continue as directed.

Split Pea or Lentil Soup

Combine and cook until tender:

- 1 cup split peas or lentils
- 8 cups water
- 1–2 cups chopped fresh or leftover meat, optional

Combine separately and fry:

- 2 tablespoons cooking oil
- 1 cup chopped onions
- 2 garlic cloves, finely chopped or grated

Add and cook a few minutes. Then add to soup:

- 2–3 tomatoes, chopped
- salt to taste

Simmer 15 minutes.

* To flavor further, add a little ground cumin, sage, celery salt, chopped bacon (fried crisply and drippings), or grated carrots.

Lentil Puree: After soup is cooked, mash or rub through a strainer.

Chicken Soup

Combine and cook until tender:

- **6 cups water**
- **1 teaspoon salt**
- **1 chicken breast, cut in cubes**
- **1/4 cup rice or barley**

Add:

- **1 cup milk or water**

Brown separately and add:

- **1–2 tablespoons margarine or cooking oil**
- **1/4 cup onions, chopped**
- **2 garlic cloves, minced**
- **fresh parsley, chopped very fine**

Heat and serve with 2–3 pieces of avocado and croutons in each bowl, if desired.

Cream of Chicken Soup: Thicken soup with white sauce.

Cuban Noodle Soup: Omit rice and milk. Add and boil until tender 8 small potatoes, quartered, 1/2 cup fine noodles, and 1 teaspoon cumin.

Curried Chicken Vegetable Soup: Add lemon juice, curry, and vegetables.

Hearty Cabbage Soup

Combine in a pan and simmer covered for 15 minutes:

- **1 cup cooked meat, cut into chunks**
- **1/4 cup finely-chopped onions**
- **1/2 cup celery**
- **1 cup diced potatoes**
- **2 cups meat broth, vegetable broth, or bouillon**

Add:

- **3 cups milk**
- **2 cups finely chopped cabbage**
- **2 teaspoons salt**
- **1/4 teaspoon pepper**
- **2 teaspoons brown sugar**
- **1 teaspoon caraway or fennel seed, tied in a cloth bag**

Bring to a boil. Simmer again, covered, for 25 more minutes. Discard caraway or fennel seed. Serve hot. Serves 6–8.

Barley Cabbage Soup: Add 1/4 cup each barley and parsley and thicken by adding 4–6 tablespoons flour or cornstarch moistened with milk or water to make a paste.

See page 240 for International Conversion Charts

Sopa a la Criolla (Peru)

Boil until meat is tender:

- 10 cups water or more
- 1 whole red pepper, optional
- 2 cups beef, cubed or ground
- 1/2 teaspoon salt
- 1 tablespoon ground or mashed fresh garlic
- 1 tablespoon cumin
- pepper to taste

Remove whole pepper, then add and cook until tender:

- 3–4 medium potatoes, cut as for french fries

Combine and add:

- 1 cup oil
- dash achiote or paprika
- 1 tomato, cut finely
- 1/2 cup tomato paste
- 3–4 medium onions, finely chopped
- 1 teaspoon oregano
- corn on the cob, cooked and sliced, optional

Add slowly to boiling soup while beating liquid with a wire whip:

- 4 eggs, beaten
- 1 2/3 cup evaporated milk

Simmer soup for a short time, then add:

- 2–3 cups angel hair or fine spaghetti

Cook until spaghetti is tender. Serve with 1 slice toast, without crust, floating in each bowl of soup.
Serves 10.

Mexican Beef Stew

Brown:

- 4 cups beef stew meat, cubed
- 1 large onion, minced
- 2 garlic cloves, minced
- 1 green pepper, chopped

Add:

- 1 cup tomato sauce
- 1 tablespoon vinegar
- 1 teaspoon oregano
- dash of salt
- 1 tablespoon chili relish, optional
- 1 bay leaf, optional
- wine vinegar, optional
- beef broth or water, optional

Sprinkle over all:

- 2 tablespoons flour

Simmer covered 1 1/2 hours or until tender. Serve with rice or noodles.

Mushroom Potato Soup

Heat in saucepan:

- **4–5 tablespoons oil**

Add and sauté:

- **1 onion, chopped**
- **3 garlic cloves, minced**

Once the onions are soft and translucent, add:

- **1 tablespoon fine flour**

To prevent the flour from burning, add and stir:

- **1 cup of water**

Add and stir thoroughly:

- **1 1/2–2 cups mushrooms (one or more varieties), wiped clean and sliced**
- **Vegeta seasoning, vegetable or chicken bouillon, or salt, to taste**
- **2 pinches of dried marjoram, optional**
- **ground black or white pepper, to taste**
- **pinch of paprika**

Add and stir again:

- **2 1/2–3 cups hot water or chicken broth**

Cover and let the soup boil for 10–15 minutes. Then add:

- **5 small white potatoes, peeled and diced**

Continue boiling. When the potatoes are soft, the soup is ready. Serves 6.

Tasty Taco Soup

Brown and drain:

- **2 cups lean ground beef**

Add:

- **1/4 cup chopped green onions**
- **2 tablespoons dry taco seasoning mix (see page 254)**

Cook 1 minute. Then stir in:

- **1 can crushed tomatoes, undrained**
- **1 cup frozen, canned, or fresh corn kernels**
- **1 cup water**

Bring to a boil. Reduce heat and simmer 10 minutes. To serve, ladle soup into serving bowls. Top with:

- **1/2 cup finely shredded cheese**

Serve with tortilla chips, if desired. Serves 4.

* *To crush your own tomatoes: Peel and quarter tomatoes. Remove excess water and seeds. Place in saucepan and crush with a spoon. Simmer for 10–15 minutes, stirring to break up any large chunks.*

See page 240 for International Conversion Charts

Shellfish Soup

Cover with water and boil 10 minutes:

- **2 cups small shellfish**

Add and bring to a boil:

- **salt and pepper to taste**
- **2 cups liquid from shellfish and milk**
- **1 cup coconut cream (see page 102)**
- **1 teaspoon curry, optional**

Serve hot. Serves 4.

Tomato and Fish Stew (Ghana)

Brown and cook until tender:

- **3–6 tablespoons oil**
- **1 onion, chopped**
- **3 cups water**
- **2 1/4 cups chopped fresh, dried, or canned fish, or alligator**
- **1/2 cup tomato paste**
- **salt and hot pepper to taste**
- **3 cups spinach leaves, cut up okra, or eggplant**

White Sauce Mix

Combine:

- **2 cups milk powder**
- **1 cup flour**
- **2 teaspoons salt**

Cut in until mixture resembles fine crumbs:

- **1 cup butter or margarine**

Store in airtight container in refrigerator up to two months. Makes about 8 cups of white sauce. Mixes into liquids well and makes smooth cream sauces with little effort.

African Peanut Butter Sauce

Brown:

- 1/2 cup onion, chopped
- 2 garlic cloves, minced
- 1–3 tablespoons oil

Mix separately and add:

- 1/2 cup each peanut butter and water
- 2 tablespoons tomato paste

Gradually add until the sauce is the consistency desired:

- 2–3 cups water
- salt and pepper or hot pepper to taste

* *Substitute 1–2 fresh chopped tomatoes for tomato paste.*
* *Add milk powder to mixture or substitute milk for some of the water.*
* *Add cooked beef, chicken, or fish to the sauce and heat thoroughly.*
* *Brown onion, beef, or chicken and simmer in sauce for 1 hour.*
* *Add chunks of cooked squash or sweet potato and heat thoroughly.*
* *Add 1–2 cups chopped greens and cook until tender.*
* *Add 1/4 teaspoon nutmeg and 1–3 teaspoons chili powder.*
* *Dissolve 1–2 bouillon cubes in sauce.*

African Peanut Butter Soup: Add more water.

All-Purpose Curry Sauce

Combine and set aside:

- 2 tablespoons coconut
- 1/2 cup boiling water

Fry:

- 2 tablespoons meat fat, shortening, or oil
- 1 onion, diced
- 1/2 cooking banana, diced, optional

Add and fry together:

- 2 tablespoons flour
- 1 teaspoon salt
- 2 teaspoons curry powder

Add slowly, stirring constantly, and bring to a boil:

- 2 cups meat broth or bouillon water

When boiling, add:

- coconut and water
- 1 tomato, chopped
- 1/3 cup raisins
- 1/2 eating banana, diced, or pulp from 1/2 orange
- 1 tablespoon vinegar or lemon juice

Cook until smooth. This sauce is very good for currying meat, fish, hardboiled eggs, sweet potatoes, or vegetables such as carrots, potatoes, beans, peas, etc. Serve sauce with rice, almonds, or other nuts, if desired. Serves 8–12.

See page 240 for International Conversion Charts

White Sauce From Mix

Combine in saucepan:

- 1/2 cup White Sauce Mix
- 1 cup cool water, meat broth, milk, or tomato juice
- pepper, herbs, and spices, as desired

Cook over low heat, stirring constantly, until thickened and smooth. Use any of the options for White Sauce.

White Sauce

Combine in saucepan:

- 2 tablespoons butter or margarine, melted
- 2 tablespoons flour
- 1/4 teaspoon salt
- 1/8 teaspoon pepper

Cook over low heat, stirring until mixture is smooth and bubbly. Boil 1 minute. Remove from heat. Stir in slowly:

- 1 cup milk

Bring to boil, stirring constantly. Boil 1 minute.

* *For a thin white sauce omit 1 tablespoon each butter and flour.*
* *For a thick white sauce add 2 tablespoons each butter and flour.*
* *For commercial condensed soup make thick white sauce.*
* *For a quicker method use powdered milk. Mix powdered milk with a small amount of cool water. Use boiling water for remainder of liquid.*
* *Use to thicken cream soups or make chowders or fillings for pot pies.*

Alfredo Sauce: Make 2 cups of thin white sauce. Add 1/2 chopped, browned onion, 2 teaspoons seasoned salt, 1/2 teaspoon basil, and 1/4 teaspoon oregano. After removing from fire, add 1/4 cup parmesan cheese and 1 cup mozzarella cheese.

White Sauce Options: Use 1 cup medium white sauce and serve any of the following options over rice, noodles, or biscuits. Or any of these options may be combined.

Bacon Sauce: Dice 3 slices of bacon and fry until crispy. Use the drippings in the cream sauce and crumble bacon into sauce.

Celery Sauce: Add 1/2 cup chopped cooked celery or celery salt.

Cheese Sauce: Add 1/4–1/2 cup grated cheese. Stir until the cheese melts. Season to taste with mustard and paprika.

Curry Sauce: Substitute bouillon, broth, or water for milk. Add 1 teaspoon curry powder.

Egg Sauce: Add 1–4 hard-cooked, chopped eggs and 1 teaspoon mustard.

Garlic Sauce: Add 1 large garlic clove, chopped, and fry in butter or season to taste with garlic salt.

Gravy: Use meat broth or water for milk and meat fat or oil for butter.

Hamburger Gravy: Use meat broth for milk and add ground beef.

Olive Sauce: Add 1/4 cup chopped ripe or stuffed olives.

Onion Sauce: Add 1/4 cup browned onions or onion salt.

Parsley Sauce: Add 2–4 tablespoons chopped parsley.

Pimento Sauce: Add 2 tablespoons browned, minced onion, and 6 tablespoons minced pimento.

Shrimp Sauce: Add 1/2 cup chopped cooked shrimp.

Tuna Sauce: Add 1 cup tuna to white sauce.

Tomato Cream Sauce: Cook 1 cup fresh, chopped, or canned tomatoes, 1 stalk chopped celery or a little celery salt, 1 sliced onion, 1/2 teaspoon salt, and a few grains red pepper together for 20 minutes. Rub through a sieve. Gradually add mixture to cream sauce, stirring constantly.

Barbecue Sauce

Combine in a saucepan:

- 1/2 cup tomato juice or ground tomato
- 1/2 cup catsup
- 1 tablespoon brown sugar
- 1 teaspoon vinegar
- 2 teaspoons Worcestershire sauce
- 2 garlic cloves
- salt
- dash of liquid smoke and Tabasco sauce, optional

Simmer about 15 minutes. Makes about 1 cup.

Spanish Sauce

Fry:

- 1/4 cup margarine or oil
- 2 cups sliced onions

Add, cover, and simmer 30 minutes:

- 1 green pepper, diced, optional
- 2 teaspoons salt
- 1/8 teaspoon pepper
- 1 bay leaf and 2 whole cloves
- 1 teaspoon sugar
- 2 1/2 cups chopped tomatoes or tomato juice

Combine separately, until smooth, and slowly add to the above:

- 3 tablespoons flour
- 6 tablespoons water

Stir until thickened. Remove bay leaf and cloves, or strain, if desired. Simmer meat or vegetables in the sauce until tender, if desired.

Mexican Tomato Sauce: Omit flour, water, cloves, and bay leaf. Add 1/4 teaspoon each cumin, pepper, and coriander or oregano, 1/8 teaspoon thyme, and 2 bouillon cubes.

See page 240 for International Conversion Charts

Chili Sauce

Fry:

- **2 tablespoons shortening**
- **1 medium onion, chopped**
- **1 green pepper, chopped**
- **1–3 garlic cloves, minced**

Add and stir until smooth:

- **2 tablespoons flour, optional**
- **1/2 teaspoon salt**
- **1 teaspoon chili powder**

Add and cook slowly until thick and smooth:

- **1 cup chopped tomatoes or tomato purée**
- **1 cup meat stock or consommé**

* *Oregano, cumin, or coriander may be added to taste.*

Fresh Chili Sauce: Wash chilies and remove the seeds. Mash, grate, or finely mince and add to sauce.

Red Chili Sauce: Add 1 teaspoon oregano and a little cumin to Fresh Chili Sauce.

Green Chili Sauce: Add 1/2–1 teaspoon coriander to Fresh Chili Sauce.

Catsup

Combine in a saucepan and cook until thick:

- **2 cups tomato sauce**
- **3/4 teaspoon salt**
- **1/3 cup sugar**
- **1/8 teaspoon cloves**
- **1/4 teaspoon allspice**
- **1/8 teaspoon cinnamon**
- **1/2 cup mild vinegar**
- **1 large garlic clove, sliced**
- **1/4 cup onion, finely chopped**
- **1/4 teaspoon paprika**

* *For tomato sauce, use tomato paste and add water to consistency of tomato sauce.*

Marinade

Combine:

- **2 tablespoons oil**
- **1/4 cup soy sauce**
- **1–3 large garlic cloves, crushed**
- **1 tablespoon powdered ginger**
- **1 1/2 tablespoons lemon juice or vinegar**
- **1 tablespoon sugar**

Marinate any meat in sauce for up to 2 hours or overnight in refrigerator. Baste several times during the cooking process.

* *Omit soy sauce, ginger, and sugar. Add 1 teaspoon salt, 1/2 teaspoon pepper, and 1/4 teaspoon each basil and rosemary.*

Papaya Seed Marinade: Omit ginger, soy sauce, and garlic. Add 1–2 teaspoons fresh papaya seeds and 1/4 teaspoon salt.

See page 240 for International Conversion Charts

Vegetable Hints

To avoid unpleasant odors: While cooking onions, cabbage, broccoli, or fish, add 1 tablespoon lemon juice or a wedge of lemon with skin. Or drop a slice of bread into pan or place a crust of bread on top of vegetables.

To make cauliflower whiter: Add a teaspoon of lemon juice to water.

To discourage sprouting of potatoes, onions, chayote, etc.: Store in a cool, dark place, with plenty of air circulation.

To improve the crispness of fried potatoes: Let raw potatoes stand in cold water for at least 30 minutes before frying.

To keep baked potato skins soft and tender: Grease skins before baking or wrap in foil.

To bake potatoes quickly: Boil in salted water for 15 minutes before putting into a hot oven.

For fluffy mashed potatoes: Sprinkle with dry powdered milk.

For a new flavor: Mash potatoes and carrots together.

To keep tomatoes and other vegetables for weeks: Bury them completely in moist sand or ashes, not allowing one to touch the other. They will dry a little but still taste the same.

To keep leftover canned pimentos from spoiling: Place in a small dish and cover with cooking oil.

To keep carrots crisp while storing: Remove tops before storing. Tops drain moisture and carrots become limp and dry.

To reduce gas in beans: Drain the water beans were soaked in. Cook beans in fresh water for 15 minutes. Drain and begin again with fresh water.

If vegetables have wilted: Let stand in very cold salted water.

When celery loses its crispness: Place in a pan of cold water with a slice of raw potato. Let stand for a few hours. Remove the celery from the water and you will find that it has regained its original crispness.

To keep onion fresh: Use the top part first, leaving the root intact, and rub the open side of the onion with butter.

To prevent onions from burning your eyes: Hold them under water when peeling or slicing, and cut from the stem end.

To remove vegetable stains from hands: Rub hands with a slice of lemon.

To remove garlic and onion smell from hands: Dampen your hands and rub salt onto them, then wash with soap and water.

To enhance flavor of any vegetables: Add 1/4–1/2 teaspoon sugar to cooking water.

Vegetable Cooking Chart

Vegetable	Steam-Minutes	Simmer-Minutes	Pressure at 15 lbs-Minutes	Water for Pressuring
Asparagus	20–30	10–15	2 (use rack)	1/2 C
Beans—string, lima	20–25	15–20	3	1/2 C
Beets	15–20	15–20	3	3/4 C
Broccoli, cauliflower	15–20	10–15	2	1/2 C
Cabbage, peas, celery, carrots	20–25	15–20	2	1/2 C
Corn on the cob	5–6	3–5	3 (use rack)	1 C
Onions	30–40	20–25	3	1/2 C
Potatoes—white, whole	40–60 bake	30–40	6–10	1/2 C
Potatoes—sweet, whole	40–60 bake	30–40	10–15	1/2 C
Pumpkin, winter squash	15–20	15–20	6–12	1/2 C
Summer squash, chard, tomatoes	15–20	5–10	1–2	1/4 C
Turnips	20–25	15–20	1–2	1/2 C

Butter-Crunch Topping for Vegetables

Melt in skillet:

- 1/4 cup margarine or cooking oil

Add and fry until brown and crisp:

- 1/2 cup coarse bread crumbs, oatmeal, or dry cereal
- 1 teaspoon finely chopped onion

Sprinkle over drained cooked vegetables.

Butter-Nut Topping for Vegetables

Fry until brown, stirring constantly, and pour over drained, cooked vegetables:

- 2 tablespoons margarine
- 1/4 cup chopped nuts

Top with lemon juice, sour cream, or pieces of cooked meats.

See page 240 for International Conversion Charts

Baked Potatoes

Wash whole, white, or sweet potatoes and peel, if desired. Prick with fork and bake at 425°F for 40–60 minutes or at 350°F for 70–80 minutes. Rub skins with shortening or wrap each in foil before baking.

Baked Bananas: Bake whole, ripe, cooking bananas in their skins in oven or on top of stove. Turn occasionally. Bananas will "pop" when done.

Baked Chayotes: Bake in pan with 1/2 cup hot water. Cover. Add more hot water if needed.

Boiled Potatoes

Wash white or sweet potatoes. Leave whole or cut in pieces. Put in pan and cover with water. Boil until tender.

Boiled Green Cooking Bananas, Green Papaya, or Yucca: Cut in small pieces and add to soups and stews. Boil until just tender. Takes on the taste of whatever it is added to.

Mashed Potatoes

Peel, dice, and cook until tender:

- **4 medium potatoes**

Drain, mash, and add:

- **1/4 cup margarine**
- **salt and pepper to taste**
- **1/4–1/3 cup milk**

* *Substitute any of the following for potatoes: cooking bananas, yams, sweet potatoes, winter squash, or chayotes.*

* *Substitute potato water and add milk powder for milk.*

* *Leave skins on potatoes.*

Scalloped Potatoes

Prepare each separately:

- **9 medium potatoes, thinly sliced**
- **2 tablespoons onion, minced**
- **3 cups medium white sauce**

In greased 2-quart casserole dish, arrange one half of the potatoes. Sprinkle with half the onion. Pour half of the white sauce on top. Repeat with remaining potatoes, onion, and sauce. Cover casserole dish and bake at 350°F for 1 hour. Uncover and bake 1 hour longer or until potatoes are fork-tender and tops are browned. Makes 10 servings.

* *Use cooked potatoes and bake for 1/2 hour.*

* *On bottom of greased casserole, place one pork chop per individual and add potato mixture to top.*

* *In place of potatoes, use 4–5 cups of any sliced or chopped vegetable such as cabbage, chayotes, onions, broccoli, green papaya, green cooking banana, etc. If the vegetable is already cooked, bake only until bubbly. Sprinkle top with cheese, if desired.*

Golden Potato Casserole: Omit white sauce. Grate potatoes. Combine 1/4 cup melted margarine, 2 cups sour cream or yogurt cheese, 1/3 cup chopped onions, 2 cups each grated cheese and potatoes. Bake in a greased 9x9 pan for 1 hour.

Potato Cheese Scallop: Omit white sauce. Layer cooked, sliced potatoes in casserole. Sprinkle each layer with flour, salt, pepper, margarine, and grated cheese. Continue layering the same. Pour 1–2 cups hot milk to cover potatoes and bake at 350°F for 30 minutes. If using uncooked potatoes, bake about 1 hour.

English Style Roasted Potatoes

Preheat oven to 400°F. Peel and cut into bite-sized pieces:

- potatoes

Place in a pot of cold, salted water. Heat to boiling and let cook for 5 minutes. Drain in colander and then shake the potatoes in the colander to soften their outsides. This is a key step to creating crispy shell. Cover the bottom of a roasting pan with:

- olive or other oil

Add potatoes and stir until lightly covered with oil. Season with:

- **salt and pepper to taste**
- **rosemary, oregano, basil, parmesan cheese, or other seasoning, optional**

Bake in oven 10 minutes, until tender, and then put under the broiler. Turn as needed, allowing to cook for 10 minutes or until the potato pieces are brown and crispy on the outside. Serve immediately.

Fried Potatoes

Cook potatoes until tender. Cool thoroughly. Slice or cut in small pieces and fry in hot oil until golden brown. Add salt to taste.

Potato options: These recipes can be used with either raw or cooked potatoes, yucca, chayotes, sweet potatoes, green cooking bananas, or green papaya.

Baked French Fries: Cut large raw potatoes in lengthwise strips and arrange on a cookie sheet or pan so they don't overlap. Pour 1 tablespoon melted fat or oil over each potato, sprinkle with salt, and bake at 450°F for 30 minutes, turning when necessary.

Banana Chips: Slice green cooking bananas thin. Fry crisp in hot oil.

French Fries: Use raw or cooked potatoes with or without skins. Cut in lengthwise strips, dry, and fry in hot fat until crispy and golden in color. Remove from pan, drain, and salt to taste.

Hash Browns: Peel and grate 2–3 raw or cooked potatoes. Add grated onion, salt, and pepper to taste, and fry.

Potato Cakes: Make as hash browns but add 1 egg and enough flour to make potato mixture hold together. Drop by tablespoons into hot oil, turn, drain, and serve.

See page 240 for International Conversion Charts

Candied Sweet Potatoes

Arrange in greased 9x9 pan:

- 6 sweet potatoes, cooked, peeled, and cut in pieces

Combine and pour over potatoes:

- 1/4 cup oil or melted margarine
- 1/2 cup brown sugar
- 1/4 cup water
- 1/2 teaspoon salt

Bake at 350°F for 30 minutes or simmer in a skillet, turning occasionally.

* *Layer sliced bananas on top of potatoes.*

* *Use any cooked yellow squash or ripe cooking bananas for potatoes.*

* *Use orange juice for oil and water. Add 1 tablespoon vanilla.*

* *Instead of making a sauce, sprinkle potatoes with water and sugar and dot with margarine. Top with marshmallows, if desired.*

Sweet Potatoes Pirado: Mash sweet potatoes. Add 2 cups cooked crushed pineapple and 1/4 teaspoon ground cloves. Combine with mashed potatoes, margarine, etc. Top with 1/2 cup bread crumbs, if desired.

Yellow Winter Squash

Baked Winter Squash: Place whole squash in pan with 1/3–2/3 cup water. Bake at 350°F for 30–60 minutes or until tender. If using halved squash, remove seeds and put 1/2 cup water in each half and cover with aluminum foil before baking.

Boiled Winter Squash: Cook peeled, cut-up squash until tender. Mash. Serve with salt, butter, brown sugar, and cinnamon, if desired.

Fried Winter Squash: Slice raw, peeled squash, and fry like potatoes.

Pressured Winter Squash: Chop into portions and pressure cook 5 minutes. After removing from cooker, spread each piece with oil and panela or brown sugar. Bake at 350°F for 30 minutes.

Squash Seeds: Fry or bake dried squash seeds, washed or unwashed. Sprinkle with salt and serve like peanuts. Can substitute for peanuts in some recipes.

Summer Squash Tomato Casserole

Layer in greased casserole, seasoning each layer:

- **2–3 medium, unpeeled summer squash or zucchini, sliced**
- **1–2 tomatoes, sliced, optional**
- **1 onion, sliced, optional**
- **1 garlic clove, chopped fine**
- **1 teaspoon salt**
- **1/8 teaspoon pepper**

Cover with:

- **1/2 cup dry bread crumbs or 1 cup cubed bread**
- **1/2 cup grated cheese**

Dot with:

- **2 tablespoons butter**

Cover and bake at 350°F for 45 minutes. Serves 6.

Italian Squash: Sprinkle squash with 1 teaspoon oregano and 1/2 teaspoon basil. Pour over 1–2 cups tomato sauce, enough to barely cover vegetables. Bake. Uncover casserole for the last 10 minutes and add bread and grated cheese.

Zucchini Au Gratin: Heat 2 tablespoons oil in skillet. Add first 5 ingredients. Cover and cook 15 minutes, stirring occasionally. Omit bread crumbs. Add cheese. Heat just until melted without stirring.

Crusty Zucchini Strips

Roll in flour:

- **3 medium zucchini, cut lengthwise in eighths**
- **1/3 cup flour**

Roll zucchini in:

- **1 egg, beaten with 1 tablespoon milk**

Roll in:

- **1 1/2 cups crushed corn flakes or dried bread crumbs**

Fry until brown in:

- **1/4 cup oil**

Drain and serve with:

- **1/2 cup plain yogurt, if desired**

Keep fried zucchini warm in an oven set at 200°F until all zucchini is cooked.

See page 240 for International Conversion Charts

Fried Zucchini

In a frying pan, heat:
- **1 tablespoon olive or other cooking oil**

Add to the pan:
- **6–7 mini zucchinis, cut into 1/2-inch thick slices**
- **1/4–1/2 medium onion, sliced into rings**

Be sure to cover the pan during cooking to keep the vegetables from drying out. Cook the vegetables until tender—about 10 minutes.

Add:
- **sea salt or other available salt, to taste**

Sprinkle over the zucchini:
- **1/2 cup shredded parmesan cheese or other fresh cheese**

Vegetables in Crumb Crust

Combine and press into 9-inch greased pie plate:
- **1/2 cup melted butter or margarine**
- **2 cups oats, rice, corn flakes, crumbs, etc.**

Place in crumb shell:
- **2 cups cooled, seasoned, cooked vegetables**

Combine and pour over vegetables:
- **2 beaten eggs**
- **3/4 cup milk**
- **3/4 teaspoon salt**

Sprinkle over all:

- **1 1/2 cups grated cheese**

Bake at 350°F for 30 minutes.

Oriental Mixed Vegetables

Prepare thin diagonal slices of three or four different vegetables. Cook the vegetables requiring longest cooking time first and add others in succession so all are tender at the same time. Cook in steamer or in boiling water. Serve as mixed vegetables. May also cool vegetables and serve as for a Cuban salad.

Scalloped Greens or Spinach

Combine:
- **2 cups cooked greens, chopped fine**
- **2 tablespoons chopped onion**
- **2 eggs, beaten**
- **1/2 cup milk**
- **1/4 cup grated cheese, optional**
- **salt and pepper**

Pour into a greased baking dish. If desired, top with:
- **1/2 cup buttered crumbs**

Bake at 350°F for 20 minutes.

Spinach or Swiss Chard

When cooking spinach or Swiss chard, add a little chopped onion and coriander for a tasty addition. Serve with vinegar, if desired.

Squash Casserole

Wash, trim, and shred or chop fine:

- **2 pounds summer squash, zucchini, chayote, or crook-neck squash**

Add:

- **1–2 teaspoons salt**
- **1 large onion, chopped**
- **1 garlic clove, chopped, optional**
- **2 beaten eggs**
- **2–4 tablespoons oil**
- **1–1 1/2 cups bread cubes**

Knead ingredients in bowl until well mixed. Place in shallow greased casserole. Bake at 350°F for 35–40 minutes. Remove from oven, cover top with:

- **1 cup grated cheese**

Return to oven for another 10 minutes. Serves 6.

* *Use whole wheat bread or other dark bread to add nutty taste.*

* *To make an excellent accompaniment dish for poultry or pork, add 1 teaspoon poultry seasoning to mixture before baking.*

Jenny's Ratatouille

In a frying pan, heat:

- **1–2 teaspoons oil, preferably olive oil**

Add and cook until soft and translucent:

- **2 onions, chopped**

Add and sauté until the vegetables begin to soften:

- **2 cups small okra, with stems trimmed off**
- **1 1/2 cups eggplant (or African eggplant), cubed**
- **1 cup sweet green pepper, zucchini, or other vegetable, chopped, optional**

Add:

- **2 cups diced fresh tomatoes**
- **4 garlic cloves, minced**
- **1 pinch each dried sage and thyme**
- **1 teaspoon dried basil**
- **1 teaspoon salt**

Cook a few minutes longer, until the tomatoes begin to fall apart.

Serve as a side dish or with couscous, fonio, or another grain for a full meal. Vegetable amounts can be varied to suit taste. Serves 4 as a side dish or 2 as a main dish.

See page 240 for International Conversion Charts

Tomato Chutney (India)

In a frying pan, heat:

- 3 tablespoons cooking oil

Add and fry for 5–10 minutes:

- 3 medium onions, chopped
- 1 teaspoon mustard seeds
- 3 green chilies, chopped
- 2 tablespoons ginger/garlic paste
- 4–5 curry leaves
- 1 teaspoon powdered turmeric
- 1/2 teaspoon chili powder

When seasonings are browned, add:

- 2 pounds fresh tomatoes, chopped and pureed

Cook until mixture is thickened and the color changes. Stir in:

- 2–3 tablespoons chopped fresh coriander leaves
- 1–2 chicken bouillon cubes, crumbled
- 1/2 teaspoon salt, or to taste

To cut the acidity, stir in:

- 1/2–1 teaspoon sugar

Cook for another 2–5 minutes. Taste before serving. Can be served with curries, meats, basmati rice, etc.

Stir-Fry Vegetables

Cut up:

- 4–6 cups vegetables

Heat in large skillet over medium heat:

- 2–3 tablespoons oil

Cook the vegetables requiring longest cooking time first and add others in succession. Cook uncovered, stirring frequently until tender-crisp. Then stir in:

- 1 tablespoon soy sauce
- 1/2 teaspoon salt
- dash of pepper

* *Use any or a combination of the following: zucchini, onion, celery, green or red peppers, fresh spinach, Chinese cabbage, broccoli, tomatoes, cabbage, bean sprouts, green beans, carrots, mushrooms, water chestnuts .*

* *Add 1–4 garlic cloves, finely diced.*

Chow Mein: Combine 2 tablespoons cornstarch, 1/4 cup soy sauce, and 1 cup cooled chicken bouillon. Add to hot stir-fry vegetables. Bring to a boil over medium heat, stirring constantly, and boil 1 minute. Serve over rice or noodles, if desired.

Nepal-Style Vegetables: Omit soy sauce. Sprinkle over the cooked vegetables: salt, ginger, turmeric and khursani, optional. Cover and let cook. Serve with chapatis, rice, and daal.

Stir-Fry Meat and Vegetables: Add chopped fish, beef, or chicken, marinated, if desired. Stir-fry meats before vegetables.

Company Broccoli Bake

Wash, chop, and cook until tender:

- **8 cups fresh broccoli**

Drain, arrange in greased 3-quart baking dish, and sprinkle with:

- **2 tablespoons finely chopped onion**
- **2 hard-cooked eggs, sliced**

Combine in pan and cook until cheese melts:

- **1 1/4 cups undiluted cream of mushroom soup or white sauce**
- **1 cup shredded cheddar or other cheese**
- **1/2 cup mayonnaise**

Pour over broccoli and sprinkle with:

- **1/4 cup buttered cracker crumbs**

Bake at 350°F for 20 minutes or until bubbly.
Garnish with:

- **1 hard-cooked egg, sliced, optional**

Serves 8.

Stuffed Tomatoes

Remove pulp and tops from:

- **3–4 tomatoes**

Add to pulp:

- **grated cheese**
- **crumbled soda crackers**
- **minced onion**
- **salt and pepper**

Stuff tomatoes with pulp mixture. Bake at 350°F for 30 minutes.

See page 240 for International Conversion Charts

Stuffed Green Peppers

Cover with water, simmer 3 minutes, and drain:

- **4 medium peppers, with tops and membranes removed**

Fry separately:

- **2 tablespoons butter or margarine**
- **2 tablespoons chopped onion**
- **2 tablespoons chopped celery**

Add and brown:

- **1 cup ground beef**

Add to meat mixture:

- **1 bouillon cube**
- **1/3 cup hot water**
- **1/2 cup cooked tomatoes**

Heat well. Fold in:

- **1 1/2 cups toasted bread cubes or cooked rice**

Stuff peppers and place in greased shallow baking dish. Bake at 400°F for 25 minutes.

* ***Add cooked kidney beans or corn.***

* ***Use 3/4 cup each grated cheese and bread crumbs or 1 1/2 cups bread crumbs only.***

Hungarian Stuffed Peppers: Put stuffed peppers in a pan. Combine and cover with equal parts tomato juice and water. Simmer at least 2 hours. Serve in soup bowls topped with sour cream or yogurt.

Harvard Beets

Combine in a saucepan:

- **1/2 cup sugar**
- **1 1/2 teaspoons cornstarch**

Add and boil 5 minutes:

- **1/4 cup vinegar**
- **1/4 cup water**

Add:

- **12 small cooked beets, sliced or cubed**

Let stand 30 minutes. Before serving, bring to the boiling point and add:

- **2 tablespoons butter**

Glazed Carrots

Combine and cook in covered pan until tender:

- **8 medium carrots, peeled and cut lengthwise into quarters**
- **3 tablespoons sugar**
- **1/4 cup water**
- **1/2 teaspoon salt**
- **1 tablespoon oil**
- **1 teaspoon lemon juice, optional**

Green Beans and Bacon

Fry until crisp:

- 3–6 slices bacon

Remove bacon. Leave 2 tablespoons of the drippings in pan.

Add:

- 4–6 cups fresh green beans, cut up

Fry beans until they turn a very bright green. Add only a small amount of boiling water and simmer until tender. Stir occasionally. When beans are almost done, add the fried bacon, broken, into small pieces, and continue cooking a few more minutes.

Green Beans Fermier: Cook green beans first. Add 1/2 cup diced onion to the bacon and brown. Add 1/4 cup flour and 1/8 teaspoon pepper to make paste with bacon grease. Gradually add 1 1/2 cups water or bean liquid in which 2 chicken bouillon cubes have been dissolved. Cook, stirring constantly until sauce is thick. Add green beans. Place in greased 1 1/2 quart casserole. Bake at 350°F for 20–25 minutes. Sprinkle with 1/2 cup almonds, bread crumbs, or cheese and continue baking 5 minutes.

Guatemalan Green Beans

Combine:

- 2 egg whites, beaten until thick
- 2 tablespoons flour
- 2 egg yolks
- 1/2 teaspoon salt

Fold in:

- 2–4 cups cooked green beans, chopped or left whole

Place green beans into hot greased frying pan and brown on both sides.

Combine separately in saucepan and heat:

- 1 cup tomato sauce
- 1/4 teaspoon oregano
- 1/4 teaspoon garlic salt
- salt and pepper to taste

Serve sauce over the green beans.

Guatemalan Vegetables: Substitute other chopped, cooked vegetables for green beans.

See page 240 for International Conversion Charts

Green Beans in Mushroom Sauce

Fry until lightly browned:

- 2–3 teaspoons butter or margarine
- 1/4 cup chopped blanched almonds, cashews or peanuts
- 1 tablespoon onion, minced

Blend in and heat thoroughly:

- 1–2 cups mushroom soup
- 2–4 cups green beans, cooked

* *Use any cooked vegetable in place of green beans.*

Corn on the Cob

Cook in boiling, unsalted water for 5–10 minutes, until tender:

- corn on the cob with husks removed

* *To keep corn from becoming tough, do not add salt to the water.*

* *Add a little sugar or lemon juice to the water.*

Corn Puff

Drain and reserve liquid from:

- 2 cups corn

Add to the corn liquid:

- 3/4 cup milk

Blend separately in saucepan:

- 1 tablespoon melted margarine or butter
- 2 tablespoons flour
- 1/4 teaspoon pepper

Separate:

- 2 eggs

Beat the egg yolks. Stir corn and beaten egg yolks into the flour mixture. Beat egg whites until stiff and fold into corn mixture. Pour into a greased 1 1/2 quart casserole dish. Bake at 350°F for 45 minutes. Serves 6.

Hominy

Combine in large non-aluminum kettle:

- **4 cups shelled corn, washed**

Add and soak overnight:

- **8 cups cold water**
- **2 tablespoons soda**

In the morning, bring the corn to a boil in the same water in which it has soaked. Cook for 3 hours or until hulls loosen. Add more water as necessary during the cooking process. Drain off water and wash corn in clean water, rubbing vigorously until all the hulls are removed. Bring to boil again in clear water and drain. Repeat.

Add:

- **1 teaspoon salt to each 4 cups of hominy**

Corn Fritters

Combine:

- **1 cup drained, cooked corn**
- **1/2 cup flour**
- **1/2 teaspoon each salt and baking powder**

Add:

- **1 egg yolk, beaten**

Fold in:

- **1 egg white, stiffly beaten**

Fry in a small amount of hot oil until brown. Drain.

Braised Cabbage

Fry until tender:

- **3 tablespoons margarine, butter, or oil**
- **3 tablespoons onion**

Add and fry until tender, yet crisp:

- **3 grated carrots**
- **2–3 cups shredded cabbage**

Add:

- **salt and pepper to taste**
- **chopped apple, optional**

See page 240 for International Conversion Charts

Baked Cabbage in Milk

Wash and boil cabbage with salt in water until nearly cooked, using very little water. Drain well and place in pie dish or casserole and cover with coconut cream (see page 102). Bake at 350°F until coconut cream sets.

* *Use 1/2 cabbage and zucchini.*
* *Use milk or cream for the coconut cream.*
* *Place cooked, finely sliced cabbage in greased casserole dish and sprinkle with 2 tablespoons each flour and onion, 3 garlic cloves diced, 2 fresh tomatoes, or 1 cup tomato sauce. Cover and bake at 350°F for 45 minutes.*

Creamed Cabbage: Boil sliced cabbage in salt water and place it in a greased baking dish. Cover with any cream sauce and 3/4 cup grated cheese, if desired. Bake at 450°F for 5–10 minutes.

Stuffed Cabbage: Boil whole cabbage and spread leaves gently to insert stuffing. Combine 1 cup cooked zucchini or other vegetable, 2 cups cooked beef or combination of cooked meat and rice, 2 beaten eggs, salt, pepper, and 1–2 tablespoons chopped parsley and onion, optional. Insert into leaves, roll up, and place in baking dish. Pour 5 tablespoons oil over rolls and bake at 350°F covered for 25 minutes.

French-Fried Cabbage

Crisp cabbage in cold water, finely shred, drain, and dry. Dip in milk and roll in flour. Fry in hot fat only a small amount at a time, drain, and salt.

Breadfruit

Boil breadfruit in salted water for 10 minutes, drain, peel, and cut into 1-inch thick slices. Fry in hot fat until crisp.

Coconut Cream Breadfruit: Bake at 350°F until tender. Peel and remove seeds. Slice, place in 9x9 baking dish, cover with coconut cream (see page 102) and bake at 350°F until cream sets.

Cactus

Cube cactus and heat in a tomato sauce or add to boiled beans or potatoes.

Fried Eggplant

Peel, slice, and soak in salt water 1 hour:

- **eggplant**

Drain well, then dip slices in:

- **beaten egg**
- **salt and pepper**

Fry until brown and top each slice with spaghetti sauce and grated cheese, if desired.

* *Dip in bread crumbs before frying.*

* *Dip in fritter batter and deep fry.*

* *Cut eggplant in small cubes. Fry until soft with 1–2 tablespoons oil, chopped onions, and tomatoes. Omit egg. Add salt, pepper, garlic, and chopped parsley. Mash and sprinkle with flour. Add boiling water to make a rich sauce. Pour into baking dish. Top with grated cheese and bread crumbs. Bake at 350°F until browned.*

Vegetables in Foil

Place any combination of vegetables in a large, heavy piece of foil and bake at 350°F until tender. Or cook directly on hot coals, 10 minutes on each side.

* *One fresh tomato cut in wedges makes a very tasty addition and also adds a little moisture to the vegetables while baking. When using cabbage, slice and bake in a separate foil package as it requires an extra 20 minutes baking time.*

See page 240 for International Conversion Charts

Extras

See page 229 for this Finger Gelatin recipe.

EXTRAS

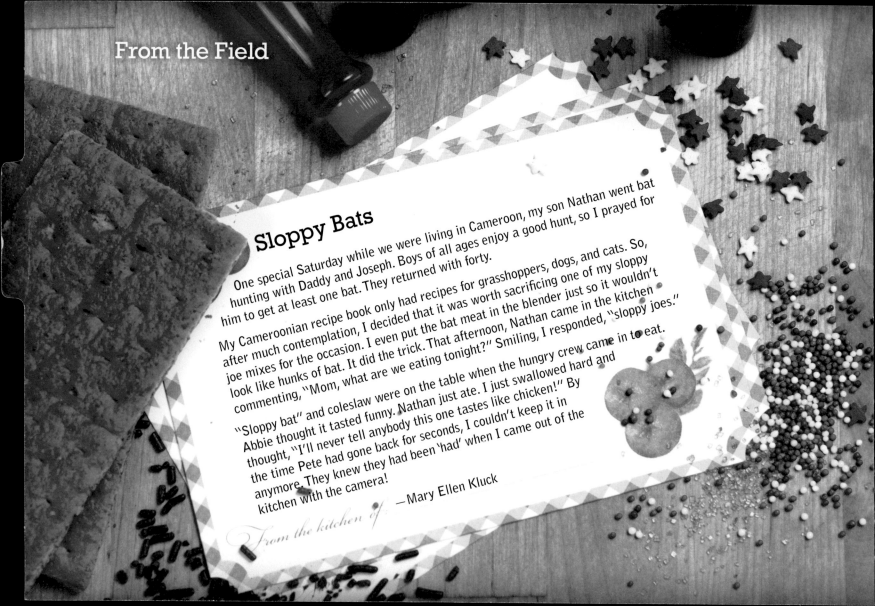

Sloppy Bats

One special Saturday while we were living in Cameroon, my son Nathan went bat hunting with Daddy and Joseph. Boys of all ages enjoy a good hunt, so I prayed for him to get at least one bat. They returned with forty.

My Cameroonian recipe book only had recipes for grasshoppers, dogs, and cats. So, after much contemplation, I decided that it was worth sacrificing one of my sloppy joe mixes for the occasion. I even put the bat meat in the blender just so it wouldn't look like hunks of bat. It did the trick. That afternoon, Nathan came in the kitchen commenting, "Mom, what are we eating tonight?" Smiling, I responded, "sloppy joes."

"Sloppy bat" and coleslaw were on the table when the hungry crew came in to eat. Abbie thought it tasted funny. Nathan just ate. I just swallowed hard and thought, "I'll never tell anybody this one tastes like chicken!" By the time Pete had gone back for seconds, I couldn't keep it in anymore. They knew they had been 'had' when I came out of the kitchen with the camera!

—Mary Ellen Kluck

From the kitchen of:

Cooking Corner
Whimsy Sculpture Bread

Use 1 ball of bread dough formed into any shape desired. Place on a greased cookie sheet. Cover with a cloth and let rise in a warm place about 45 minutes. Brush with beaten egg yolk. Bake at 350°F for 30 minutes.

Monster or Sun: Roll dough into a circle. Place a bowl, bigger than the dough, upside-down in the center of the dough to form circle. Cut strips of dough going straight out from bowl. Remove bowl. Twist strips into sun rays or monster hair. Make small round dough balls for nose and eyes. Form arms, legs, or antennae by rolling dough between your palms. Join to face by pinching the two parts together.

Teddy Bear: Divide dough in half. Use one half to shape the body. Divide the other half in half. Use 1 part to form the head. Divide the other part in 7 equal balls for arms, legs, ears, and nose. Attach parts by pinching dough together. Use raisins for eyes, nose, and bellybutton. Let rise until double. Brush with beaten egg and bake at 350°F for 30–35 minutes until dough is well browned. Cool. When cool, eat or tie a ribbon around neck and mount on cardboard cut to bear shape. Hang as an ornament.

Baked Monster Pancake

Combine:

- 1/2 cup each milk and flour

Beat in:

- 2 eggs

Melt in a 9x9 pan at 400°F:

- 3 tablespoons margarine or butter

Pour egg mixture into the pan and bake about 15 minutes or until edges are golden brown and the middle is puffy. Baked pancake looks like a monster's face. Sprinkle with lemon juice or powdered sugar or drizzle with syrup. Use raisins for eyes and nose, if desired. Serves 2–3.

Happy Face Pizza

Knead on a floured board:

- 1 ball of bread or biscuit dough

Roll or press as thin as you can onto a baking sheet. Spread dough with sliced tomatoes or tomato sauce. Make a face or other design using cooked meats, olives, or whatever is available. Cover with shredded cheese. Pour a little oil on top, if desired, and bake at 425°F for 20 minutes.

Bright Bean Salad

Combine in a bowl:

- 1 cup mixed cooked beans
- 1 tomato, cut In quarters
- 1 small sliced onion, optional

Combine in a cup and pour over beans:

- 1 tablespoon oil
- 1 teaspoon vinegar
- 1/2 garlic clove, crushed
- dash of salt and pepper

Place on a lettuce leaf and serve.

Honey Bee Butter

Combine and mix well:

- 1/4 cup softened butter
- 1/4 cup honey
- 1/4 teaspoon cinnamon, optional

Spread on toast, waffles, or pancakes.

Ox-Eye Eggs

For each person, place in greased baking dish:

- 1 slice toast with hole cut in center

In each hole put:

- 1 raw egg

Add to the top of each egg:

- 1/4 teaspoon butter or margarine
- salt and pepper

Bake at 325°F for 10 minutes.

Decorated Eggs

Boil eggs 12 minutes until hard boiled. Cool and decorate as below:

1. Draw bright, happy, funny, sad, or mad faces with marking pens.

2. Glue hair, beards, mustache, tissue paper, or small pictures on eggs.

3. Paint eggs with glue, then wrap with rows of colorful yam. Or roll eggs in any kind of seeds after painting with glue.

4. Make dye with food color or crêpe paper soaked in water. If desired, stick a pattern of masking tape on the eggs securely. Then dip eggs in dye. After it dries, remove tape. Dip egg again in a lighter color.

See page 240 for International Conversion Charts

5. Draw pattern on egg with crayon. Dip egg into dark dye, put egg in oven to melt crayon marks, wipe dry, and dip eggs a second time in a lighter color.

Easy Peanut Butter Cookies (flourless)

Beat together:
- 1 egg, beaten
- 3/4–1 cup sugar
- 1 cup peanut butter

Bake on greased cookie sheet at 350°F for 8 minutes.

Cake Cones

Fill flat bottom ice cream cones 1/2 full with cake batter. Bake at 375°F for 20–30 minutes, until toothpick comes out clean. Cool and decorate with icing.

Crispy Critter Cookies

Combine in a saucepan:
- 2 1/2 tablespoons sugar
- 1 tablespoon butter
- 1/4 cup cocoa

Add and cook until melted. Do not boil:
- 1 heaping tablespoon corn syrup or honey

Remove from heat and add:
- 1 cup corn flakes, rice crispies, or other suitable cereal

Drop by spoonfuls onto greased dish. Shape into animals and serve.

Alpha's Alphabet Cookies

Use any cookie dough that can be rolled out. Roll out dough on a floured surface. Cut in strips. Roll each strip between the palms of your hands to make "ropes." Cut "ropes" and form the alphabet or have each person make the letters for their names. Place formed letters on a greased cookie sheet. Flatten to 1/4–inch thick. Brush with Egg Yolk Paint (recipe follows) or sprinkle with colored sugar. Bake at 300°F for 30 minutes.

Animal Cookies: Follow recipe above. Roll dough very thin. Cut out animal shapes with a knife or cutters. Arrange legs, arms, and heads so the animals look like they are running. Brush with Egg Yolk Paint (recipe follows). Use raisins, cherries, and nuts to make eyes, nose, and mouth. Bake on greased cookie sheet at 375°F for 10 minutes.

Mobile or Christmas Tree Decoration: Put a hole in each cookie 1/2 inch from top before baking. Put string through hole when baked.

South Sea Banana

Place in a cereal bowl:

- **1 peeled and sliced banana**

Sprinkle with:

- **1 tablespoon shredded coconut**
- **1 tablespoon milk**
- **1 tablespoon honey or brown sugar**
- **1/2 teaspoon cinnamon**
- **1/4 cup chopped nuts, optional**

Pioneers' Delight: Place 2 cookies or a piece of cake in bowl, then add a sliced banana. Top with milk, if desired, or sprinkle with the above ingredients.

Egg Yolk Paint

Combine:

- **1 egg yolk, beaten**
- **1/4 teaspoon water**

Divide mixture into 4 or more small containers. Add different food colors to each. Paint cookies before baking.

See page 240 for International Conversion Charts

Frozen Peanut Butter Treat

Combine in a bowl and mix well:

- **1 cup yogurt, sour cream, or whipped cream**
- **1/2 cup peanut butter**
- **1/2 cup sugar**

Place mixture in freezer for 24 hours, scoop onto plates and put jelly on top, if desired.

Fruit Juice Ice Pops

Pour into ice pops molds or paper cups:

- **any fruit juice**

Freeze 30 minutes, then insert sticks into ice pops and freeze until firm.

* *To keep ice pops from thawing rapidly: Add to 3–4 cups of juice, and 1 tablespoon unflavored gelatin mixed with 1/2 cup cool water.*

* *Add milk powder or yogurt to juice before freezing, if desired.*

Frozen Banana Ice Pops: Omit fruit juice. Slice ripe bananas lengthwise, spread with peanut butter, and put banana back together. Wrap with plastic wrap and freeze.

Finger Gelatin

Mix together:

- **1/3 cup gelatin powder, any flavor**
- **1 tablespoon unflavored gelatin**

Pour in and stir thoroughly:

- **1 cup boiling water**

Pour into flat pan. Let set. Cut into squares with a sharp knife or cut with cookie cutters. Peel out of pan with fingers. This will be very firm. Kids love to eat it with their fingers. If the weather is cool, this will set without refrigeration.

Sugar-Free Finger Gelatin: Combine 3 tablespoons unflavored gelatin and 3 cups juice. Soften and bring to a boil. Add extra sweetener if needed. Pour into lightly-greased pan and chill until firm. Cut into shapes or cubes and store in airtight container.

Baby Foods

Introduce only one new food every three days and keep a record to see if baby is digesting it well or has an allergic reaction. If no reaction, continue with the new food and add another. The first food baby eats, besides mother's milk or formula, is a little formula mixed with cereal and blended.

After your baby is eating cereals, begin on puréed vegetables, fruits, yogurt, and small amounts of puréed meat. A good idea is to freeze the puréed foods in ice cube trays. At dinner, heat the different cubes in an egg poacher or double boiler.

Blend foods together for variety.

If you live in the tropics, bananas, guavas, and avocados are easy to prepare and digest. Avocados supply iron and other minerals as well as vitamins A, C, and E.

Baby Oatmeal

Blend:

- 1/2 cup oatmeal
- 1/3 cup wheat germ, optional
- 1 2/3 cups milk or boiled water

Cook until creamy and add:

- 1/4 cup banana, applesauce, or other fruit, mashed

Craft Corner
Baker's Clay

Combine to make a stiff mixture:

- 1 cup flour
- 1/2 cup salt
- 1/4–1/2 cup water

Break in small amounts and add food coloring now, or paint before or after baking. Roll out dough and cut into desired shapes (see suggestions below). Bake flattened shapes at 200°F until hard. Check and turn after 5 minutes. Bake molded or formed objects at 350°F for 1 hour or until hard. Cool and paint with any water-based paint or food coloring.

* *Use a pattern and cut shapes with a knife.*

* *Use a cookie cutter: You can flatten these forms by hand and bend their arms, legs, or heads. Or you can prop them up with foil and bake in a sitting or active position.*

* *Mold dough as if it were clay.*

* *Roll into strips and weave or braid dough.*

* *Remember to make holes 1/2 inch below the top in beads, pendants, puppets, and Christmas tree ornaments. A plastic straw makes a uniform hole.*

* *Create a landscape scene in a shoe box by molding trees, clouds, sun, birds, animals, and hills. Remember to put a hole in the top of the clouds, sun, and birds so you can hang them.*

* *Make a Christmas tree by using a clay base for a small branch.*

Play Dough

Combine:

- 2 cups flour
- 1/2 cup salt
- 3/4–1 cup water
- 1/2 teaspoon food coloring
- 2 teaspoons cream of tartar or alum to smooth dough, optional
- 2 tablespoons oil, for a more elastic dough, optional

Knead on floured board until playdough consistency. Cover and store in refrigerator.

See page 240 for International Conversion Charts

Paddy's Paste

Combine in a saucepan and mix to a smooth paste:

- 1/2 cup each water and flour

Cook over low heat and stir, then add:

- 1/2 cup water

Cook, stirring constantly, until glue thickens. Store in jar with lid.

Mosaics

Use any kind of beans, seeds, pasta, rice, crushed colored egg shells, torn colored paper, cereal, or yarn. Draw a design on any size plywood, cardboard, wood panel, box, or frame. Brush a small area of your design with glue or paste and fill the design with seeds, beans, or pasta. Continue with glue and beans until design and background are covered. Allow to dry and paint with varnish or plastic coat, if desired.

Hints: Separate different seeds or beans in egg cartons or shallow dishes. Pasta and rice can be colored by adding food coloring to a little water. Dip rice or pasta in water to color. Dry on cookie sheets.

Necklaces

Soak assorted beans in hot water until soft enough for needle to go through. Drain and blot. Thread needle with string long enough to tie and fit over head. String beans and/or pasta of contrasting colors and shapes. Tie ends. Allow to dry. Spray with plastic coating or shellac, if desired.

Christmas Tree Ropes: Use longer pieces of string.

Pasta Ornaments

Glue different sizes of pasta together to make ornaments. Some possibilities include: trees, butterflies, snails, angels, snowflakes, flowers, etc. When glue is dry, pasta can be painted with food or water colors. Dry. Spray with clear protective coating, if desired.

Apple-Head Dolls

Carve a face on a peeled apple. Insert and glue in rice teeth and raisin or peppercorn eyes, then insert a stick or popsicle-stick neck. Dip apple in lemon juice and allow to dry in a warm room for about a month. Shape features as it dries. Make body by stuffing a stocking around the stick neck. Place glue at neckline and tie with a string. Tie waist with a string. Use yarn or cotton for hair and scraps for clothes.

Fruit Turkey

Combine:

- 1 orange, cut in half with fruit scooped out
- 1 apple, chopped
- 1 banana, chopped

Refill orange half with fruit. Stick toothpick out for turkey's neck. Put a carrot slice on top of the toothpick for the head and a small piece of toothpick sticking out for a beak. Use a celery top for a tail. Use as an edible table decoration.

Fruit and Vegetable Characters: Make dinosaurs, farm animals, and monsters using any vegetables or fruit available. Cut and shape vegetables and fruits with blunt scissors or knives. Use shish kabob sticks or strong toothpicks to hold pieces together.

Peanut Finger Puppets

Break off one end of a fat peanut shell and remove the peanut so that you can stick your finger inside the shell. Paint a miniature face on the shell with a felt-tip pen and glue on yarn for hair. Make enough shell faces to fit on all your fingers. Make up a story for the peanut puppets. Tell the story as you act it out with your fingers.

* *No peanuts? Draw faces on your fingers. Attach hats (bottle caps, cotton balls, paper) with tape rolled in circles with sticky side out.*

Vegetable and Fruit Stamps

The following vegetables and fruits can be dipped in paints or stamp pads and used as stamps:

- pumpkin wedge or potato, sliced and carved with pictures or letters of the alphabet. (Remember, these need to be made backwards.)
- ear of corn
- 1/2 cabbage tied with string to hold it loosely together
- fruit, such as apples, pears or oranges, cut in half

Finger Paint

Combine and stir until dissolved:

- 1 tablespoon cornstarch
- 1/2 cup cold water

Stir constantly while cooking over medium heat until mixture comes to a boil, loses whiteness, and starts to thicken. Lower heat and continue stirring about 2 minutes, until mixture is very thick and smooth. Cool slightly. Divide mixture into separate jars and color with tempera or food coloring. Leftover paint can be stored in a covered jar in the refrigerator for a week.

To paint: Moisten surface with a sponge. Deposit a tablespoon of paint on surface and spread by hand. Make designs in the paint using knuckles, fingertips, and front or back of hands or wrists. You can also use string, yarn, sponges, or paint brushes. Cleanup requires only a wet sponge or paper towel.

See page 240 for International Conversion Charts

Face Paint

This face paint is easy to make, apply, and clean off.

Combine in a small bowl:

- **3 tablespoons cornstarch**
- **1 tablespoon flour**

Add gradually and mix until smooth:

- **3/4 cup light corn syrup or honey**
- **1/4 cup water**

Divide into 4 containers.

Add 1/2 teaspoon liquid food color or 1/4 teaspoon paste color to each container. Stir just before use.

Basic application: Do not paint eyelids. Paint a generous coat of untinted makeup on the forehead. Place a single sheet of facial tissue over the painted area and brush on additional base to cover all areas of tissue. Continue painting and covering face with tissue. Let dry 15 minutes.

To remove: Peel off tissue and wash face with warm soapy water.

Painted Faces

After applying the basic Face Paint, fix face in one of the following ways:

Clown: Make large yellow arches above eyebrows and put red on nose and around mouth.

Ghost: Paint tissue with untinted base and dust with flour.

Monster: While basic application is still wet, apply cotton to build up nose, forehead, and chin. Paint with tinted makeup.

Freckles or moles: Stick puffed wheat on face with untinted base and paint, if desired.

Beard: Apply cotton along jawline and chin. Paint with brown, blue, red, or black.

Papier-mâché

Combine gradually and stir until all lumps are gone:

- **1 cup water**
- **1/2–1 cup flour**

Dip in paste and wring out excess by pulling strips through fingers:

- **1x3–inch strips of torn newspaper**

Begin with hard-to-reach areas and apply overlapping layers of pasted strips on a form (balloons work well.) Or make your own form by molding newspaper strips together. Let dry 3–4 days, then paint. For best results, paint on a base coat of white paint, allow to dry, then paint design. Dry and spray with a clear protective coating, if desired.

Papier-mâché Maracas: Wrap newspaper strips around a light bulb. Coat entire bulb with several layers. Let dry. If desired, cover handle of maraca with beige tissue paper strips dipped in paste, and coat bulb with brightly colored tissue paper. Let dry 1 day. Hit maracas gently against a hard surface until light bulb inside breaks and maraca makes a good rattle sound.

Bubbles

Make bubbles by combining equal parts of water and liquid dish detergent. Make your own bubble machine by poking a pencil into the side of a paper cup, 1 inch from the bottom, to make a hole. Stick a drinking straw halfway through the hole into the cup. Add bubble mixture. Blow until bubbles froth over the rim of the cup and float away.

See page 240 for International Conversion Charts

Health Precautions

Background: In remote and underdeveloped areas, soil, water, and certain foods are often contaminated with bacteria, viruses, and eggs of parasites that cause disease. Much contamination comes from human and animal excreta. The following procedures must be followed.

Hands

Clean hands and nails are a major protection against food contamination. Use a brush to scrub hands and nails. Use anti-bacterial soap, if available, and air dry or use a clean towel.

Water Purification

Use Purified Water for the Following: Ice, beverages, all uncooked foods, foods cooked under 15 minutes or baked less than 30 minutes, and for washing foods to be eaten raw.

Boiling: Maintain at a rolling boil for the time listed in the following chart.

Elevation	Water Boils	Minutes to Boil Water
0	212°F	5
500	211°F	6
1,500	209°F	8
2,500	207°F	10
5,000	202°F	15
6,000	200°F	17
7,000	198°F	20
8,000	196°F	23
9,000	194°F	27
10,000	192°F	32

Pressure Cooking: Pressure cook water at 15 pounds for 5 minutes. Pressure cookng is more efficient than boiling, especially at heights over 7,000 feet.

Filtering: Use Katydine water filters. People with kidney disease or arthritis are not to use filters over a long period of time. If filters are not available in your area, write to: JAARS, P.O. Box 248, Waxhaw, NC, 28173, U.S.A.

Iodine: Add 1 drop of iodine to 4 cups of water and let stand for 20 minutes.

Dishes

Add 1 tablespoon bleach to detergent and dishwater. Pour boiling water over the washed dishes and allow to dry rapidly. Store in a covered area.

Dairy Products and Meats

Fresh Milk: Milk is a potential health hazard unless you are certain of the reliability of the source, handling, and pasteurization. It is best to pasteurize your own by bringing milk to a scald or simmer temperature for 30 minutes, cooling, and refrigerating.

Cheese: Only eat cheese made from pasteurized milk.

Eggs: Never eat eggs raw as they are a common source of typhoid fever and hepatitis. No eggnogs or soft-boiled eggs. Yolks and whites must be completely coagulated. Use only meringues baked at 350°F for over 15 minutes. No underbaked food.

Meats: Never eat raw, freshly-salted, pickled, or undercooked meats. This is true for all kinds of meat, poultry, fish, or shellfish. Meat that is green, slippery, or has a bad odor is spoiled and must be thrown out.

Raw Fruits and Vegetables

The most reliable method to avoid parasites is to cook all vegetables, but the following methods are possibly as effective.

Wash all fruits and vegetables with liquid detergent, rinse in purified water, and dry. Then use one of the following methods:

1. Peel all fruits and vegetables before eating, when possible.

2. When fruits or vegetables are delicate, leafy, or have many external seeds, wash and rinse. Then soak for 20 minutes in cold, purified water to which enough iodine has been added so that the water remains yellow at the end of the 20 minutes. Or use other products such as potassium permanganate that are specifically designed for purifying foods. Rinse in cold, boiled water. Leafy vegetables are best done in this manner. Strawberries and other berries with many external seeds may be handled in this manner or rinsed and brought to a boil for 5 minutes in purified water.

3. Immerse non-delicate vegetables and fruits briefly in boiling purified water.

After purifying fruits and vegetables, dry well and store in refrigerator, cool dry place, or in closed but not sealed plastic or paper bags to avoid air-borne contamination.

See page 240 for International Conversion Charts

Food-Borne Illness

See Health Precautions and Canning and Food Preparation to prevent the following diseases.

DISEASE AND SOURCE	SYMPTOMS	ONSET/ DURATION	TREATMENT	PREVENTION
Amebiasis (Dysentery)—all contaminated food	diarrhea, cramps	24 hours–10 days/variable	Metronidazole, Tinidazole, Iodoquinol	Cook foods. Purify raw foods and water. Wash hands before eating.
Botulism—canned low-acid foods, smoked fish, honey (for infants)	double vision, difficulty speaking, swallowing, and/or breathing, high fatality	12–36 hours/ variable	Allow to vomit and have diarrhea to remove toxin from system, then control symptoms and support respiratory system. Visit a doctor if at all possible.	Bacterial spores in food are destroyed by high temperatures obtained only in the pressure cooker. More than 6 hours is needed to kill the spores at boiling temperature (212°F). The toxin is destroyed by boiling 10–20 minutes (exact time required depends on kind of food).
Brucellosis— fever (undulant) milk and cheese	intermittent low-grade fever	6–21 days/ variable	Tetracycline, Streptomycin	Pasteurize milk.
Hepatitis "A" Virus— fecal-oral contamination	tender liver, yellow color	15–45 days/ variable	Rest, high calorie diet, control fever.	Purify raw foods and water, cook foods, wash hands, Gamma Globulin shots.
Traveler's Diarrhea (Montezuma's Revenge)— fecal-oral contamination	nausea, vomiting, cramps, diarrhea	5–72 hours/24–36 hours	Restrict food and fluids until pain is gone, then when vomiting stops, give Rehydration Drink (page 238).	Eat only hot cooked foods when eating out and drink purified water.
Salmonella—poultry, red meats, eggs, dried foods, dairy products, sausages	headache, vomiting, diarrhea, cramps, fever	8–48 hours/ variable	Restrict food and fluids until pain is gone and system is flushed, then treat symptoms and give Rehydration Drink (page 238).	Salmonella in food is destroyed by heating the food to 140°F and holding for 10 minutes or to higher temperatures for less time (for instance, 155°F for a few seconds). Refrigeration at 40°F inhibits the increase of Salmonella, but they remain alive in foods in the refrigerator or freezer and even in dried foods.
Giardiasis—unsterilized water, fecal-oral contamination	intermittent diarrhea, abdominal distention	1–3 weeks/1–7 days but will recur unless treated	Metronidazole, Quinacrine, Tinidazole	Purify food and water.
Staph—custards, egg, potato, chicken or macaroni salad, ham, salami, cheese, mayonnaise	vomiting, diarrhea, cramps, prostration	6–12 hours/1–2 days	Allow body to purge until pain subsides, then treat symptoms and give fluids. Give Rehydration Drink (page 238).	Growth of bacteria that produce toxin is inhibited by keeping hot foods above 140°F and cold foods at or below 40°F. Toxin is destroyed by boiling for several hours or heating the food in a pressure cooker for 30 minutes.

Rehydration Drink

Combine:

- **4 cups water**
- **2 tablespoons sugar**
- **1/2 teaspoon salt**
- **Kool-Aid or lemon to cover the taste, optional**

Chill and give to sick person every 15 minutes, as follows, to relieve or prevent dehydration. Make a fresh solution every 24 hours.

Age	Amount every 15 minutes	Maximum per day
6 months–3 years	2 teaspoons	4 cups
4–6 years	1 tablespoon	5 cups
7 years–adult	2 tablespoons	8 cups

* *The information in Health Precautions and Food-Borne Illness has been included for people who live in remote locations overseas without easy access to medical help.*

All medical information in the book has been researched and checked by several medical professionals. Despite our attempts to provide accurate up-to-date information, the authors disclaim any responsibility for the outcome. We advise checking with your personal physician before using the medical material, if possible.

Pest control

To stop an ant invasion: Wash or spray counter tops, cabinets, and floors with equal parts vinegar and water.

To keep ants out: Sprinkle baby powder or cleanser where they enter. Ants won't walk through powder. Or plant peppermint at entrances to your house. Crushed peppermint leaves release mint oils that deter ants.

To keep ants out of cupboard: Set cupboard legs in lids filled with powder.

To seal off bats: Never swing at or chase a bat because it can turn on you and bite. Wait outside at night and determine where the bat exits the house. Seal that spot. Wear protective clothing and gloves for this procedure as bat feces can contain rabies.

To kill beetle (weevil) and moth eggs: Place foods such as grains, cereal, or dried fruit on a cookie sheet and bake at 140°F for 30 minutes. Cool and store in covered jars or cans. Or freeze for four days.

To keep beetles from entering or their eggs from hatching: Store foods in a sealed container that contains a bay leaf.

To kill cockroaches with paste: Combine 1 cup each borax and cornmeal, 1/2 cup flour, and 1/3 cup powdered sugar. Add milk to make paste, smear on pieces of cardboard, and set where needed. Form paste into balls and put in drawers. If desired, omit flour and cornmeal and add 1/4 cup powdered non-dairy coffee creamer and decrease the sugar to 1 tablespoon.

To kill cockroaches with powder: Combine 2 cups boric acid powder, 1/2 large onion (grated), 1 tablespoon sugar, and 1/2 cup

See page 240 for International Conversion Charts

flour. Sprinkle in many hard-to-reach places. Roaches are killed when they clean themselves after walking through the powder.

* *Use cucumber peels or bay leaves to repel cockroaches.*

* *Use a house gecko (lizard) to get rid of roaches.*

To get rid of fleas: In late summer, clean house by vacuuming and washing all floors, rugs, etc. Throw away the vacuum cleaner bag immediately and give your pet a good flea bath. This will eliminate adult fleas and developing larvae. Sprinkle diatomaceous earth, if available, in the heavily affected area to destroy any remaining larvae.

To get rid of mice: Place squares of camphor gum where mice invade, but keep children and pets away. Or use mouse traps.

For termites or firewood ants: Store firewood off the ground.

To get rid of a wasp: Wet wasp's wings with spray bottle. Wasp will drop and you can kill it.

Preparation for Emergencies

The following preparations should be made by all those living in areas of political unrest and in areas where devastating storms, typhoons, and earthquakes are likely to occur.

Always contact your home country's embassy or consul as soon as you enter a country so they will have your current address, phone number, and someone to contact in the event of an emergency.

Prepare a suitcase for rapid evacuation for each member of the family: Include a small Bible, money, documents, medicine, bandages, matches, warm clothes, dried foods, and a flashlight. Stuff a blanket and some plastic bags in a laundry bag or a bag that is easy to carry. The blanket and bags can be used to protect you from the weather.

Keep at least a two-week supply of the following items because stores, market places, banks, and money changers may be closed:

1. Matches, candles, flashlights, batteries, battery-operated radio.

2. Plastic containers of drinking water.

3. Fuels or charcoal for cooking, as electricity may be off.

4. Foods that keep for a long period of time, are easily transported, and require no refrigeration or cooking:

CANNED OR DRIED	STAPLES	PERISHABLES
meats	rice	green tomatoes
vegetables	flour	whole squash
milk	beans	green peppers
fruits	lentils	beets
crackers	sugar	eggs
coffee	salt, cooking oil	turnips
tea, cocoa	baking powder and soda	green bananas
flavored drink mix	dried yeast	papayas, oranges
soups	cornmeal	firm apples
seeds for sprouting	oatmeal and other cereal	potatoes

International Measurements

Liquid and Dry Measures

IMPORTANT: Milliliters (ml) are being used to represent grams and cubic centimeters because the recipes are written according to volume rather than weight. They have been rounded to the nearest convenient equivalent.

Abbreviations that are not noted elsewhere: pt=U.S. pint and lb=U.S. pound.

U.S. CUPS	T=TABLESPOON t=TEASPOON	ml=MILLILITER	OUNCES
	1/8 t=pinch	1/2	1/40
	1/4 t	1	1/20
	1/2 t	2	1/10
	1 t	5	1/5
	1 1/2 t=1/2 T	7	1/4
	3 t=1 T	15	1/2
	2 T	30	1
	3 T	45	1 1/2
1/4	4 T	60	2
1/3	5 T	80	2 1/2
3/8	6 T	90	3
	7 T	105	3 1/2
1/2	8 T	120	4
	9 T	135	4 1/2
5/8	10 T	150	5
2/3	11 T	170	5 1/2
3/4	12 T	180	6
	13 T	195	6 1/2
7/8	14 T	210	7
	15 T	225	7 1/2
1	16 T	250	8
1 1/4	20 T	310	10
1 1/2	24 T	370	12
2	1 lb/pt	500=1/2 liter	16
3	1 1/2 lb/pt	750=3/4 liter	25
4	2 lb/pt	1,000=1 liter	33
16	8 lb/pt	3,800=4 liters	114

See page 240 for International Conversion Charts

Temperature

Temperatures are to the nearest convenient equivalent.

Celsius: This is the international term and is the same as centigrade.

To convert Fahrenheit to Celsius: Subtract 32, multiply by 5, then divide by 9.

To convert Celsius to Fahrenheit: Multiply by 9, divide by 5, and add 32.

Fahrenheit	Celsius
80	29
100	38
110	43
115	46
135	57
140	60
150	66
160	71
165	74

Fahrenheit	Celsius
170	77
180	82
190	88
200	95
205	96
212	100
225	110
250	120
275	135

Fahrenheit	Celsius
300	150
325	165
350	180
375	190
400	205
425	220
450	230
475	245
500	260

Linear Measure

Inches are to the nearest convenient equivalent.

To convert inches to centimeters, multiply inches by 2.54.

To convert centimeters to inches, multiply centimeters by 39.

Inches	Centimeters
1/16	1/4
1/8	1/2
1/4	3/4
3/8	1
1/2	1 1/2
3/4	2
1	2 1/2
1 1/2	4
2	5
2 1/2	6 1/2
3	8
3 1/2	9
4	10

Inches	Centimeters
5	13
6	15
7	18
8	20
9	23
10	25
12=1 ft	30
14	35
15	38
16	40
18	45
20	50
24=2 ft	60

Alternate Cooking Methods

Pressure Cooking

For specific pressure cooking times: Refer to charts in the specific food group.

To pressure cook foods: Pressure cook directly in cooker or use small empty cans for custards and to separate items when pressuring a complete meal. All cooking may be done at 15 pounds pressure. Exhaust steam for 4 minutes without the stop cock or weight, close the stop cock or apply the weight, raise the pressure to 15 pounds, and time according to the charts in individual sections. When cooked, remove cooker from the heat, allow pressure to return to zero, open stop cock or remove weight, and remove lid away from you.

To pressure cook above sea level: Add 1 pound pressure to chart figures for every 2,000 feet above sea level. Processing time remains the same or you can increase the cooking time 5 percent for every 1,000 feet above 2,000 feet.

To cook grains and beans at the same time: Place grain in a bowl or can inside the pressure cooker and cover with water to 1 inch above the grain. Put 2–3 inches of water in cooker and place beans in this water. Cook according to the chart for the longer cooking food.

Roasting over an Open Fire

Skewer small pieces of meat on an opened coat hanger or stick and cook over a fire. Do not use a stick from an Oleander bush or tree which has sweet smelling pink or white flowers. Use only sticks from trees and bushes that have edible fruits, since others may be poisonous. Roast larger pieces by cooking on a rotisserie.

A rotisserie is made by placing forked sticks upright in the ground 1–2 feet apart and placing skewered balanced meat across the forked ends. Build the fire toward the back and place a pan for drippings at the front. Turn the meat periodically using the pan juices for basting.

* *See also Biscuits on a Stick and Foil Dinner.*

Frying over an Open Fire

Frying on a griddle: Place four stones around your fire to support a piece of metal or some heavy aluminum foil to be used as a griddle. A refrigerator or oven rack may be used to make a grill.

Frying on a stone: Flat, heated, greased stones may be used to fry eggs and thin strips of meat. Heat stones as hot as the fire allows. Then use a stick to move the stones to the edge of the fire, grease stones, and fry food.

Skillet Cooking

Use an iron or heavy skillet or a pressure cooker with a flat metal lid. Anything may be cooked or baked in a skillet. Use coals, a reflector oven, or the top of any stove from mud to modern.

* *To keep baked goods from sticking or burning, use a maximum of 6 cups of flour. Liberally grease pan and sprinkle with cornmeal, or line pan with banana skins or several layers of foil.*

* *If the bottom cooks faster than top, put coals on the lid or cook slower.*

* *If rising too high, place a stick or spoon between the lid and the skillet.*

* *If the bottom is cooking unevenly, even out the coals or move pan around.*

See page 240 for International Conversion Charts

* *Skillet bake custards, bread puddings, soufflés, and casseroles.*

* *See also Stove Top Baking, Fried Biscuits, and Frying Pan Cookies.*

Skillet Bread: Use any bread recipe. Form loaves into three balls which can be split apart during the cooling process. Set balls of dough into a well-greased heavy pan, pressure cooker, or skillet, and let rise until doubled in bulk. Cover pan with a lid and put on low heat. If cooking with coals, cover lid with hot coals and place in a cool place in the fire. After 1/2 hour, when bread is firm and dry on top, gently tip bread out onto a clean towel, turn it over, and slip it back into the pan for another ten minutes. Check for doneness with a clean straw from a broom or piece of uncooked spaghetti. Turn loaves out on a board to cool and split into three loaves.

Cinnamon Rolls, Cakes, and Quick Breads: Put batter into greased pan, making sure the sugar doesn't touch the inside of the pan. Cover and cook over low heat until done.

Quiche and Custard or Pumpkin Pie: Line greased skillet with crust. Fill with filling, cover, and cook over low heat until set.

Pizza: Line greased skillet with crust. Cook a few minutes, then turn crust. Add toppings, cover, and cook until done.

Stove-Top Baking

Pressure Cooker Bread: Prepare any yeast dough and allow to rise until double. Grease all inside surfaces of a metal or oven-proof mixing bowl, casserole dish, or baking pan with sides. Choose one that will fit loosely inside the pressure cooker with 1-inch space around the edges and is at least 3 inches lower than the lid.

Form dough into a ball or other desired shape and place in greased bowl, turning to grease the top. Use only enough dough to fill the bowl or pan half full, to allow space for bread to rise.

Place rack in cooker and add 1 inch warm water. Place bowl of dough in the cooker on the rack and cover with the lid and weight. Allow to rise in a warm place until double in bulk. Gently move cooker to stove and heat until weight begins to jiggle. Lower heat if necessary and process 8 minutes at 15 pounds pressure for a 5–6-inch round loaf, or longer for a larger size. Remove cooker from heat. Do not remove weight. Allow cooker to cool before opening lid.

Test for doneness by gently touching top of loaf. If it seems firm, bread is done. Remove from pan immediately. If dough seems soft to the touch and raw in the center, return to heat and process a few minutes longer.

A ring mold works well for cinnamon or dinner rolls.

Soup Kettle Bread: Prepare as for pressure cooker, using a large kettle with a tight-fitting lid. Place a large canning jar ring, or several small ones, in kettle in place of a rack and add 2 inches of water. Allow dough to rise in kettle, then place covered kettle over medium heat and boil gently for about one hour for an 8-inch round loaf. Be careful not to allow water to boil dry. Add more if necessary. This method may also be used for baking cakes, custards, and puddings.

While waiting for small batches of dough to cook, store leftover dough in a cool place and punch down when it rises to double in bulk.

* *See also Steamed Cake.*

Cooking in a Hole

This is an excellent way to cook beans, soups, stews, meats, and vegetables. For cooking meats, wrap meat in banana or papaya peels, or leaves or similar leaves from edible plants, or aluminum foil. Also wrap the vegetables. If cooking a soup or stew, place all ingredients in a coffee can or similar container. Proceed as follows.

1. Dig a hole that is larger and deeper than the container or size you need.

2. Place hot coals in the bottom of the hole.

3. Place food to be cooked or the covered container of soup on these coals.

4. Bury the container or wrapped meat with coals. Be certain there are plenty of hot coals covering meat or container.

5. Cook overnight or start in the morning for supper meal.

Food Preservation and Storage Pressure Canning

1. Assemble and clean materials and equipment.

2. Check rim of jars and lids for any irregularities.

3. Prepare only as much food as can fit into pressure cooker at one time.

4. Keep jars, lids, and food to be canned hot while packing, except raw foods.

5. Prepare foods according to charts.

6. Fill warm jars to within 1 inch of top with broth, juice, syrup, or water and insert a knife inside jar to release trapped air. Clean jar rims.

7. Apply self-sealing lid and ring and tighten, using only hand pressure. Place jars on rack or can lids in cooker and add warm water to the halfway mark.

* *Add 1 tablespoon vinegar or 1 teaspoon cream of tartar to the cooker water. This prevents stains from forming on the jars or the cooker.*

8. Close and seal the pressure cooker, heat on high, and exhaust the steam for 10 minutes before tightening the stop cock or applying the pressure weight. Begin timing when cooker reaches 15 pounds pressure. Process for the time stated on the chart. Keep pressure constant.

9. At the end of processing time, remove from heat and allow pressure to return to zero.

10. When pressure reads zero, open the cock or remove the weight and allow the remaining steam to escape. Loosen lid clamps and remove the lid away from face.

11. Remove jars, place on a well-padded surface, and cool at room temperature, away from drafts.

12. Allow 24 hours to set seal. Test by tapping lid with a fork. If a high-pitched sound occurs, it is sealed. If a "thud" or empty sound occurs, it is not sealed and you need to refrigerate the product and eat it within the week. Sometimes jars do seal in the refrigerator, so you can retest it after 24 hours in the refrigerator.

See page 240 for International Conversion Charts

13. Label and date your jars. You may remove the rings now and store your jars. If you are going to travel, leave rings in place.

IMPORTANT: BRING ALL HOME-CANNED PRODUCTS TO A FULL, HARD BOIL BEFORE EATING.

Pressure Canning Meats

Pack meat prepared in the following ways into hot jars and add 1 teaspoon salt per pint. Fill jars with broth, bouillon, or water to within 1 inch of the top, if indicated. Process at 15 pounds pressure for 75 minutes for pints and 90 minutes for quarts.

Roasted and Fried Meats: Roasts, steaks, meatballs, and patties of any meat can be roasted at 350°F for 20–40 minutes or fried and packed into hot jars. Add salt and broth, bouillon, or water.

Simmered Meats: Simmer cubed meats in water for 45–60 minutes. Pack in hot jars and add salt and broth.

Raw Beef: Pack raw meat (cubed, ground, etc.) into clean, cold jars. Do not add water. Use boiling-hot canning lids.

Raw Fish: Add 1–2 teaspoons salt (pickling salt is best) and 1 tablespoon olive, peanut, or cooking oil. Do not add water and can only in pints at 15 pounds pressure for 90 minutes.

Alligator, poultry, and wild game are all excellent when canned.

Leftover, processed, or other cooked meat may also be canned.

Frying is the least desirable method of precooking meat for canning, as it gives a very dry product.

Pressure Canning Vegetables

Pack vegetables prepared in the following ways into jars, adding 1/2 teaspoon of salt per pint and filling with water. Time is in minutes for pressuring at 15 pounds.

Vegetable	Preparation	Pints	Quarts
Asparagus, carrots	Wash, trim, and cut.	25	30
Beans—green or wax	Wash, trim, and cut.	20	25
Lima beans, green peas	Shell and wash.	40	50
Beets	Boil, remove skins, leave whole, slice, or dice.	30	35
Corn	Cut corn from cob.	55	85
Summer squash	Wash, slice, and boil 2 minutes.	30	40
Winter squash	Wash, remove seeds, slice, steam, or bake and blend pulp.	65	80

Water Bath Canning Fruits and Tomatoes

1. Assemble clean materials and prepare fruit according to chart

2. Pack fruit into warm or hot sterilized jars and add hot syrup (see following chart) or water to within 1 inch of top. Or follow Hot Pack instructions below.

3. Remove air bubbles, wipe rim, seal with hot lids, and hand tighten.

4. Place filled jars on rack or jar lids in canner or large pan 1/3 filled with hot water. Add hot water to cover jar lids by 1/2 inch, bring to boil, begin timing, cover canner if desired, and reduce heat to keep a steady but gentle boil.

* *Note: For every 1,000 feet above sea level, add 2 minutes to processing time.*

5. Remove jars and cool on padded surface. Test for seal (see #12 under Pressure Canning), label, and store.

DO NOT USE WATER BATH OR OVEN PROCESSING FOR MEATS OR VEGETABLES!

* *Add ascorbic acid (a vitamin C tablet) to fruits that tend to discolor.*

* *Fruits and tomatoes need to reach boiling temperature in order to kill any organisms that might cause spoilage or illness.*

Hot Pack: Fruits are cooked at a rolling boil in syrup or juice. Hot sterile jars are filled with the hot fruit and syrup and hot sterilized seals are applied. The product is then processed using the Water Bath method (see page 245).

* *Tomatoes and high-acid fruits do not need to be processed in the water bath if the hot pack method is used.*

Syrup: Allow 1–1 1/2 cups of syrup for each quart. Combine sugar and water, bring to boil, dissolve sugar, and keep syrup hot until used.

Syrup	Sugar	Juice/Water	Yield
Thin (sweet fruits)	1C	3C	3 1/2C
Medium (most fruits)	1C	2C	2 1/2C
Heavy (sour fruits)	1C	1C	1 1/2C

Sugar-Free Water Pack: Use hot water instead of syrup. Add ascorbic acid (vitamin C tablet can be used) and artificial sweeteners, if desired.

Fruit Processing Chart

Prepare fruit in the following ways. Follow method for water bath canning using the times in this chart. For every 1,000 feet above sea level, add 2 minutes to the time.

Fruit	Basic Preparation	Pints	Quarts
Apples	Wash, peel, core, slice, boil in syrup, and pack in jars.	15 min.	20 min.
Applesauce	Pack boiling hot in jars.	10 min.	10 min.
Apricots, cherries, plums, and prunes	Wash, pit, and pack.	20 min.	25 min.
Berries	Wash, stem, and pack.	10 min.	15 min.
Cranberries and rhubarb	Wash, stem, cut, and cook to tender in heavy syrup.	10 min.	10 min.
Juice—fruit and tomato	Crush fruit, heat, strain, add sugar or salt. Heat to boiling and pack.	10 min.	10 min.
Peaches and pears	Peel, pit, and halve, or slice pack.	25 min.	30 min.
Pineapple	Slice, peel, remove eyes, core, boil in medium syrup 5–10 min., pack in jars, and add more syrup.	30 min.	30 min.
Tomatoes	Peel, quarter, pack into jar, and add 1 teaspoon salt per quart.	35 min.	45 min.

See page 240 for International Conversion Charts

Smoking Meat

To smoke meat: Prepare meat as for Easy Jerky (see page 137). Place rack over a slow smoky fire where smoke will reach it. Check and turn often until thoroughly dried. Cooking takes 3–4 hours. Meat may be eaten at once or kept for a few days to a month under refrigeration, depending on how dry you can get it. Dryer meat keeps longer. Tastes delicious in beans and barbecues.

Dutch method of keeping smoked fish: After smoking, remove the skin, break into pint-jar lengths, and pack into warm sterilized jars. Add hot vegetable, olive, peanut, or cottonseed oil until all the spaces between the fish pieces are filled and you have a layer of oil on top of the fish pieces. Place hot sterilized lids and rings on the jar and store in a cool place. Fish keeps many months if prepared in this manner.

Curing Ham or Bacon

Rub with salt and drain overnight in refrigerator. Then wash:

- **4–6 pounds meat**

Combine and divide in half:

- **1 cup salt**
- **3/8 cup sugar**
- **1 tablespoon saltpeter, optional**

Add to 1/2 the mixture and cool:

- **4 cups boiling water**

Add washed meat and refrigerate overnight. Drain but retain the water and salt mixture (brine). Rub remaining 1/2 of mixture into the meat and return meat and brine to a large container that will not rust or taint the meat. Make certain the meat is covered.

Place a weight on top of the meat so it will remain immersed in the brine. If the brine becomes slimy, dump it. Wash meat and cover with new brine. Remove meat from brine after 5 days and wash with hot water, then cold. Drain in the refrigerator for 12 hours and then smoke over a slow smoky fire for 6 hours.

Curing Fish: Clean, wash, and rub dry salt over the fish and place in the above salt mixture overnight. In the morning, rinse and make a new cleaning brine using 1 cup of salt to 16 cups of water. Leave the fish in this brine for 30 minutes. Rinse and roll each fish in salt to coat and place in an oven to dry (procedure explained in drying of fruits and vegetables) or smoke over slow smoky fire for 3–4 hours.

Drying

Oven method: Place cake racks on top of cookie sheets and place food to be dried on the racks, or place on cookie sheets. Place in oven at 225°F with the door slightly open for 2–3 hours, or until dry and crisp. Cool and pack in sterile jars with tight lids and store in a dry, dark place.

Dehydrated vegetables: Once dehydrated, a year's supply of vegetables would not weigh over 10–20 pounds and would fit in a suitcase. The process is simple and could be adapted for use with vegetables bought in any market and using a homemade drier placed over a charcoal fire. For full information write for "Farmer Bulletin No. 984" and "Farm and Home Drying of Fruits and Vegetables" from the US Department of Agriculture, Washington, DC.

Dried beef: Rub strips with lemon juice, then salt. Dry in oven or over slow fire or see Easy Jerky in meat section.

To use dried beef or jerky: Pressure cook with beans, lentils, or peas, making sure that no salt is added. If beef is hard to cut, soak for several hours in warm water. Or soak overnight, drain water, and grind for hamburger. Or cut meat into chunks and simmer for 3 hours. Or pressure at 15 pounds for 30–45 minutes. Add barbecue sauce and simmer for 30–45 minutes longer. Or brown in a small amount of oil and use in white sauce, tomato sauce, soups, etc. Or slice very thin and fry for a few minutes and add to eggs.

Food and Equipment Storage Hints

To keep leftovers: In warm or moist climates, it is best not to keep leftover foods for more than 24 hours without refrigeration, especially if foods contain milk. To use leftovers, boil or reheat thoroughly for several minutes before using.

To store foods: In moist climates food should not be stored in cloth or paper bags or cardboard containers for a very long time, as they deteriorate and rats and roaches can eat through them.

Containers for storing cornstarch, soda, baking powder, etc: Store in glass jars with tight fitting lids. Lids should be oiled against rust. Cans with tight fitting lids may be used if rust is not a problem. It is best to store an unopened package inside the can so that if the can does rust, it won't touch the food. It also gives added protection from weevils, etc. Tupperware is good for food storage, but rats can eat through it.

To remedy stale food: Items such as flour, cocoa, cold cereals, crackers, etc., may be heated in the oven or a frying pan. When using a frying pan, stir constantly. Sufficient heating will cause stale odors to disappear.

To prevent rust: When canned foods are to be stored over a long period of time in damp climates, oil the tops and bottoms of the cans with a small amount of cooking oil. Equipment such as can openers, knives, meat grinder parts, etc., should also be oiled before storing.

Seasonings

Begin adding 1/8 teaspoon dry or 1/4 teaspoon fresh herb. Use any or a combination of the following seasonings with foods listed.

Alligator: Basil, marjoram, oregano, parsley, rosemary, saffron, garlic, curry, cilantro, ginger, onion, chives.

Beans: Chives, cumin, dill, marjoram, savory, thyme, sage, basil, onions, peppers, chili, cilantro.

Beef: Basil, bay leaf, chervil, dill, marjoram, oregano, parsley, lemon, onion, rosemary, saffron, sage, savory, tarragon, thyme, cumin, peppers, cilantro, curry, chili, garlic, ginger.

Beets: Basil, savory, thyme, caraway, cloves, ginger.

Breads: Poppy, anise, caraway, sesame, rye, onion, dill, cumin, coriander, ginger, nutmeg.

Broccoli: Oregano, tarragon, mace.

Cakes: Vanilla, allspice, nutmeg, ginger, cloves, cinnamon.

Candy: Cardamom, anise, poppy, cassia, coriander, fennel.

Cookies, Puddings, Pastry: Mace, poppy, sesame, caraway, anise.

Cabbage: Oregano, caraway, dill, ginger, mint, fennel.

Carrots: Parsley, bay leaf, mint, oregano, rosemary, sage, thyme, marjoram, cloves, curry, ginger, chives.

Cheese: Chives, sage, caraway, basil, sweet marjoram, thyme, tarragon, dill, cumin, parsley, onions, mint, chervil, peppers, chili, cilantro, anise, garlic, poppy.

Chayote: Same as potatoes.

Eggs: Capers, chives, shallots, tarragon, thyme, rosemary, basil, chervil, dill, marjoram, oregano, parsley, chilies, saffron, sage, savory, peppers, cilantro, curry, onion.

Eggplant: Basil, dill, marjoram, parsley, rosemary, thyme, sage.

Fish: Basil, bay leaf, chervil, dill, marjoram, oregano, parsley, rosemary, saffron, sage, savory, tarragon, thyme, onion, tomato, chili, peppers, curry, fennel, garlic, mace, nutmeg.

Fruits and Drinks: Cassia, ginger, nutmeg, cinnamon, cloves, mace, mint.

Lamb: Basil, bay leaf, dill weed, oregano, mint, rosemary, saffron, sage, marjoram, thyme.

Pasta: Lemon, parsley, rosemary, dill, onion, chervil, cilantro, oregano.

Peas: Basil, chervil, marjoram, mint, nutmeg, rosemary.

Pickles: Allspice, anise, cardamom, cassia, chili, cloves, dill, garlic, onion, ginger, mace, saffron, turmeric, tarragon, rosemary, fennel.

Pork: Basil, dill, marjoram, onion, rosemary, sage, tarragon, caraway, coriander, curry, fennel, garlic.

Potatoes: Bay leaf, chervil, parsley, mint, rosemary, tarragon, mace, chives.

Poultry and Game: Basil, bay leaf, chervil, dill, marjoram, oregano, parsley, rosemary, sage, savory, tarragon, thyme, curry, garlic, onion, ginger.

Rice: Chives, cumin, oregano, parsley, saffron, savory, rosemary, thyme, shallots, capers, dill, caraway, cilantro, curry.

Salads: Basil, chervil, dill, marjoram, oregano, parsley, mint, saffron, savory, tarragon, thyme, capers, chives, onion, garlic, poppy.

Soups: Basil, bay leaf, chervil, dill, marjoram, oregano, parsley, mint, rosemary, saffron, sage, savory, tarragon, thyme, onion, cilantro, cumin, chili, peppers, cheese, garlic.

Spinach: Chervil, dill, marjoram, rosemary, tarragon, nutmeg, mint

Squash and Sweet potato: Basil, rosemary, saffron, cinnamon, nutmeg, allspice, cassia.

Tomato: Basil, bay leaf, chervil, oregano, onion, parsley, tarragon, garlic.

Zucchini: Marjoram, mint, saffron, thyme.

Cooking Terms

Bake: To cook by dry heat in an oven. Also called roasting, when referring to meats.

Baste: To pour liquid by spoonfuls over food while it is cooking.

Blanch: To pour boiling water over a food or to immerse briefly in boiling water, then drain and rinse with cold water.

Braise: To cook in low moist heat with fat and water or other liquid (usually used for meats). The meat is browned quickly in the fat, the liquids added, the pan covered, and the heat turned low to cook.

Bread: To cover or coat food with bread crumbs.

Brine: Liquid of salt and vinegar, used for pickling.

Brown: To give the outer surface of a food a brown color by frying, toasting, broiling, or baking at a high temperature.

Candy: To cook syrup until transparent or to glaze with sugar or syrup.

Combine: To mix thoroughly two or more ingredients.

Deep Fry: To fry in a large kettle in deep fat which completely covers the food being prepared. Fat should be hot to brown foods quickly.

Flour: To cover completely with a thin layer of flour.

Fold: To add ingredients, usually beaten egg whites or whipped cream, gently to a mixture by cutting through the mixture and folding it over the ingredients.

Fry: To cook in hot fat. When a small amount of fat is used, the process is called pan-frying or sautéing. When food is partially covered with oil it is called shallow frying, and when food is completely covered it is deep frying.

Grease: To rub inside of a dish with shortening, margarine, butter, or oil.

Knead: To work dough by repeatedly stretching it with the hands, folding it over, and pressing it with the "heel" of the hand.

Parboil: To boil until partially cooked. Cooking is then usually completed by some other method.

Parch: To brown by means of dry heat. Applied to grains.

Pasta: A dough such as macaroni, noodles, or spaghetti.

Poach: To cook in a simmering liquid.

Render: To heat any solid animal fat to melting point.

Sauté: To cook in a skillet in a small amount of fat or liquid.

Scald: To heat just below the boiling point. Also to pour boiling water over the food or to dip food briefly into the boiling water.

Sear: To brown the surface of food, usually meat, by exposing it to high heat for a comparatively short time.

Set: A term applied to gelatins, baked custards, or puddings when they have congealed.

Simmer: To cook just below the boiling point so that only an occasional bubble appears on the liquid's surface.

Skim: To remove foam, fat, or a solid substance from a mixture's surface.

See page 240 for International Conversion Charts

Steam: To cook over, but not in, boiling water.

Sterilize: To destroy microorganisms with boiling water, dry heat, or steam.

Stock: The liquid in which meat, fish, or vegetables have been cooked.

Whey: A nutritious liquid that is drained off in the process of making cheese, or the liquid that forms on yogurt.

High-Altitude Adjustments

For Cakes, Cookies, and Biscuits

Adjustment	Ingredient at Altitudes 3,000–7,000 ft
Decrease	Sugar per cup, 1–3 tablespoons
Increase	Flour, 2 tablespoons
Increase	Temperature, 15–25 degrees°F
Decrease	Cooking time
Decrease	Beating time of egg whites: soft peaks only

For Yeast Dough

Adjustment	Ingredient at Altitudes 3,000–7,000 ft
Decrease	Rising time
Increase	Liquid

For Stove-Top Cooking

Adjustment	Ingredient at Altitudes 3,000–7,000 ft
Increase	Boiling point by adding salt
Increase	Liquid and cooking time
Increase	Cooking time for deep frying and cook at lower temperature
Maintain	Cooking time for candies, jellies, and syrups

For Pressure Canning

Adjustment	Ingredient at Altitudes 3,000–7,000 ft
Increase	Pressure 1 pound for every 2,000 feet above sea level, or increase time by 5 percent.

For Water Bath Canning

Adjustment	Ingredient at Altitudes 3,000–7,000 ft
Increase	Time 2 minutes for every 1,000 feet above sea level.

Substitutions

Ingredient	Substitute
apples or applesauce	green mangos, guavas, or green cooking bananas
baking powder— 1 teaspoon	1/4 teaspoon soda and 1/2 cup sour milk, or 3/8 teaspoon cream of tartar, or 1/4 teaspoon soda and 1 teaspoon cream of tartar
bean sprouts	shredded cabbage
bread crumbs	cracker, corn flake or tortilla crumbs, or oatmeal
candied fruit	dried bananas
chocolate—1 square	3 tablespoons cocoa and 1 tablespoon shortening
chocolate chips	chopped candy bar
condensed soups	see White Sauce, page 201
cornmeal	oatmeal powdered in blender
cornstarch—1 tablespoon	2 tablespoons flour
corn syrup—1 cup	1 cup honey or 1 1/4 cups sugar and 1/3 cup liquid boiled to syrup
cream, coffee	7/8 cup milk and 3 tablespoons butter
cream, heavy—1 cup	1/3 cup butter and 3/4 cup milk
cream, whipping—1 cup	1 cup cream and 1 tablespoon softened gelatin
cream, whipped—1/2 cup	1/3 cup evaporated milk, whipped
cream cheese	ricotta cheese, yogurt, tofu, cottage cheese, or blend 1 banana and 1 cup cottage cheese
cream of tartar—1/4 teaspoon	4 teaspoons vinegar
egg—1 whole	2 yolks, or 1/4 cup liquid plus 1–3 tablespoons oil and 1 teaspoon baking powder, or 2 tablespoons oil plus 1 tablespoon water

Ingredient	Substitute
flour, to thicken—1 tablespoon	1/2 tablespoon cornstarch or 2 teaspoons quick tapioca
flour, all purpose—1 cup	3/4 cup wheat flour, or 1 cup plus 2 tablespoons cake flour
flour, cake—1 cup	7/8 cup all-purpose flour plus 2 tablespoons cornstarch
garlic—1 clove	1/8 teaspoon garlic powder or 1/2 teaspoon garlic salt
honey—1 cup	1 1/4 cups sugar plus 1/4 cup water
margarine or butter—1 cup	7/8 cup oil, shortening, or lard plus 1/2 teaspoon salt
mayonnaise	yogurt or sour cream
meat tenderizer	milk from papaya skin or leaf
milk, evaporated—1 cup	1/2 cup powdered milk plus fill to 1 cup with water
milk, sour—1 cup	1 cup milk plus 1 tablespoon lemon juice or vinegar
milk, whole—1 cup	1/2 cup evaporated milk plus 1/2 cup water
milk, whole fresh—1 cup	1 cup powdered milk reconstituted plus 2 teaspoons butter
molasses—1 cup	3/4 cup brown sugar plus 1/4 cup liquid
mustard, dry—1 teaspoon	1 tablespoon prepared mustard
nuts, chopped—1/2 cup	1/2 cup crushed corn flakes plus 1/4 teaspoon almond extract, or use toasted coconut, pumpkin, squash, or sesame seeds plus almond or walnut flavor
potatoes, mashed—1 cup	1/2 cup each cooked rice and potatoes, or 1 cup mashed chayote
sour cream—1 cup	1 cup milk plus 1 tablespoon white vinegar or lemon, let stand 5 minutes, or 1 cup yogurt or 1/2 cup each cottage cheese and yogurt plus 2 tablespoons milk and 1 tablespoon lemon juice
seasoning substitutes	see page 253
sugar, powdered—1 cup	1/2 cup white sugar, blended
sugar, brown—1 cup	1 cup white sugar plus 2 tablespoons molasses

See page 240 for International Conversion Charts

sugar substitutes	see following chart
sugar, white—1 cup	Add 1/2 teaspoon soda per cup plus 1/2 cup honey, decrease liquid by 1/4 cup or use 1 cup brown packed or 2 cups powdered
tomatoes, canned—1 cup	1 1/2 cups cooked tomatoes
tomato, sauce	3/4 cup tomato paste plus 1 cup water
tomato, juice	1/2 cup each tomato paste and water
vinegar	lemon juice
water chestnuts	diced jicama
yeast, dry—1 package	1 tablespoon dry active yeast or 1 yeast cake

Artificial Sugar Substitutes

The following are equivalents for sugar substitutes. Check the equivalents on your package to be certain. Add sweetener after recipe has been cooked, if possible. For best flavor use half sugar and half sugar substitute.

(t=teaspoon, T= tablespoon, and pkg=package)

Tablets	Dry	Liquid	Equal to sugar
1/3	1/10 t	1/8 t	1 t
1	1/4 t (1 pkg)	1/3 t	1 T
2	1/2 t	3/4 t	2 T
4	1 t	1 1/2 t	1/4 cup
7	1 1/3 t	3 t	1/3 cup
8	2 t	4 t	1/2 cup
16	4 t	8 t	1 cup

Artificial sugar substitutes can be used in cooking, baking, canning, in hot or cold drinks, on cereals, in granola, pancakes, sweet sauces, dressings, breads, ice cream, milk shakes, puddings, etc.

Sugar substitutes may be used on a hypoglycemic or diabetic diet. Sweet 'n' Low contains 1/2 gram of carbohydrate to the teaspoon, and 2 calories. Concentrated fruit juices may be used in place of sugar. Reduce fluid in the recipe and remember fructose is also concentrated.

Seasoning Substitutes

Allspice: 1/4 teaspoon each nutmeg and cinnamon plus 1/2 teaspoon cloves.

Anise: Fennel, dill, cumin, or caraway.

Basil: Tarragon or summer savory.

Bay Leaf: Thyme.

Caraway: Fennel or cumin.

Cardamom: Cinnamon or mace.

Chervil: Parsley, tarragon, or cilantro.

Chili: Cayenne pepper, cumin, oregano, and garlic, to taste.

Cilantro: Coriander leaf, celery leaf, or parsley.

Cinnamon: Allspice or cardamom.

Cloves: Allspice, nutmeg, or mace.

Cumin: 1/3 anise plus 2/3 caraway, or use fennel.

Curry Powder: Combine 2 tablespoons each coriander, black pepper, cumin, red pepper, turmeric, and 1 1/4 teaspoons ground ginger. Or use a combination of allspice, cinnamon, fennel, garlic, and mace, and adjust to taste.

Dill: Celery seed.

Fennel: Anise or caraway.

Garam Masala: Combine 1/4 teaspoon each of cloves, cinnamon, and nutmeg, 1/2 teaspoon each of cardamom and black pepper, and 1 teaspoon each of coriander and cumin.

Mace: Allspice, cloves, nutmeg, or nutmeg plus cardamom.

Marjoram: Oregano or thyme.

Nutmeg: Allspice, cloves, or mace.

Oregano: Marjoram, rosemary, or thyme.

Parsley: Chervil, tarragon, or cilantro.

Pumpkin Pie Spice: Combine 1/2 teaspoon cinnamon, 1/4 teaspoon each, cloves and nutmeg, and 1/8 teaspoon each, cardamom and allspice.

Rosemary: Marjoram or oregano.

Sage: Rosemary or oregano.

Savory: Thyme.

Sesame: Finely chopped almonds.

Taco Seasoning: Combine 1 tablespoon chili powder, 1 teaspoon onion powder and 1 teaspoon salt. Then add any or all of the following: 1 teaspoon ground cumin, 1 teaspoon garlic powder, 1 teaspoon paprika, 1/4–1/2 teaspoon cayenne pepper, and 1/4–1/2 teaspoon black pepper.

Tarragon: Chervil or parsley.

See page 240 for International Conversion Charts

Bibliography of Additional Books

The following are other helpful books on specific topics and from specific locations.

Topics

Bread: Pilkinton, Marcelle. *Take Our Bread*. Distributed by the Pilkinton Family, 15 Jillett St. Titahi Bay, New Zealand.

Children's: *Fun to Cook Book*. Printed by the Carnation Company, Los Angeles, CA 90036, 1982.

Economy: Longacre, Doris Janzen. *More-with-Less Cookbook*. Scottdale, PA: Herald Press, 1976.

Meatless: Lappé, Frances Moore. *Diet for a Small Planet*, Revised Edition. New York: Ballantine Books, 1975.

Missionary Minded: Pugh M. Neva and Jan Cunningham. *Cooking From Scratch on the Missionfield*. Waseca, MN: Walters Publishing Co., 1981.

Mixes: Eliason, Karine, Nevada Howard and Madeline Westover. *Make-a-Mix Cookery*. Tucson, AZ: H. P. Books, 1978.

Substituting Ingredients: Epstein, Becky Sue and Hilary Dole Klein, *Substituting Ingredients*. Charlotte NC: The East Woods Press, 1986.

Locations:

Australia: Morrow, Aileen. *More Food for Thought*, Second Edition. *Kangaroo Ground*, Australia: Wycliffe Bible Translators, 1986.

Bolivia: Women's Auxiliary of the "Hospital Metodista." *Epicuro Andino, High Altitude Cooking*. La Paz, Bolivia: Cooperativa de Artes Graficas E Burillo Ltda., 1973.

Colombia: Meehan, Carole and Joni Roraff. *Mejores Malocas y Chagras*, Cookbook for "Lomalindans." Complied by Explorer Pioneer Girls, 1985.

Mexico: Villalobos, Maria. *Maria's Culinary Secrets, Zapotec Cookery from Southern Mexico*.

Nigeria: International Women's Club. *From the Crocodiles*. Kaduna, Nigeria, 1979.

Pacific Islands: British Red Cross Society. *Island Recipes*. Vila New Hebrides, Hong Kong: China Translation and Printing Services, 1979.

Philippines: Weaver, Marilou. *The Plain and Fancy Cookbook, An Adventure in Eating in the Philippines*. **Philippines:** The Summer Institute of Linguistics, 1978.

South America: Baker, Mary. *Jungle Cooking*. South American Indian Mission, 1966.

See page 240 for International Conversion Charts

Index

*The **Updated** Wycliffe Cookbook—Index*